EARLY CHILDHOOD EDUCATION SERIES

Sharon Ryan, *Editor*

ADVISORY BOARD: *Celia Genishi, Doris Fromberg, Carrie Lobman, Rachel Theilheimer, Dominic Gullo, Amita Gupta, Beatrice Fennimore, Sue Grieshaber, Jackie Marsh, Mindy Blaise, Gail Yuen, Alice Honig, Betty Jones, Stephanie Feeney, Stacie G. Goffin, Beth Graue*

(continued)

To look for other titles in this series, visit www.tcpress.com

THE
EARLY
YEARS
MATTER

Education, Care, and the
Well-Being of Children, Birth to 8

MARILOU HYSON and
HEATHER BIGGAR TOMLINSON

Foreword by Jacqueline Jones

Teachers College
Columbia University
New York and London

National Association for the
Education of Young Children
Washington, DC

Published simultaneously by Teachers College Press, 1234 Amsterdam Avenue, New York, NY 10027 and the National Association for the Education of Young Children, 1313 L Street NW, Suite 500, Washington, DC 20005

Copyright © 2014 by Teachers College, Columbia University

All rights reserved. No part of this publication may be reproduced or transmitted in any form or by any means, electronic or mechanical, including photocopy, or any information storage and retrieval system, without permission from the publisher.

Library of Congress Cataloging-in-Publication Data

Hyson, Marilou.
    The early years matter : education, care, and the well-being of children, birth to 8 /
        Marilou Hyson, Heather Biggar Tomlinson ; foreword by Jacqueline Jones.
            pages cm. – (Early childhood education series)
    Includes bibliographical references and index.
    ISBN 978-0-8077-5526-6 (pbk. : alk. paper)
    ISBN 978-0-8077-7310-9 (e-book)
        1. Education, Preschool–United States. 2. Early childhood education–United States.
    3. Preschool teachers–Training of–United States. 4. Early childhood teachers–United
    States. 5. Child development. I. Title.
    LB1140.23.H97 2014
    372.21–dc23   2014003018

ISBN 978-0-8077-5558-7 (paper)
ISBN 978-0-8077-7310-9 (ebook)

NAEYC item # 1122

Printed on acid-free paper
Manufactured in the United States of America

21   20   19   18   17   16   15   14   8   7   6   5   4   3   2   1

Contents

Foreword

Over the past few years, early childhood education has undergone an extraordinary transformation. The unprecedented federal focus on early learning in the Obama administration, coupled with increased state and local funding for preschool programs, has brought the care, development, and education of young children to the forefront of the national discourse. In a period of extreme partisan rancor, early childhood education has been one of the few issues to achieve bipartisan sponsorship.

Yet supporting young children's development and learning has become a complex endeavor. Spanning the age range of birth through 8 years, early childhood education in the United States has evolved into a fragmented set of services that are often segmented into age ranges such as birth to 3 years; preschool for children aged 3 and 4 years; and school-based kindergarten through 3rd-grade programs for children aged 5–8 years. These services are often delivered through a variety of agencies (including Head Start, family child care, home visiting, state and local programs, and private providers) that, historically, have been funded by a patchwork set of federal, state, local, and private sources. There are wide variations in program-funding levels; eligibility criteria; and the preparation, professional development, and compensation requirements for the adults who work with young children. Individual children may receive services that are supported by multiple funding sources within a single program that is trying to meet many program requirements. Or they may be attending more than one program each day, as their family tries to balance work schedules with child care availability. The result is a system that varies in program quality within and across providers.

Hyson and Tomlinson cut through this complex picture and present a coherent and insightful view of the field through the eyes of young children, their families, and the adults who work in their behalf. Beginning with a look at children across the birth to 8 years age range, the authors follow children and their families in home visiting, family child care, preschool, and 1st-grade settings. The real-life issues facing families who are trying to support their children—while dealing with low-income wages, violence and multiple stress factors, children with special needs and challenging behaviors, immigrant status, and life in developing countries—are woven tightly with a variety of effective early childhood programs and practices that can help children grow, develop, and learn. Rather than treating children with special needs as an afterthought, Hyson and Tomlinson take the reader into the world of a child with disabilities and reveal the person she has become, the services she receives across the early childhood continuum, and the joy she brings to her family. The discussion of children with challenging behaviors is a topic of great interest to early childhood educators, regardless of funding source or service delivery model. Hyson and Tomlinson present this issue through the eyes of a child who is struggling and the teachers who desperately want to implement strategies that will help him adjust to his environment. The reader is also given a view into the life of an immigrant family that is trying to adapt to a different culture and hoping to provide their child with the tools for a successful future.

In addition, Hyson and Tomlinson introduce the reader to the wide-ranging ways in which actual early childhood professionals, such as classroom teachers, college professors, researchers, and program administrators, provide services to young children across a variety of program settings. For those who are new to early childhood education, the text provides an overview of the field and a unique insight into the many opportunities for early childhood professionals to promote the well-being of young children and their families.

While there is a good deal of agreement that high-quality early education is important to children's growth and development, we seldom get a glimpse into early childhood education programs from so many personal perspectives. Hyson and Tomlinson do not simply provide a straightforward and comprehensive view of this field of practice, they humanize it through the experiences of children, families, and early childhood professionals. They leave the reader with a clear understanding of the myriad of ways in which high-quality early childhood education programs matter in the early years, and they matter a lot.

–Jacqueline Jones, Ph.D.

Acknowledgments

We are enormously grateful to the many individuals and early childhood groups that—whether they were aware of it or not—have contributed to *The Early Years Matter: Education, Care, and the Well-Being of Children, Birth to 8.*

First are the young children and families whose experiences inform the central themes of this book. Although the anecdotes that frame each chapter represent composites and not actual people, the descriptions capture the realities of those whom we have worked and played with, observed, and studied over many years. We also acknowledge and admire the countless early childhood professionals who spend every day improving outcomes for young children and their families, often without recognition or adequate compensation.

Specifically, we thank the 19 early childhood professionals who are featured in Chapters 2 through 10: Nilofer Ahsan, Lindy Buch, Lacy Carter, Jim Clay, Michele Dandrea, Cathy Grace, Amer Hasan, Mary Louise Hemmeter, Donald Hernandez, Diane Horm, Cindy McCann, Beatrice Wambui Muriithi, Stephen O'Connor, Margo Okapal, Sharon Ritchie, Rosa Milagros Santos, Yulianti Siantayani, Donna Widmaier, and Anna Yu. When we discussed the possibility of including a "Professional Profiles" feature, we had no idea whether people would be willing to take time to share their lives and professional commitments with us and with readers of this book. Their responses exceeded our expectations and will help readers envision the scope and rich diversity of the early childhood field.

We could not possibly list all of the early childhood researchers and policy leaders whose work has informed *The Early Years Matter.* Throughout, we have relied on the knowledge of countless experts who together provide the best available evidence about why the early years matter and about the kinds of supports and services that young children and their families require. Because we wanted this book to be concise and accessible, we have selected from and greatly simplified this knowledge base, and take responsibility for any resulting omissions or misinterpretations.

The original concept for *The Early Years Matter* was generated by Marie Ellen Larcada and Sharon Ryan of Teachers College Press; their enthusiasm and thoughtful feedback have continued to support our progress at every stage of the book's development. From NAEYC, Kathy Charner joined in supporting the book's copublication and its inclusion as an NAEYC comprehensive member benefit. NAEYC has also contributed to this book by providing a professional home for us, authors Marilou and Heather, whose years of collaboration in Washington nurtured the values, vision, work style, and friendship that have led to this coauthored publication. We also appreciated the suggestions of those who reviewed the original proposal and of other colleagues in higher education. The book's final form owes much to Wendy

Schwartz's editing expertise and Karl Nyberg's careful oversight of every detail of production.

Finally, both of us are indebted to our families and other providers of personal support. Marilou thanks her family for their unfailing patience, encouragement, and vicarious enjoyment of her never-boring life: Jeff, Juliette, Sam, Ellie, Dan, Jess, and most of all John. She offers a special dedication to her compassionate, committed, and courageous sister, Susan Carey Biggam. Heather thanks Joanna for helpful edits, traveling around the globe multiple times to provide child care (warm and responsive, of course), and modeling how to write between the cracks; Robert for writing about cancer, AIDS, and magical circuses, and for a lifetime love of books; Hugh for deftly shortening the word count, teaching her that every word matters, and saying yes to every request for swims and bike rides; Rob Biggar for making introductions; Buster Bars, Ibu Nengsih, and Ibu Desi for keeping her household moving so she could sit still and write; Kevin Tomlinson for logistical support and his own brand of one-line poetry; and Tatum, Finn, and Clara for providing an endless supply of sunshine even during the monsoons.

CHAPTER 1

Introduction:
Opening Doors to Learning for
Young Children and Their Families

©Ellen B. Senisi

© Niderlander

© Marilyn Nolt

copyright © NAEYC®. Reprinted with permission

Welcome! You are beginning or renewing an exploration of the world of Early Care and Education, also known as Early Childhood Education, or ECE. You may be a student, teacher, program director, teacher educator, policymaker, parent, or simply someone who cares about the lives of the very youngest members of our society. Let's look into some of these lives through fictional, composite stories of four children and begin to think about how early childhood services can make a difference to them and their families.

THE EARLY CARE AND EDUCATION EXPERIENCES OF FOUR CHILDREN

Nico and Home Visiting

A knock on the door alerts Nico's mother, Ana, that Miriam has arrived for a home visit. Ever since Nico came home from the hospital, the home visiting program has sent Miriam, a specially trained professional, to spend time each week with Ana and her baby. Nico was born prematurely and even at 6 months is still not developing like her friends' infants. Miriam has become a warm, trusted support for Ana, whose parents are back in the country from which she emigrated 5 years ago. At first Ana thought that Miriam would act like an expert, telling her exactly what to do with Nico. Instead, Miriam has become a valued friend. She often spends most of her visit watching Ana and Nico play traditional games that Ana used to enjoy when she was a child. Miriam has told Ana all the things that Nico is learning from playing with his mother, which surprises and pleases Ana. Now she is eager to play the games more often. Miriam shows Ana how she can use everyday activities like bathing Nico or taking him for walks to strengthen his body, mind, and spirit. Ana can already see how well Nico's developing, and she feels proud of what she's doing as his mother.

Julia and Family Child Care

Julia peeks around the corner of the front door of Ms. Abbott's family child care home. Every day, Ms. Abbott and her sister-in-law care for six children from ages 1 to 5. Most of the children have been attending the Wee Care program for a long time, but today is 2-year-old Julia's first day to stay without her mother, who has just started a full-time job at a bank in their suburban town. Ms. Abbott has visited with Julia's family and knows Julia's routines, but she also knows that this will be a hard day for her. Ms. Abbott used her experience, education, and training to help her think about how to make the transition easier—that's why Julia is holding her favorite stuffed animal as well as a photograph of her parents. "Julia, we are so happy to see you today," says Ms. Abbott. "If you want to watch us from there, that's just fine. See, Eric is putting the dolls to sleep; maybe later you would like to play with him. I'm going to start fixing our morning snack: you can think about whether you want to come into the kitchen and help me with that." Julia settles into a corner and watches.

Rachel and Prekindergarten

Last fall Rachel began attending the prekindergarten (pre-K) program at the local public school. Rachel is almost 5 and she had never gone to child care or any other preschool. Most days she stayed home with her mom, who has been looking for work in their low-income rural community without success. With nothing else to do, Rachel spent a lot of time watching television and playing with her two younger brothers. When she started pre-K, it was a big surprise for Rachel. The only children Rachel had played with were her younger brothers, and she was used to just grabbing things from them. The children in her class did not seem to like that, but she kept doing it because it worked at home. Rachel's teacher, Mr. Jackson, understands that Rachel is not "bad." Having Rachel in his class has been challenging for Mr. Jackson, but he has some help. His school has been using a special program to coach all of the teachers in how to prevent and deal with what they call "challenging behavior." As part of that program, Mr. Jackson has gotten to know Rachel's mom, and they are working together to help Rachel learn new ways of getting what she wants and making friends at the same time. Now it's April and Rachel almost never grabs and yells. With Mr. Jackson's and her mother's support, she has found new ways to make friends and be a friend.

HENRY AND 1ST GRADE

First-grader Henry bounces in his place in the class's circle on the rug, hand waving in the air. "Ms. Roberts, Ms. Roberts! I have a great idea!" His teacher turns and smiles at Henry. "What's your idea, Henry?" Henry proceeds to tell his teacher and the class about how they can make a birdhouse for their class project, in which they have decided to learn all about birds. As the children get paper to draw their designs for birdhouses, his teacher thinks about how far Henry has come this year. Ms. Roberts' use of projects based on the children's interests has certainly given her new ways to strengthen the children's literacy and math skills, but it has also captured the enthusiasm of a few children like Henry, who began the year discouraged and disengaged. Henry used to enjoy only the outdoor climbing and free play opportunities. Not any more: Henry is one of the most enthusiastic young learners in Ms. Roberts' class. His parents have been really supportive of his excitement about the projects, too. Henry and his father, who is a carpenter, picked out a good spot in the tree in their tiny urban yard, and together are working on making a birdhouse. Henry plans to paint it when they finish, using a new painting kit his mother has already bought for him.

Nico, Julia, Rachel, and Henry are different from one another in many ways. They range in age from 6 months to 7 years. They live in cities, suburbs, and rural communities. Some of their families have very low incomes and other families are well-off. The four children are diverse in their cultures and home languages. Yet they have one important thing in common: They all participate in some kind of early childhood program.

- For Nico, it is a home visiting program funded by the federal government. The goal is to start as early as possible to partner with parents in encouraging the positive development of babies and toddlers whose families have low incomes or who are at risk because of disabilities or other developmental problems.
- For Julia, it is a private family child care home that offers care and stimulation for a small group of children of different ages whose parents work full-time.
- For Rachel, it is a state-funded pre-K program. The program provides a half day of classroom activities to support the development and learning of children whose families have low incomes.
- For Henry, it's a public school 1st-grade classroom—one where the children are mastering important academic skills but doing so in a way that fits their early childhood way of learning: playful, social, and intellectually challenging, yet not intimidating.

Each of these programs is making a huge difference for the children and their families.

THE NATURE OF EARLY CARE AND EDUCATION

The Goal of Services for Young Children and Their Families

The goal of all early childhood services is to enhance the development and learning of young children from birth to 8, including their physical well-being, health, and safety; their social and emotional competence; their thinking skills and knowledge of the world; and their enthusiasm for and engagement in learning—skills that are also known as "approaches to learning." In the short run, these competencies contribute to children's well-being and school readiness; in the longer run, they prepare children for success in life.

Early Care and Education Settings and Auspices

As these examples show, services for children in the early years may take place in multiple settings. Many of these services are programs for groups of children: these might be called center- or classroom-based preschools, child care programs, family child care homes, prekindergarten programs, public school kindergarten, and primary-grade classrooms. Group programs also include after-school programs or "school-aged child care." Other early childhood services may be home-based, like the visits that Nico and his mother receive every week. And these are just a few of the settings you will learn more about as you read this book.

Some services are free to parents and paid for through government funds; for example, public school kindergarten and primary grades are funded primarily by taxes levied on property owners, with the resources varying depending on the value of property in a given school district. Some state-funded prekindergarten programs use state tax dollars to support services for children in low-income families; the Head Start program does the same with federal government funds. But, unlike many other countries, in the United States families generally pay the full expense of services for children birth to age 5 out of their own pockets. In later chapters we'll see the problems that these expenses present to many families, especially in a challenging economic environment.

DEFINING THE EARLY CHILDHOOD YEARS AND EARLY CARE AND EDUCATION

The early years or "early childhood" extend from birth through age 8, according to organizations such as the National Association for the Education of Young Children and the United Nations. "Early childhood education," also known as "early care and education"—both "ECE"—includes educational programs and a wide array of other services that support development and learning across the early childhood years. Depending on the state, "early childhood" teacher certification may span birth to age 5, preschool to grade 2, prekindergarten to grade 4, or one of many other configurations.

How Early Childhood Education Got Started

Discussing how early care and education began could take a book in itself. The idea that the early years are a uniquely important period of life goes back centuries. As communities recognized the need to support young children, early childhood services evolved, often with differing goals. Historically, early childhood services primarily protected children's health and safety, especially if their families were unable to care for them. Other services focused more on giving children opportunities to play, explore their environment, and socialize with other children. Still other programs targeted specific academic skills that children need for school success. Even though most people agree that early childhood programs should pay attention to all areas of children's development (the "whole child" or "holistic early childhood services"), to some extent these different emphases have continued today, reflecting debates over the primary purposes and desirable outcomes of services for children birth to 8 and their families.

The timeline in Figure 1.1 shows just a few milestones in the long and fascinating history of this field–a field to which you may make important contributions.

ABOUT THIS BOOK

Why is it important for young children and their families to have access to the kinds of services received by Nico, Julia, Rachel, and Henry, as well as to the many other educational and developmental programs for children birth through age 8? What difference might those services make in their lives, now and in the future? And how can we know what should be included in those services? These kinds of questions are the focus of this book.

The Book's Central Claim:
The Early Years Matter for Young Children and Their Families

After this introductory chapter, a series of chapters will help you take a closer look at why the years from birth to age 8 matter so much, why programs and services during these years are important for all young children and their families, and why these programs and services can have an especially powerful impact on some groups of young children and their families.

Chapters 2–4: What Happens in the Early Years Is Important for All Children from Birth Through Age 8. We will begin with three chapters that show how all children and families benefit from early care and education programs, and how professionals and programs support the development of children as they grow from infancy through age 8. Across these years, children's lives, as well as the lives of their families, can be enriched by many kinds of early childhood services, tailored to each child's developmental, individual, and cultural characteristics. We present the evidence for three age groups:

Figure 1.1. 20 Important Events in the History of the Early Childhood Field

1801	Johann Pestalozzi wrote *How Gertrude Teaches Her Children,* emphasizing home education and learning by discovery.
1816	Robert Owen set up a nursery school in Great Britain at the New Lanark Cotton Mills, believing that early education could counteract bad influences at home.
1837	Friedrich Froebel established the first kindergarten in Blankenburgh, Germany. Froebel is known as the father of the kindergarten.
1856	Mrs. Margaretha Schurtz established the first kindergarten in the United States in Watertown, Wisconsin; the school was founded for children of German immigrants, and the program was conducted in German.
1873	Susan Blow opened the first public school kindergarten in the United States in St. Louis, Missouri, as a cooperative effort with superintendent of schools William Harris.
1907	In Rome, Maria Montessori started her first preschool, called Children's House; she based her now-famous teaching method on the theory that children learn best by themselves in a properly prepared environment.
1911	Margaret and Rachel McMillan founded an open-air nursery school in Great Britain in which the class met outdoors; the emphasis was on healthy living.
1919	Harriet Johnson started the Nursery School of the Bureau of Educational Experiments, later to become the Bank Street College of Education.
1921	Patty Smith Hill started a progressive laboratory nursery school at Columbia Teachers College.
1926	Patty Smith Hill, at Teachers College, Columbia University, founded the National Committee on Nursery Schools, now called the National Association for the Education of Young Children; it provides guidance and consultation services for educators.
1933	The Works Project Administration (WPA) provided money to start nursery schools so that unemployed teachers would have jobs.
1940	The Lanham Act provided funds for child care during World War II, mainly for day care centers for children of mothers working in war-related industries.
1955	Rudolf Flesch's *Why Johnny Can't Read* criticized the schools for their methodology in teaching reading and other basic skills.
1965	The Head Start program began with federal money allocated for preschool education; the early programs were known as child development centers.
1968	The federal government established the Handicapped Children's Early Education program to fund model preschool programs for children with disabilities.
1975	Congress passed Public Law 94-142, the Education for All Handicapped Children Act, mandating a free and appropriate education for all children with disabilities and extending many rights to the parents of such children.
1990	The United Nations Convention on the Rights of the Child went into effect, following its signing by 20 nations.
1995	Head Start reauthorization established a new program, Early Head Start, for low-income pregnant women and families with infants and toddlers.
2002	President George W. Bush signed Public Law 107-110, the No Child Left Behind Act of 2001. NCLB contains four basic provisions: stronger accountability for results, increased flexibility and local control, expanded options for parents, and an emphasis on teaching methods that have been proven to work.
2007	Congress passed the Improving Head Start for School Readiness Act of 2007, which reauthorized the Head Start program through 2012.

Source: Adapted from Morrison, 2012.

Chapter 2: The Early Years Matter for Babies and Toddlers
Chapter 3: The Early Years Matter for Preschoolers
Chapter 4: The Early Years Matter for Children in Kindergarten Through 3rd Grade

Chapters 5–10: What Happens in the Early Years Is Especially Important for Vulnerable Children. In every age group, some children have circumstances or characteristics that challenge their development. For these children and their families, early childhood programs have special value. In the next six chapters, you will see how early childhood professionals and programs can be an essential resource, respecting children's and families' strengths and creating environments where every child can flourish.

Chapter 5: The Early Years Matter for Children in Low-Income Families
Chapter 6: The Early Years Matter for Children Who Experience Violence and Stress
Chapter 7: The Early Years Matter for Children with Disabilities
Chapter 8: The Early Years Matter for Children with Challenging Behavior
Chapter 9: The Early Years Matter for Children in Immigrant Families
Chapter 10: The Early Years Matter for Children in Developing Countries

We have organized these ten chapters to emphasize that there are general truths about how children develop and learn and about the environments that allow them to blossom, but also that children have distinctive strengths and needs that early childhood programs can and should respond to in individualized ways. No one path is ideal for all children and all families. The endless variety of riches and difficulties each child and family bring to a program makes the early childhood field delightful, complex, and intriguing. Not every toddler is like every other toddler–although if you have spent time with 2-year-olds you know that there is such a thing as "toddlerness." The same could be said for preschoolers, kindergartners, and children in 1st through 3rd grade. And then there are groups of children and families whose life circumstances may require special support, such as children of immigrant families, or children who face violence and stress. While good early childhood professionals understand what is generally true about each group, and use that knowledge to create wonderful, enriching environments, we never forget that each child and family is unique and there is not one pattern into which each child must fit. On the contrary, our job is to find out what families want and value for their children, to learn from them, and to use that knowledge, as well as the best available research, to adapt services to individual, family, and cultural characteristics.

Chapter 11: What Happens in the Early Years Is Important for Our Future. The preceding chapters tell the stories of individual children and diverse groups of children whose lives can be enhanced and whose families can be supported by early childhood services. In the last chapter we consider a broader, longer-term perspective. What happens in the early years does not stay in the early years; it contributes to the quality of later education, to society as a whole, and to our future.

Chapter 11 summarizes a great deal of evidence showing the long-lasting benefits of early-years services. Certainly teachers and principals in the later grades benefit when children enter school well prepared to meet new academic and social challenges–not only ready to learn but *excited* to learn.

On a very practical level, spending money on programs in the early childhood years can save taxpayers money in the long run, whether or not those taxpayers have young children. Economists have shown that for every dollar that a society spends on early childhood services, it can save between $7 and $20 in later years, with the greatest returns provided by children from low-income families (Grunewald & Rolnick, 2010).

How can this be such a good investment for society? As later chapters will document, these economic benefits emerge because children who participate in high-quality programs early in life are less likely to be involved in delinquency or substance abuse in later years. They are also less likely to have to repeat grades in school or to drop out of school before graduation (Belfield, Nores, Barnett, & Schweinhart, 2006). These positive outcomes mean that in the long run society has to spend less money on individuals who received care and support in the early years, who are more likely than non-participating children to grow up to be independent, productive citizens.

As early chapters will suggest and the last chapter will strongly emphasize, however, there are no guarantees of success. All programs are not created equal. The most important message of all this research is that early childhood services–whether they are provided through child care centers, preschools, or 1st-grade classrooms–need to be high-quality in order to lead to those lasting benefits. Leaving a young child in a bad early care and education program, cared for by adults who are unqualified and unmotivated, will do little to enhance that child's current or future development, no matter what environment that child lives in. Families, professionals, and countries do the right thing when they support and demand high-quality early care and education services, especially for our most vulnerable young children and families. We all reap the rewards that come from caring for one another, which leads to a more stable, peaceful, and productive society.

Chapter Features to Support Understanding and Application

Each chapter has features that will help you understand and apply new insights about young children and families. These features include:

- An opening story about one child (a fictional composite created from the lives of many real children) whose life is, or could be, impacted in positive ways by effective early childhood programs and services.
- Information about the lives, development, typical characteristics and unique strengths, and potential of various groups of young children and their families.
- A description of the challenges generally facing various groups of children and their families, along with a description of the opportunities that high-quality early childhood services can provide, expanding the potential of all children to develop and learn to their full capacity.
- Professional Profiles: First-person narratives from real professionals who make a difference as classroom teachers, research leaders, early childhood policymakers, and more. You will get a sense of what these remarkable professionals do every day, and you may get some new ideas about your own career.

- "Reflection, Dialogue, and Action," a feature with questions and suggested activities to use with classmates, colleagues, or on your own.
- A set of resources called "Information to Explore and Share," pointing the way to key websites and other easy-to-access information that will supplement the content of each chapter.

PROFESSIONALS LIKE YOU MATTER TO CHILDREN IN THEIR EARLY YEARS

Early childhood professionals hold many positions and perform many functions. But whatever their specific roles or functions, these professionals share a strong foundation of knowledge, skills, and dedication that our field urgently needs. And you just may find, if you do not yet know it, that the early childhood profession matters to you as much as it does to young children and their families.

The Professionals Who Support Young Children and Their Families

Each of the fictional examples that began this Introduction featured not just a child but also a professional who made a difference: a home visitor, a family child care provider, a pre-K teacher, and a 1st-grade teacher. Other early childhood professionals do not appear directly in these examples, but they perform essential behind-the-scenes work. One may be a researcher who studies what kind of "challenging behavior" program works best for children like Rachel. Another helped to design the home visiting program that benefits Nico. Another is an early childhood specialist in a state department of education, who helped to develop the requirements and funding for the state's prekindergarten programs. And still another is an elementary school district superintendent whose knowledge of early education has supported the use of project-based learning in the district's primary-grade classrooms. All of these professionals are part of the early childhood workforce–a diverse, dedicated group who often need more support than they receive, but who stay dedicated to children and families and find deep satisfaction in their work.

You may fill one or more of these positions now or in the future. You may be using this book in a college or university course. Some of you already have decided to be teachers of young children, and you may even know what age group you like and what setting you prefer to work in. Some of you may already work in the early childhood field and are taking classes or doing other professional development activities to expand your future opportunities. Some of you may not be at all sure that this is what you want to do as a career, but are exploring the option of being involved in this profession. Just as early childhood services help young children, families, schools, and society, being an early childhood professional can have great benefits for you.

What It Takes to Be a Competent Early Childhood Professional

Although they may not say so, some people think that those who work with young children are babysitters, or they think that if early childhood educators were more capable people they would be doing something else. Those people would be mistaken. Reread the four vignettes at the beginning of this introduction and think

> ## THE MEANING OF *TEACHER* FOR CHILDREN IN THE EARLY YEARS
>
> The early childhood field includes a variety of professionals who work with young children and their families, sometimes directly and sometimes indirectly. To simplify our language, in this book we use the term *teacher* to refer to all the professionals working directly with young children: classroom teachers, infant and toddler caregivers, family child care providers, early interventionists, and many others—only occasionally using a more specialized professional title when a distinction is needed.

about the competencies that those teachers needed to be successful early childhood professionals. Within these vignettes, where might you find evidence of the professional knowledge, skills, and dispositions that are outlined here?

Knowledge

- Understands what kinds of things help children develop well.
- Understands that each child develops differently, lives in different circumstances, and needs different things to help his or her development.
- Understands the role of early childhood professionals in promoting children's positive development and learning.

Skills

- Creates opportunities for children to gain new knowledge and practice emerging skills.
- Builds close relationships with children to create security and motivation to learn.
- Assesses each child's development to identify strengths and learning needs.

Dispositions and Attitudes

- Respects each child's and family's language and culture.
- Believes that each and every child has the ability to learn.
- Reflects on her or his work as an early childhood educator with the goal of continuous improvement.

These are just a few of the competencies that early childhood professionals need. We will see more of these in action in the chapters that follow.

Why You Might Want to Be an Early Childhood Professional

Few careers have the satisfactions, potential for growth, and intellectual and emotional challenges of the early childhood field.

- Being an early childhood professional gives you a chance to use your unique gifts and skills—perhaps you have a playful spirit that attracts children to you; perhaps you have an analytical mind that can organize lots of information into meaningful experiences for children; perhaps you have a drive to tackle challenging problems like those facing early childhood researchers and curriculum developers.
- Being an early childhood professional will broaden and deepen your existing talents and knowledge.
- It will put you squarely in a community of like-minded but extremely diverse professionals who will become your friends, mentors, and collaborators. You will be part of a strong, inspirational network.
- It will give you abundant career choices. You may start in one position, say a kindergarten teacher, and later become a business owner, a university instructor, or a master coach for other teachers—or you may return to a preschool classroom after years as a program director. Whatever the path, you may surprise yourself.
- It will give you a chance to make a difference for a child—or a parent—who desperately needs the careful, loving attention that you will give him or her, and that could alter the trajectory of the child's and family's life far into the future. Child by child, over your career you could impact hundreds or thousands of lives.

CONCLUDING THOUGHTS: OUR HOPE FOR YOU

Just as you aim to make a difference for young children, we hope that *The Early Years Matter* can make a difference for you. As you read the chapters, reflect on the stories of children and professionals, and work with others to apply the book's content, we hope you will:

1. Develop an understanding of the many reasons why early childhood education matters for children, families, and society.
2. Understand and respect young children's strengths and unique, fascinating characteristics.
3. Gain a realistic sense of the challenges of implementing early childhood services and what it takes to make these services effective.
4. Broaden your knowledge of potential careers and ways to contribute to the well-being of young children from birth through age 8 and their families.
5. Develop or renew an informed commitment to the field of early care and education.

The Early Years Matter is a small book with big ambitions. We want to expand your perspective, encourage your excitement about the early childhood field, and sharpen your appetite for more knowledge and skills. Good luck as you continue your journey.

REFLECTION, DIALOGUE, AND ACTION

1. What has been your personal experience with early care and education, either when you were growing up or in the work you do now? Share these experiences with others.

2. Choose two of this Introduction's opening vignettes and think about each program's goals in light of the section *The Goal of Services for Young Children and Their Families.* In what way do the two programs' goals seem the same? Are there any ways in which they may be different?

3. Begin to explore a few of the thousands of studies that have been done on early childhood education and related services by going to www.researchconnections.org. Browse or search any topic that interests you. You might also see what kinds of things were written about that topic this year, 5 years ago, and even 15 or 20 years ago (it's easy). Then pool your new knowledge with that of others.

4. Learn more about the fascinating history of the early childhood field by (a) looking at the detailed description provided in Morrison's textbook (2012) and (b) doing an internet search for more information on one of these events.

5. Early childhood programs serve children of different ages and take place in many different settings. At this point, reflect on which age groups, specializations, or settings you are most interested in, and what strengths you might bring to this work. Begin to keep notes on your preferences—but keep an open mind, as you will learn much more about the field's opportunities.

INFORMATION TO EXPLORE AND SHARE

Child Care and Early Education Research Connections

This should be your go-to site for research and reports about the early childhood field. You'll find that it is very user-friendly, and can be searched by keywords or browsed by topic or author. www.researchconnections.org

A Global History of Early Childhood Education and Care by Sheila Kamerman (2006)

This resource, published by UNESCO, is especially interesting because it introduces you to the history of early education and care, not only in the United States and Europe, but also in a number of developing countries in Asia and Africa. unesdoc.unesco.org/images/0014/001474/147470e.pdf

Research on Early Childhood Education Outcomes by the Public Policy Forum

This chart summarizes and provides links to research that demonstrates benefits of early childhood education in many areas of children's development, as well as broader benefits to society. publicpolicyforum.org/Matrix.htm

CHAPTER 2

The Early Years Matter
for Babies and Toddlers

© Sebastian Czapnik

Ellen and Andy are excited and nervous. They have recently learned that they are
expecting twins—a girl and a boy, whom they've decided to name Teresa and Trevor.
There have never been twins in their families, and Teresa and Trevor will, in fact, be
the first grandchildren. Everyone is thrilled and looking forward to the babies' birth in
just a few months.

Yet caring for the babies is already a big concern for the twins' parents. Both
Ellen and Andy work full-time. Neither of their employers gives much paid time off
for new parents, and they can't afford for either of them to stay home long, especially
with the extra expense of having two babies at once. They would love to rely on the
grandparents-to-be to help out, but that won't be possible, since Ellen and Andy have
recently moved to another state because of a job transfer. Friends and relatives have
described many different kinds of child care services, such as day care centers and in-
home care, but at this point Ellen and Andy aren't even sure what these are, whether
they exist in their community, and how they will be able to know what would be good
options for Teresa and Trevor. They've heard some worrisome stories.

Besides figuring out child care, Ellen and Andy have lots of questions about childrearing in general. Ellen is an only child and never babysat. And Andy's family—even though he's one of six—thinks caring for babies is "women's work," an opinion that neither Ellen nor Andy agrees with. Yes, there is the Internet, and they have bought some books, but like most parents-to-be, they don't know how to sort out good information from bad and decide between the sometimes conflicting advice: Should they let their babies "cry it out" to get back to sleep or follow an "attachment-parenting" style with everyone sleeping in the same big bed? They don't have a lot of confidence that they will know what to do to help Teresa and Trevor become healthy, happy, caring, and capable children.

HOW BABIES AND TODDLERS GROW

With Ellen and Andy's concerns in mind, this chapter explores early childhood services for babies and toddlers–what those services may be, what effects they may have on children and families, how the services can be enhanced, and what roles early childhood professionals have and may have in the future. But first we should begin by describing who babies and toddlers are and how they develop.

Ask parents and teachers what children are like before they turn 3 and you'll get something like this: always changing, curious, loving and lovable, expressive, needing to explore, needing to move, needing comfort, needing security, becoming a person, unique, frustrated and frustrating, active, intense, sweet, eager, full of contradictions, and full of life.

Typical Changes from Birth to Age 3

A lot happens in the first 3 years. The changes that occur month-by-month, and sometimes day-by-day, are hard to believe. Living far away, Teresa and Trevor's grandparents will probably see them only every few months. They'll be amazed at what happens between visits.

When their grandparents see them at 2 months, Teresa and Trevor will probably be able to do the following:

- Smile
- Coo
- Follow moving things with their eyes
- Hold up their heads

When the children get to the age of 4 months, they may add new skills to their repertoire:

- Babble and copy sounds that they hear
- Reach for toys
- Show that they recognize their grandparents when they come in the door
- Roll over

By the time they are 6 months old, the twins are likely to:

- Show that they enjoy playing with other people
- Make sounds to show that they are happy or not happy about something

- Show curiosity about many things
- Begin to sit up without support

At 9 months, they will probably:

- Show some fear of people they don't know (even Grandpa, if they don't see him often)
- Point at things and play peek-a-boo
- Crawl
- Stand while holding on

On their 1st birthday, Teresa and Trevor may:

- Show that they have favorite things or people
- Say "mama" and "dada"; try to say what they hear others saying
- Explore things in different ways, like shaking, banging, and throwing
- Follow simple directions, like "pick up the toy"

At 18 months, the children can probably:

- Play simple pretend games, like feeding a doll
- Say several single words
- Scribble with a crayon
- Walk unassisted

And by their 2nd birthday, Teresa and Trevor may:

- Copy things that other children and adults do
- Say sentences with 2–4 words
- Point to and name pictures in a book
- Play simple make-believe games

By the time they turn 3, the children are likely to be able to:

- Follow instructions that have several steps
- Carry on a conversation
- Do simple puzzles, copy a circle, and build block towers
- Climb, run, and pedal a tricycle

[Adapted from the Centers for Disease Control and Prevention's summary of developmental milestones (CDC, 2013)]

The Many Influences on Babies' and Toddlers' Development

During these years children change rapidly in every area of their development: social and emotional; language and communication; cognitive (thinking, learning, problem-solving); and movement and physical skills. There's no other time of life in which change is so rapid and dramatic. A baby is born with about 100 billion brain cells, but at birth there are few circuits or connections among these cells. With astonishing speed, connections begin to be made: By the time Teresa, Trevor, and other children are 3 years old they have hundreds of trillions of connections among the cells within each of their toddler brains.

But development from birth to age 3 is more diverse than this description suggests. Each child develops in a somewhat different way. Teresa may learn to talk earlier than Trevor; Trevor may be more fearful around strangers. Most of these variations are to be expected and celebrated. They're normal. Trevor may be born with a more "slow to warm up" temperament; it is simply part of who he is. And Teresa's somewhat earlier language development and larger vocabulary are typical of many girls. However, other differences in development can be early signs of difficulties that may—without effective intervention—create negative outcomes later on.

Researchers have shown that the "First 1,000 Days"—from the start of a mother's pregnancy to her child's 2nd birthday—set the stage for lifelong health, largely through nutritional inputs during pregnancy and infancy. Both for very poor families in the United States and in developing countries, under-nutrition is a significant risk, and the effects can be lifelong (1,000 Days Partnership, 2013).

Beyond the effects of nutritional inputs, all kinds of early experiences—with people, objects, language, interesting sights and sounds—can literally build the architecture of the developing brain, creating, shaping, and strengthening neural connections that in turn provide a foundation for later development and learning (National Scientific Council on the Developing Child, 2007).

Among all of these critically important experiences, the greatest influence on development is the relationship that Teresa, Trevor, and all babies and toddlers have with their families.

THE HEART OF BABY AND TODDLER DEVELOPMENT: RELATIONSHIPS WITHIN FAMILIES

Although there are disastrous exceptions, such as in the case of abandoned and orphaned children in Romania (Zeanah, Smyke, Koga, Carlson, & the BEIP Core Group, 2005), most children spend their early years as members of a loving family, like the family that will welcome Teresa and Trevor. These may be biological families, adoptive families, or extended families in which many people have close relationships with their youngest members. Babies usually bring out the best in grown-ups: We seem to be programmed to respond to them with delight and caring concern—playing games, encouraging them to try out new skills, spontaneously using "baby talk," and almost instinctively giving infants and toddlers what they need to thrive.

Yet many families find it difficult to establish and sustain growth-promoting relationships with their babies. Work pressures; the challenges of being a teen parent; the stress of poverty, family conflict; or the absence of an extended family network and other social supports—all of these stressors and others can create significant challenges. Most expectant and new parents need encouragement and lots of helpful tips as they move into this new phase of their family life. Many parents, like Ellen and Andy, will also need out-of-home care for their children at least part of the time. Some parents will also need specialized services, for example, if their baby has a disability.

These are large needs, and we are a long way from being able to meet them with the services that the majority of parents can find and afford. But let's take a look at what is currently available, and what the gaps or barriers may be.

SERVICES FOR FAMILIES AND CHILDREN BIRTH TO AGE 3

There are 12 million children under age 3 in the United States (Murphey, Cooper, & Forry, 2013). Whether or not parents of babies and toddlers are working outside the home, they need information and support. First we describe some services that support parents (or others such as grandparents or foster parents). Then we will look at services for the children themselves.

Caring for Parents

Even before their twins are born, Ellen and Andy are looking for information and support. Here we describe what *may* be available, although access is limited in some communities and for some groups of parents (we will discuss how to address those gaps later).

First, most communities do offer prenatal classes, often through physicians' offices or hospitals. These typically give information, not only about the physical care of babies, but also about the many other things that children may need to develop well. Once Ellen's and Andy's babies arrive, some encouragement, information, and support may be offered at the hospital, although most hospital stays these days are relatively brief.

If Trevor and Teresa arrive prematurely, however (as many twins do), they're likely to spend additional time in the hospital as they gain weight and their development is carefully monitored. Although this can be a scary time, it can give parents more opportunities to learn about early development. Help is generally available through specialized hospital staff in the neonatal intensive care unit and also from family-to-family groups, swapping tips and giving practical support.

It's one thing to learn about baby care in the hospital, it's another to be hit with reality when the new parents and baby come home. What help is available? One source of information for new parents like Ellen and Andy may be the health care providers to whom they take their babies for checkups. Of course, the value of this help will depend on whether those providers are prepared to discuss broad questions of child development, not just physical health. The training of pediatricians and pediatric nurse practitioners has traditionally focused on physical health, but it is becoming more holistic.

Young couples in the military often deal with a great deal of stress, and becoming a parent may create even more. The Department of Defense offers assistance through the New Parent Support Program, which helps expectant and new parents to nurture their babies while coping with their other challenges.

Whether they are military families or not, most American parents also like to gather printed or online information and resources. Early childhood professionals can help families gain access to these resources. Most state departments of education have websites with relevant materials. For example, the Massachusetts Department of Education has downloadable videos, brochures in many languages, and tips on topics such as sharing books with babies and toddlers, talking with an infant, and promoting children's health and well-being (Commonwealth of Massachusetts, 2013).

Finally, home visiting programs (Stoltzfus & Lynch, 2009) are a source of help for at least some new parents. The United States has not historically been a leader in providing home visiting programs compared to other countries: In many European countries (e.g., Denmark, Great Britain, Ireland, and the Netherlands), for example, almost all families of infants, regardless of income, routinely receive free visits from a public health nurse who offers social support as well as health education (Cawthorne & Arons, 2010). In the United States, although 40 states have home visiting programs, services are usually available only for families living in poverty or otherwise at risk. For many immigrant families, home visits by trained community members who share the family's language and culture may help reduce isolation and support the development of their babies and toddlers (Di Lauro, 2009). Home visiting is also a major component of Early Head Start programs. Looking to the future, many researchers and advocates recommend expanding successful home visiting models, with well-trained and well-supervised professionals, as part of a universal "system of care" for everyone with a young child (Astuto & Allen, 2009). Political support for expanding home visit programs appears to be growing, with recent proposals for increased funding of visits to new parents by nurses, social workers, and others.

New parents need lots of help to understand, enjoy, nurture, and stimulate the newest members of their family. This help may or may not be available, depending on where families live, what their income is, and how well-trained are the professionals with whom they interact. Whatever their situation, parents should not feel alone as they make this important transition.

Caring for Babies and Toddlers While Parents Work

About half of all children under age 3–6 million out of 12 million infants and toddlers–regularly spend time in some kind of child care program, with half of them spending 25 hours a week or more in out-of-home care (Lally, 2013; National Women's Law Center, 2013). Like many other parents, Ellen and Andy will need child care, because both of them will be returning to work shortly after the twins' birth. The challenges they will face would be fewer if they lived in most other countries: Compared with the 33 other relatively wealthy countries that are members of OECD (Organisation for Economic Co-operation and Development), the United States is the only one with no provision for paid parental leave to support working families (Damme, 2011; Heymann, Earle, & Hayes, 2007). The federal Family and Medical Leave Act does give parents time off after the birth of a child; however, that leave is not paid, and half of all working parents are not covered (Damme, 2011). So within a few months at most, Trevor and Teresa's parents will be faced with a set of difficult choices.

Types of Early Child Care

First, parents need to think about various forms of child care and which approach may be the best fit for them and their babies (Ehrle, Adams, & Tout, 2001). They have at least three options to consider.

Family, Friends, and Neighbor Care (FFN). Especially when their children are very young, most families that need child care rely on informal arrangements with grandparents or other relatives (an arrangement not possible for Ellen and Andy), a friend, or someone else in the neighborhood. Sometimes this care is provided in the child's own home and sometimes in the home of the relative or friend. This form of child care is usually called Family, Friends, and Neighbor Care (FFN) or, sometimes, Kith and Kin Care. Most of the time, parents do not pay for this care, as they consider the caregiver part of their extended family. One-third to one-half of all employed American families use FFN care, and it's the most common form of care among those with babies and toddlers (Susman-Stillman & Banghart, 2008).

Home-Based or Family Child Care. A second option is licensed family child care, a paid service provided to a small group of children by someone, not a relative, in the provider's own home. If Trevor and Teresa were in a family child care home, the group might include a few other babies and toddlers but also some preschool-age children—somewhat like siblings in a family. Before and after school hours, the group might also include some older children from the neighborhood.

Rather than enrolling their infant or toddler in a child care center, many parents of children this age (17% of those who are employed) prefer family child care homes (Morrissey & Banghart, 2007). One reason may be that parents see a family child care environment as more homelike. Activities might include folding laundry or a walk to the store or a visit to a neighborhood park, and parents may feel that the provider will know them and their child very well.

Child Care Centers. Ellen and Andy may also think about enrolling their twins in a licensed child care center. Twenty-two percent of children under age 3 attend centers as their primary child care arrangement, but the need for such care exceeds the supply. Not all centers provide care for infants and toddlers—in fact, there is a critical lack of such care, especially for infants (Lombardi, 2003; Murphey, Cooper, & Forry, 2013; Schumacher & Hoffman, 2008). Unlike family child care homes, centers generally divide the children into separate age groups, with children moving up to a different classroom as they get older, usually but not always with different teachers. Regulations vary by state, but include what the ratios of children to adults must be, health and safety requirements, staff qualifications, and requirements about what is provided in the program.

Whatever the age of the child, the cost of care is a big concern for families, as discussed in detail in the next chapter, and the highest cost is for infant-toddler care. Fees vary, however, and subsidies may be available for families with lower incomes.

It is important to know that families' child care arrangements often change considerably over time, complicating the process of making these arrangements, and often adding stress to families' lives. Many families cannot rely on only one child care arrangement, so the baby or toddler might spend part of the day or week with a relative, part in a center, and part with a neighbor. And as children get older, both their needs and the family's may change; parents more frequently use child care centers after children turn 2 or 3. Chapter 3 provides more detail on arrangements for older children.

THE EFFECT OF EARLY CHILDHOOD SERVICES ON THE DEVELOPMENT OF BABIES AND TODDLERS

Do early childhood services support babies' and toddlers' positive development? Or can these services actually be harmful? Or do they make any difference at all?

Because the services and the characteristics of children and their families vary so much, it's difficult to give a simple answer to these important questions.

Child Care Arrangements and Children's Development

Ellen and Andy, and other parents, should probably not worry too much about needing to enroll their very young children in some form of child care as long as the quality is good. A study that followed more than 1,300 children over many years (National Institute of Child Health and Development [NICHD] Early Child Care Research Network, 2002) showed that the average development of children who spent time in good-quality out-of-home care from an early age was not much different from children who stayed home. If children spent especially long hours in child care centers, however, there was some evidence of more aggressive behavior in the later preschool years, but not at a level of great concern. As shown in the following section, there can be significant benefits for the many infants, toddlers, and families who are at risk because of poverty or other difficult circumstances—again, as long as the services are of high quality.

The Special Benefits of High-Quality Services for Disadvantaged Babies and Toddlers

Most of the news on the positive side comes from studies of programs that have targeted low-income families living in poverty, whose children are especially vulnerable to delayed development, problem behaviors, maltreatment, and other concerns. Good services for infants and toddlers are especially important because almost half of all children under age 3 now live in low-income families, with 1 in 8 living in deep poverty (Murphey, Cooper, & Forry, 2013), and research demonstrates that the earlier programs start, the more effective they are. Below are two examples of interventions for low-income babies and toddlers and their families.

Nurse-Family Partnership. This home-visiting intervention brings trained nurses into the homes of vulnerable first-time mothers, often single teen parents, from pregnancy until their children turn 2. Building relationships and sharing information, the nurse home visitors aim to improve children's physical health and overall development, while strengthening families. Implemented in communities across the country for 30 years, the program served 20,000 families in 2014. Large-scale evaluations have consistently demonstrated improvements in prenatal health, improvements in children's cognitive and academic outcomes, fewer childhood injuries, and increased employment of mothers (Coalition for Evidence-Based Policy, 2012; Olds et al., 2007).

Early Head Start. Figure 2.1 describes the background and key components of Early Head Start (EHS), an intervention for low-income infants, toddlers, and their families. Early Head Start's impact on children and families was rigorously evaluated using a sample of sites around the country (Love, Chazan-Cohen, Raikes, & Brooks-Gunn, 2013). Some programs offered center-based services, some home-based, and some a combination. Most families enrolled when their children were under 1 year

Figure 2.1. Early Head Start: Comprehensive Services for Families Living in Poverty

Head Start, the U.S. government's program for low-income preschool children, has been around since the 1960s. But as researchers evaluated the program, early childhood advocates and policymakers realized that starting to intervene at age 3 (when Head Start began) could be too little, too late. Thus, in 1995, the government created Early Head Start to serve pregnant women and families with children under 3 living in poverty. These programs now exist in every state.

Early Head Start services are comprehensive, aiming to improve every aspect of children's development, empower and strengthen families, collaborate with and enhance community services, and develop skilled, caring staff. Services may be provided in one of three patterns: home-based (using trained Early Head Start home visitors), center-based, or a combination of both. As promising as this sounds, limited resources mean that less than 4% of eligible babies, toddlers, and their families are able to participate (National Women's Law Center, 2013; Schmit & Ewen, 2012), although 20 states are expanding access to Early Head Start.

old; children whose families that had enrolled in EHS services during pregnancy (about one-quarter of the families) had especially positive outcomes. When researchers assessed the children's development at ages 2 and 3, they found many positive effects on cognitive, language, and social-emotional development. And at age 5, children who had been in EHS continued to show better social and emotional outcomes (such as fewer behavior problems) and greater engagement in learning activities—although other language, cognitive, and academic benefits did not persist after children left EHS. Families enrolled in EHS were also more likely to support their children's language and literacy development through the preschool years.

The Problem: There Are Not Enough High-Quality Programs

The programs described above produce positive results, but their services have been well planned and implemented by well-trained staff with many resources. Only a small number of such services are available; research shows that there are not enough high-quality programs for infants and toddlers in the United States.

For example, a large study of child care centers conducted in the 1990s found that 90% of programs serving infants and toddlers were observed to be less than good quality (Cost, Quality, and Child Outcomes Study Team, 1995). Researchers in a similar study focusing on family child care programs rated only 9% of them as good—and 35% were deemed inadequate to support positive development and learning (Howes, Galinsky, Kontos, & Shinn, 1995). As far as FFN care is concerned, quality is difficult to study because such services are not regulated, and the concept and measurement of quality may differ from other child care settings (Susman-Stillman & Banghart, 2011). Although different studies have come up with different ratings, one thing is clear: On the whole, child care quality is poor (Halle, Anderson, Blasberg, Chrisler, & Simkin, 2011), and it is poorest in programs serving children under age 3. Children from low-income families and ethnic minority children tend to be enrolled in the lowest-quality programs (Morrissey & Banghart, 2007), unless they are among the few able to attend Early Head Start.

PROFESSIONAL PROFILE

Margo Okapal, Lead Infant-Toddler Teacher, Early Head Start, Tulsa, Oklahoma

Planning is a central part of Margo's work. Lesson plans are due every Wednesday for the following week. Margo has to integrate every area of infant-toddler development and learning and specify how to individualize in response to each child's interests and needs in her lesson plans. She does home visits to find out more about these individual characteristics and has meetings with other team members, including the program's Instructional Coach, about activities and classroom management issues. This week, Margo talked with several behavior and mental health specialists who help staff meet the needs of the four toddlers who have disabilities. Developmental assessment is another key part of Margo's work in Early Head Start. Earlier in the year, screening was conducted using the Ages and Stages Questionnaire (ASQ) (Squires & Bricker, 2009) to identify potential difficulties, and now she and the team will refer several children for further mental health evaluation on the basis of the ASQ results. Margo collaborates with the specialists to use the ASQ and other assessment findings to ensure that the program meets each child's learning and development needs.

After earning an associate's degree in art, Margo Okapal found her passion to work with young children while raising her own children and volunteering in Head Start. As a returning adult student, she pursued her bachelor's degree and teacher certification in ECE at the University of Oklahoma, at the same time working as a lab school infant-toddler teacher and supervising college students.

INITIATIVES TO IMPROVE THE QUALITY
OF SERVICES FOR BABIES AND TODDLERS

These discouraging statistics have prompted action by individuals, states, and federal agencies. Many efforts are under way to improve the quality of infant-toddler care, whether it is provided in homes or centers.

As highlighted in Figure 2.2, adults' caregiving behavior is at the heart of quality, and is the focus of most quality improvement efforts. Below are a few examples of quality improvement efforts; keep in mind that the scale of most of these innovations is small, and that more research is needed to see how effective they may be.

Staffed Family Child Care Networks

One of the difficulties for a family child care (FCC) provider is isolation. Unlike a person working in a child care center with many colleagues, an individual providing care in his or her own home works alone, or perhaps with one assistant. Opportunities to learn new skills are few, and no funds are available to attend conferences or other professional development events–and, of course, there is no one to care for the children in the family child care provider's absence. Research shows that providers who are part of a support group, such as a family child care network, offer higher-quality infant-toddler care (Zero to Three, 2012).

Figure 2.2. What Do Caregivers Do in Quality Programs for Babies and Toddlers?

Of course, young children need to be kept safe, healthy, and well-nourished. Beyond that, research emphasizes these quality features of the interactions between adults and the babies and toddlers they care for:

- Respond sensitively to children's needs and behavior
- Stimulate children's language and cognitive development
- Have warm relationships and positive feelings about the children
- Guide their behavior in positive ways
- Help them interact with other children in positive ways
- Avoid being detached, intrusive, or negative in interactions with the children

Source: Halle, Anderson, Blasberg, Chrisler, & Simkin, 2011.

Staffed FCC networks are designed to help, enhancing quality by supporting those who provide family child care. Twenty-two states have at least one such network, although many of these networks serve only a small geographical area. Often the networks are part of a child care resource and referral agency. Specially trained, paid coordinators may visit the homes in the network, giving one-on-one guidance and feedback within a supportive relationship. Research suggests that for these networks to be successful, it is important that the coordinator have experience with very young children and that the coordinator visit the family child care provider at least once a month (Bromer, Van Haitsma, Daley, et al., 2009; Zero to Three, 2012).

Home Visiting Partnerships with Family, Friend, and Neighbor Caregivers

Earlier in this chapter we looked at how home visiting programs can support new parents—programs such as the Nurse-Family partnership or the home visiting component of Early Head Start. Yet many babies and toddlers are not in their own homes for most of the day; instead, they are being cared for by relatives, friends, or neighbors while their parents are at work. Recently, creative thinking has gone into developing a "Home Away from Home" tool kit to help states, early childhood organizations, and others use home-visiting services to reach out to children in FFN care (Johnson-Staub & Schmit, 2012). Some of these programs can also help FFN caregivers join informal playgroups, reducing caregivers' isolation and giving the babies, toddlers, and older preschoolers some new, stimulating experiences. Other promising initiatives to improve the quality of FFN care are now being implemented; a recent literature review summarizes the emerging evidence of their effectiveness (Weber, 2013).

State Initiatives to Improve Quality in Child Care Centers

As summarized by Schulman (2011), a number of states have created new ways to improve both the availability of infant-toddler care and the quality of that care. For example, Utah's Baby Steps project gives centers grants to begin the process of quality improvement, with additional funds provided if the program meets annual goals for improvement, including training infant-toddler staff. Similarly, the District of Columbia helps child care providers start up or expand infant-toddler services and gives them technical assistance as they do so. A number of other states are helping teachers obtain specialized training in infant-toddler care, including higher education courses and certificates. New Hampshire gives full tuition assistance to those who are taking an infant-toddler course at a state college or university.

PROFESSIONALS IN THE INFANT-TODDLER FIELD: MANY ROLES, MANY PATHWAYS

Even more than in other areas of early care and education, the infant-toddler field offers multiple roles and pathways to service and leadership, and new professionals in this field are urgently needed. The emerging practices and policy innovations discussed above suggest new career paths for those interested in working in this sector.

Supporting Families

One career option is supporting families of babies and toddlers, whether through prenatal and newborn support, parenting education, or home visiting. Preparation for these roles is varied; some home visitors, for example, have a nursing background, while others have specialized child-development training, with a focus on the first 3 years. Another pathway might be to become a developer of resources for parents, ranging from brochures to websites to videos.

Working with Babies and Toddlers in Early Childhood Programs

Early childhood professionals may work directly with babies and toddlers in family child care homes or in child care centers, including Early Head Start programs. These professionals need specialized preparation to respond to the unique developmental and learning needs of the very young, in partnership with families and with respect for their cultures and preferences.

Providing Professional Development

Another career pathway, coming almost always after gaining firsthand experience with children, is to help infant-toddler caregivers become more skilled in their work. Providing professional development—whether as a coach, mentor, or trainer, or as a faculty member in a college or university—is a key role in improving quality of care.

Despite the urgent need for quality care and interventions for children 0–3 and their families, early childhood degree programs often fail to provide in-depth, multidisciplinary knowledge, skills, and supervised practice. In its latest position statement on standards for early childhood professional preparation, NAEYC (2009) points out the "tendency for teacher education programs to give inadequate attention to children's critical early years, especially the birth-to-age-3 period" (p. 6). The result is that graduates may not effectively support babies' and toddlers' development because the curriculum and teaching strategies they were taught to use are more effective with

---

PROFESSIONAL PROFILE

Diane Horm, University of Oklahoma at Tulsa, George Kaiser Family Foundation Endowed Chair of Early Childhood Education, and Founding Director of the Early Childhood Education Institute (ECEI)

Diane currently wears two hats: college professor and early childhood researcher. Mondays usually include work with the ECEI's leadership team to plan and monitor their applied research initiatives conducted with community agencies serving young children, birth to age 4, and their families. Tuesdays are typically teaching days, with Diane preparing lectures and class activities, as well as evaluating and communicating with her undergraduate and graduate students. Wednesdays and Thursdays typically include meetings with the ECEI's research teams and external partners to discuss research findings and their practical implications. Fridays are often filled with department-, college-, and university-level meetings in which Diane and her colleagues discuss enhancing infant-toddler content within the university's early childhood academic programs. Throughout the week, Diane devotes considerable time to the development of a new, exciting project—the IT3 (Infants, Toddlers, Twos, and Threes) Research Center—which aims to understand and inform very young children's development and learning within early care and education settings through research, dissemination, and application.

Diane Horm began her career as a school psychologist in a public school system and returned to graduate school to learn more about early development and learning, especially for children living in poverty. Since earning her Ph.D., she has held faculty, administrative, and research positions, including 15 years as the director of a university-affiliated child development center.

---

older children. This situation may be changing for the better, with some higher education programs now offering infant-toddler specializations or certificates, and with some states creating incentives to improve professional development opportunities (National Infant and Toddler Child Care Initiative, 2010).

CONCLUDING THOUGHTS:
THE JOYS AND CHALLENGES OF SUPPORTING BABIES AND TODDLERS

The first 3 years of life are uniquely important. Early developments in children's bodies, brains, and spirits can have a lasting impact. It is both exhausting and exhilarating to be the parent of a baby or a toddler. Those who work with children from birth to 3 feel a similar mix of exhaustion and exhilaration as they work hard to enhance children's progress and provide children and their families with encouragement and support.

Putting these personal feelings into a broader context, this chapter draws an often-discouraging picture of the current situation in the United States for babies, toddlers, and their families. We have shown that services for these youngest of our young children remain limited, with high costs and low quality compounding the stress for parents who need out-of-home care. Innovative approaches to early intervention, especially for the poorest and most vulnerable children, still reach only a tiny fraction of those in need of such supports.

As our title states, indeed the early years matter, and the time from birth to age 3 may matter most. As emphasized in a recent Child Trends statistical report (*The Youngest Americans*) on infants and toddlers in the United States, "there are compelling reasons to focus on our youngest children. This period provides a foundation, increasingly resistant to alteration, for much of subsequent health, learning, emotional expression, and social relationships; and, accordingly, it is the time when, for many interventions, the 'return on investment' is greatest" (Murphey, Cooper, & Forry, 2013, p. 102).

Those who want to contribute to this foundation have many exciting opportunities, whether as an infant-toddler child care teacher, administrator, researcher, professional development specialist, or policymaker. Thanks to a rapidly expanding body of child-development research, we know an enormous amount about how babies and toddlers develop, and what they need to lead toward positive outcomes. That is good news. Currently, however, most of our programs and policies fail to put that knowledge into practice.

Our society needs a renewed sense of collective responsibility and commitment to children from birth to age 3. In the words of Child Trends' report, "Every baby is a new beginning—an invitation to reimagine what it means to be human, to be in relationship, to guide and to be guided. That is the promise of the youngest Americans, and the challenge to the rest of us" (Murphey, Cooper, & Forry, 2013, p. 103).

Trevor, Teresa, and 12 million babies, toddlers, and their families are waiting!

REFLECTION, DIALOGUE, AND ACTION

1. Do you know a parent of an infant or toddler (or perhaps you are a parent yourself)? Explore some of the issues discussed in this chapter—support for new parents, child care decisions, quality concerns—and share with others.

2. Identify an early childhood professional in your community who works with infants and toddlers or with their families. Interview this person about his or her work, and share your insights with others. Or, if this is the focus of your own work, describe your work to others.

3. Search Research Connections, www.researchconnections.org, for recent "Fact Sheets and Briefs" using the search term "infants and toddlers"—or, if you have a specific interest, use terms such as FFN Care, Family Child Care, or Early Head Start. You might team up with a classmate or coworker. Look at the brief descriptions of some of these reports, download a few, read, and share.

4. What is your state doing to improve the quality of care for babies and toddlers? Again, use Research Connections as a source, in this case filtering your search by state.

INFORMATION TO EXPLORE AND SHARE

Zero to Three

A nonprofit organization that aims to promote the health and development of infants and toddlers. Publications, podcasts for parents, policy briefs, e-newsletters, other resources for families, practitioners, policymakers. Zero to Three also houses the Early Head Start National Resource Center. www.zerotothree.org

Center on the Developing Child at Harvard University

The Center has played a key role in creating clear messages and resources about early brain development and the role of early experiences in later development. www.developing-child.harvard.edu

Program for Infant Toddler Caregivers

Helps infant-toddler teachers develop loving relationships; provide responsive, stimulating care; and partner with families. PITC videos, guides, manuals, and training programs are widely used. www.pitc.org

New Parent Support Program

Helps military families, who are often under considerable stress, to develop skills that will create a nurturing environment for their infants and toddlers. www.militaryonesource.mil/parenting?content_id=26661

CHAPTER 3

The Early Years Matter for Preschoolers

© Marko Tomicic

BREE'S STORY

Bree is the youngest of three girls living in suburban Albany, New York. Her older sisters are 6 and 8; Bree is a small but feisty child who is about to turn 4. Her parents are both employed by the state government, Randy as a social worker and Joy as an accountant, and they live a comfortable middle-class life in many respects, or they did before putting three children in child care, preschool, and after-school programs. They adore their children but are relieved to be almost finished with the early childhood years because of the burden it has put on their pocketbook. Paying for child care and after-school programs for three children on their modest salaries has been a painful stretch.

   Bree, smart and a bit of a clown, is excited to start at "the big kids' school." The neighborhood elementary school opened a free pre-K classroom. However, Bree's placement in the new classroom depended on their luck with a lottery system, since the class only has 18 openings. Randy and Joy just found out Bree did not get a spot. Before telling her, they want to decide on their "plan B."

They consider Romp'n'Roll Academy, the child care center their other daughters attended, which they found only okay—the staff were nice but they did not seem to know any more than Joy and Randy about child development. Also, the program ends at 3 p.m., and both parents work full-time. From a colleague Randy learned of a good private program near his downtown office, but that would mean Bree would be away from home from 7 a.m. to 7 p.m. every day to commute with her dad, and they did not like that idea. Ms. Nina's small, private art-and-nature program is only five blocks away, but it would be a costly $1,400 a month.

As an imperfect but creative solution, they consider rearranging their schedules. Joy's supportive boss agreed to let Joy work from 6 a.m. to 2:30 p.m. each day, meaning that Randy can feed, dress, and transport the girls in the morning, and Joy can pick up Bree at 3 p.m., then meet the other two at the bus stop at 3:20. They will enroll Bree at Romp'n'Roll, and keep their fingers crossed for getting lucky with pre-K next semester. When they tell Bree, she is excited to start "school" and happy knowing she can be home with Mom every afternoon.

THE PRESCHOOL OPTIONS

Randy and Joy struggled with the issues of location, transportation, quality, and cost that almost every U. S. family with young children has to think about. Because there are many funding sources and administrators for preschools in America, the early childhood education system is not exactly a *system*, but more like a disorganized patchwork quilt, with pieces added here and there of various colors and designs, and each added by a different source—federal and state governments, private corporations, nonprofits and faith-based institutions, and individuals. In Chapter 2 we considered what is available for babies and toddlers; this chapter considers what is available for preschool-age children.

Types of Care

There are 7.6 million 3- and 4-year-olds in the United States, and the majority of them have working parents who need child care coverage (Laughlin, 2013). The options for preschoolers are similar to those for infants and toddlers. National census data for 3- and 4-year-olds show the following patterns (Laughlin, 2013):

- *Family, Friend, and Neighbor (FFN) or Kith and Kin Care:* Grandparents, older siblings, aunts and uncles, cousins, and friends who are part of the extended-family network are an important source of care when parents work. Over 71% of preschoolers of employed mothers spend at least some time with a relative as part of the family's child care arrangement; 20% of preschoolers of non-employed mothers are in relative care on a regular basis.
- *Home-Based Child Care (sometimes called family child care or family day care):* About 15% of preschoolers of employed mothers and 4% of preschoolers of non-employed mother receive care from a non-relative in someone's home.

- *Child Care Center:* This category includes various types of licensed group programs usually held somewhere other than a home, such as in a stand-alone building or privately owned space, on school grounds, in a section of an office building, or at a house of worship. Center-based programs include preschools, prekindergarten classrooms, day care centers, or Head Start programs. About half (51%) of preschoolers with an employed mother, like Bree, go to center-based care, and about 26% of preschoolers of non-employed mothers go to a center-based program some hours a week.

The percentages in the above list add up to more than 100%. This is because many families use multiple types of care, trying to wrap around the edges of the day to provide coverage for the hours of care needed. The Census Bureau reports that 27% of families with employed mothers and 9% with non-employed mothers use at least two types of care; and 14% of families with employed mothers and 69% of families with non-employed mothers have no regular child care arrangement (Laughlin, 2013). This does not mean that no one takes care of the child, but rather that the family has no stable arrangement.

Some parents prefer to keep their children at home in the early years, but most want their child to be in a preschool program, either because they need care while they work, they want the benefits of preschool for their child, or both. Families' decisions and opportunities vary depending on programs in their area, their needs and preferences for out-of-home care, whether relatives can help, and logistical factors such as location, hours, and age groups served. For Bree's family and others, another major factor is cost.

THE DIFFERENCE BETWEEN *PRESCHOOL* AND *PRE-K*

Preschool could describe any program for children before kindergarten, usually designed for 3- to 5-year-olds. These programs may be open anywhere from a few hours a day to 9 hours or more. Preschools are located in community centers, homes, churches and mosques, office buildings, and elementary schools. They may be funded by for-profits, non-profits, private individuals, school districts, faith-based organizations, community-based organizations, cities, states, or the federal government in the case of Head Start. Families generally pay for preschool, except in the case of Head Start or some state-supported pre-K. Other terms used in similar ways include nursery school, day care, child care, preprimary, and prekindergarten.

Pre-K is often used to describe *public* programs, meaning run by the local school district using government funds and typically involving no fees for families. In many cases, pre-K programs are targeted to children in low-income families. Cities and states use different sources for the funding, such as school funding formulas, lottery revenues, "sin taxes" on cigarettes or tobacco, and public-private partnerships. The programs usually are located on the grounds of an elementary school, although occasionally they are located with a Head Start or community-based program. Pre-K programs are one type of preschool program, which is the broader term.

The Options Depend on What Families Can Afford

Child care is not cheap, nor should it be necessarily. Having well-trained and adequately paid professionals, ensuring high-quality materials and spaces, and providing comprehensive services—inputs that correlate with good child outcomes—takes money. The burden of paying for preschool typically lands on families in the United States. Head Start and some public pre-K programs are free but usually only serve families living under the poverty line (see Chapter 5). In 2011, on average, center-based programs for 4-year-olds cost $3,900 per year in Mississippi and $11,700 per year in Massachusetts, and home-based care ranged from $4,100 in South Carolina to $9,600 in New York. These costs may not reflect families' full costs when before- or after-school care is factored in. This "wrap-around care," as it is sometimes called, ranges from $1,800 to $11,000 per year (Child Care Aware, 2013a).

One might think that the more money parents make, the more likely they are to be able to afford preschool, but that is not always the case. It is true that families earning a great deal of money—say, more than $60,000 a year—are more likely than others to send their child to preschool (77% or more use preschool). However, families earning about $25,000 a year are half as likely to send their 3-year-old to preschool (20%) than families earning less than $10,000 (42%) (Child Care Aware, 2013a). This is because a family must be considered truly *poor* in order to qualify for subsidized programs such as Head Start. This leaves many working-poor and low-income families—those for whom early childhood programs have the biggest impact—at a big disadvantage.

No matter what their income level, most American families feel weighed down by the costs of early care and education. The costs are one reason that there is much discussion nowadays about whether states should provide a year of preschool education to all families who want it.

CHOOSING A PROGRAM: THE QUALITY ISSUE

One of the struggles parents face is how to know if a program that seems good actually is. If there are a couple of options in their neighborhood, how do they know which one will be the best place for their child to grow, have fun, learn, and make friends? Parents often have to rely on intuition—they decide on a place if it *feels* like a good fit for their family—or on word-of-mouth from neighbors. Likewise, ECE professionals want to know whether they are taking a job in a high-quality, well-run program. There is no single system in the United States that gauges quality of ECE programs—those for preschoolers as well as for babies and toddlers like those described in Chapter 2—but below are some examples of ways to determine quality:

- The National Association for the Education of Young Children (NAEYC) runs a national, though voluntary, accreditation system. It evaluates preschools and other ECE settings to see if they meet the standards for high-quality programs, meaning they have knowledgeable and caring teachers and a safe and engaging environment, use a developmentally appropriate curriculum and assessment techniques, involve families, and so forth. Programs either are or are not accredited, depending on careful reviews and observations from ECE professionals not related to the program. Accredited programs are given a "stamp of approval."

- Some states monitor the quality of early childhood programs using a Quality Rating and Improvement System (QRIS). States began using QRISs in the 1990s as a way to recognize and encourage high-quality programs. Similar to rating systems for restaurants and hotels, the QRIS assesses and communicates quality to potential customers—the parents—and supports programs' quality improvement efforts. As of February, 2014, 37 states and the District of Columbia had implemented a QRIS (QRIS National Learning Network, 2014).

- One observation tool schools and programs can use to measure caregiving quality is the Classroom Assessment Scoring System (CLASS), which provides feedback on teaching and adult-child interactions (Pianta & Hamre, 2009). Head Start, states, and local programs use the tool for their own purposes, such as to support teachers' professional development needs, set schoolwide goals, and shape systemwide reform at various levels. The tool can be used in elementary school classrooms, kindergartens, preschools, and infant-toddler programs.

These and other quality rating efforts help administrators and teachers know what they need to do to improve, and the ratings also help parents gain an objective sense of how good a program is. The news is not usually great; as suggested previously, studies show that the quality of caregiving in American early care and education programs is generally mediocre, with low quality found even in some accredited programs. A national study conducted by leading scholars and the National Institute of Child Health and Human Development (NICHD) found that only 6% of programs provide excellent caregiving; the rest are only so-so or not good (NICHD ECCRN, 2006).

THE EFFECT OF HIGH-QUALITY SERVICES ON THE DEVELOPMENT OF PRESCHOOLERS

If parents have complete freedom to choose whether to stay home or work (which they mostly do not), is it a good idea to enroll a preschooler in child care? It depends. Because the early care and education system in the United States is not very organized or consistent, one child can have a vastly different experience than another. For example, Bree's experience in Romp'n'Roll Academy may be very different from that of the child down the street who got into the pre-K program, or a friend who spends three mornings a week with a neighbor and her son. And they will have different experiences than the girl who spends 40 hours a week at Head Start or the boy who goes to a Montessori-inspired center.

It is impossible to say which of these programs will lead to better child outcomes than the others simply by type of program or setting. What matters is the *quality* of the program. High-quality programs lead to improvements in children's development in all domains, and this is true for middle-class as well as disadvantaged children. The following findings come primarily from two sets of studies: (1) the NICHD Study of Early Child Care and Youth Development, which followed over 1,300 children from before birth until 9th grade (see NICHD ECCRN, 2006); and (2) recent evaluations of urban prekindergarten programs in Tulsa and Boston.

Cognition and Language

The first thing people often think of when asked about school readiness is, does the child know the ABCs? Knowing the letters of the alphabet is a part of the cognitive domain, which also includes thinking skills, attention, memory, vocabulary, problem solving, mathematics, reasoning, and learning strategies.

After 1 to 2 years of developmentally appropriate, high-quality, center-based preschool, children, regardless of family background, have improved language, literacy, and mathematics skills to a level that is equal to about one-third of a year of additional learning above and beyond what would have occurred without preschool. These results are robust and have been replicated across dozens of rigorous studies, including a meta-analysis of 84 studies (Camilli, Vargas, Ryan, & Barnett, 2010). The Tulsa and Boston pre-K studies showed even stronger effects, equal to about half to one full year of additional learning (Weiland & Yoshikawa, 2013).

The NICHD Early Child Care Research Network (NICHD ECCRN, 2002) and others confirm that cognition and language gains depend on program quality. Children who go to high-quality programs, regardless of type, setting, or hours of care, have better cognitive and language outcomes than other children—although children in center-based care show the greatest benefits. In other words, preschoolers in good programs do learn "pre-academic" math and literacy skills that help them be ready for school—and a much broader array of critical skills, like paying attention, increasing vocabulary, and learning to plan and problem-solve.

These positive effects last beyond kindergarten and persist at least into the teenage years (Vandell et al., 2010). That is, good preschool has long-lasting benefits for all children, whether they are from poor, middle-class, or affluent families, although benefits are biggest for children from low-income families (see Chapter 5).

There are potentially tremendous gains in cognitive development if a 3- or 4-year-old has at least one full year of good preschool. And adding a second year of preschool leads to added benefits—although not always at such a high level as the first year, perhaps because children's knowledge and skills build sequentially on what has already been learned (Yoshikawa et al., 2013). In short, for maximum growth in development and learning, children benefit from at least a year or two of high-quality preschool experience.

Getting Along with Others: Social Skills

Many parents want their children to go to preschool to "socialize them," or have them learn to get along with others. The data are not as clear in this domain as in cognitive and achievement areas, in part because fewer studies of general programs have looked at social outcomes, and in part because the measures are more varied in content and quality. However, the overall finding is that children in high-quality programs do improve their social skills; children practice sharing, learn to wait and follow rules, use words to communicate needs and play with others, become more empathic, and make friends with children with different skin colors, accents, home environments, and food preferences.

The NICHD study found that children in high-quality programs were more likely to be cooperative and compliant, less disobedient, and better able to play with peers than other children (NICHD Early Child Care Research Network, 2006). In addition, compared to non-participants, children in the Tulsa pre-K had lower levels of timidity and higher levels of attentiveness, suggesting more engagement in the classroom (there were no differences in aggression or hyperactivity levels) (Gormley, Phillips, Newmark, Welti, & Adelstein, 2011). Grade-school teachers often say they can tell which children went to preschool based on their social skills.

Very long days in child care may not be ideal for children, though. Some research shows that even when quality of care is good, by age 4½, children who spend long days every day at a child care center are somewhat less cooperative and more disobedient than other children, according to teachers (Belsky, 2002). The behavior problems are not extreme, and the children's parents do not usually see problems at home. However, long hours in center care may be stressful for 3- and 4-year-olds. Good teachers can counteract the stress with calm, predictable environments and intentionally teaching social skills (see Chapter 8).

Keeping Children Healthy

Some parents understandably worry that children will get sick when exposed to many other young children. Children in regular care arrangements with more than six children may be more likely to have ear infections, stomach illnesses, and upper respiratory infections than children in smaller groups. However, exposure to minor illnesses increases immunity, and preschoolers seem to become less susceptible over time. Children who were in large-group care at age 2 or 3 were found to be less likely than others to get a cough or stomach illness later in preschool (NICHD ECCRN, 2003a). Programs directly targeting health outcomes, typically for low-income children in particular, show increased immunization rates, reduced child mortality, increased access to dental care, and better health screening for whooping cough, respiratory illnesses, diabetes, and other child health concerns (Currie & Thomas, 1995).

Parents Still Matter Most

In some ways, Bree's mother, Joy, regrets having to send Bree to *any* child care program; she likes her job well enough but worries that a great preschool teacher will make her youngest feel less attached to her. Alternatively, Joy worries that a bad teacher will discourage her daughter and start her down a negative path. Teachers can emphatically reassure parents that no matter what happens in preschool, what happens at home is even more important. Even if children spend many hours in child care, most of them continue to have close bonds with their parents, and the power of parents' attention, conversation, activities with the child, and role modeling is generally far stronger than anything a teacher does or does not do. Bree will likely be just as attached to her mother and father as before, no matter how much time she spends in preschool (NICHD ECCRN, 2003b).

In sum, the NICHD study team and other researchers tell us that high-quality preschool not only causes no harm, but actually helps children from all different backgrounds develop well in all different domains. So why are school districts and states not investing more in preschool?

QUESTIONS ABOUT PUBLIC PRESCHOOL
THAT DECISION-MAKERS FIND HARD TO ANSWER

For whom and by whom should preschool-age services be provided? When, where, and for how long is ECE a good idea? What should the focus of instruction be, and how much structure should there be? These types of questions, discussed in depth in a book called *The Pre-K Debates* (Zigler, Gilliam, & Barnett, 2011), are especially important for state and school-district policymakers who must decide whether and how many taxpayer dollars should go toward preschool. Increasing public funds for education the year before kindergarten increases the number of children who can participate, the quality of programs, or both. Many researchers, educators, and parents believe this year of schooling should be free and available to all families who want it because there is so much evidence that it helps children succeed in school.

Among 4-year-olds in 2012, 28% attended a state pre-K, 11% attended Head Start, and 3% received other state-funded special education support; the remaining 58% attended a private program or no program (Barnett, Carolan, Fitzgerald, & Squires, 2012). Over the last decade, enrollment rates in public programs have increased, and most families served are poor or low-income. However, since the 2008 recession, there have been lower levels of spending for each child. In 2002, states on average spent $5,020 per year for each child in pre-K; in 2012, states spent $3,841 for each child (Barnett, Carolan, Fitzgerald, & Squires, 2012). Enrollment rates in public programs did not increase for 2011–2012, the last year for which data are available, an unfortunate historic first.

For All Families or Those Who Can't Afford It?

Policymakers have to decide whether to provide pre-K for all families who want it (universal) or only for low-income families (targeted). Some people feel that more affluent families should pay out of their own pockets, saving public dollars. On the one hand, there is abundant research showing the greatest benefits from ECE, including economic benefits to society, are for those children whose parents cannot afford it (see Chapter 5). On the other hand, early care and education is beneficial for all children and most American families are middle-class families who need child care coverage in order to work. When public dollars are limited, there can be a trade-off between opening more programs that are not necessarily great or having fewer programs (serving fewer children), but making them excellent programs. One possible solution is to provide public pre-K on a sliding-scale fee system; those who earn more pay more, while those earning less pay little or nothing.

Who Should Be Eligible to Educate Preschoolers?

In recent years there have been efforts to recognize the complexity and professionalism needed by requiring preschool teachers to have college degrees. Do children learn more if their teachers have degrees? The research is mixed (Early et al., 2007). Nonetheless, Head Start now requires 50% of lead teachers to have a bachelor's degree, and all other teachers and teacher aides to have an associate's degree (57% of lead teachers have a bachelor's). In 2012, 58% of state pre-Ks required the lead teacher to have a bachelor's degree (Carolan, 2013).

Implementing degree requirements poses some problems. In some areas, no colleges offer early childhood education degrees; college programs that do offer an early childhood degree do not always do a good job of preparing teachers (Burchinal, Hyson, & Zaslow, 2011); current professionals may not be able to take time off to go back to school or cannot afford it; and preschools sometimes have a hard time keeping teachers with degrees, who can often make more money teaching in public schools.

Research can help policymakers as they make decisions that will impact education and jobs in their communities. First, college-level programs should have a greater emphasis on field experiences and courses that help teachers learn specific, effective practices such as skilled interactions with young children. Second, even a great college degree is not enough: equally important is *ongoing* professional development (Pianta, 2011). Third, better wages and working conditions are likely to help preschools keep highly competent teachers (Hyson, Horm, & Winton, 2012).

Where Should Public Pre-K Operate?

Most pre-K programs (68%) are physically located in the building or on the grounds of a public elementary school (Gilliam, 2008). This location has advantages: Children and parents can easily get there and become familiar with the school; professionals can more easily align curriculum, teaching approaches, transition into kindergarten, and professional development activities of pre-K and elementary teachers, with benefits discussed further in Chapter 4. The rest of pre-K programs take place in other settings, such as in Head Start programs, private child care centers, and

---

PROFESSIONAL PROFILE

Lindy Buch, Director of Early Childhood Education and Family Services,
Office of Great Start, Michigan Department of Education

As is typical for many in similar positions, Lindy's recent week was full of meetings—sometimes six to eight in a day. Between meetings, she wrote and edited a variety of documents related to standards, grant guidance, grant applications, and presentations. Email messages flew back and forth. Monday started with a Leadership Team meeting in the department, bringing together managers of all the initiatives related to the development and learning of children and youth from birth through high school graduation. Tuesday was "internal meeting day," when Lindy met with the different teams under her leadership who manage early education initiatives, out-of-school time grants, and other projects. Later in the week she walked across the state campus to meet with managers in other state departments, and drove to a meeting with local early childhood administrators from around the state. A conference call with her colleagues in similar positions in other states allowed for sharing of solutions to common problems. The end of the week found her presenting to early childhood practitioners on revised early learning expectations at a statewide conference.

Lindy Buch began her career as a preschool and preschool special education teacher. She taught in local colleges before returning to graduate school to earn a Ph.D. in early childhood education and developmental psychology. After spending time as a university administrator, she has worked almost 2 decades as an early childhood specialist at the Michigan Department of Education.

faith-based settings (Gilliam, 2008). Advocates of the latter approach (that is, providing pre-K in various venues) cheer that diversity of settings, which they say can better reflect the unique dimensions and desires of each community, including diversity in languages and cultures. Nonetheless, experts overall see public schools as a good hub for providing most pre-K programs, with diverse settings welcome as long as programs exist under the leadership of a department of education or similar agency (McCartney, Burchinal, & Grindal, 2011).

How policymakers answer these questions influences early childhood professionals' hours, locations, compensation, training requirements, and collaboration opportunities, all essential to doing a great job for children.

HOW PRESCHOOL PROFESSIONALS MAKE A DIFFERENCE

As we have shown, children develop better in high-quality early education programs, and the quality of teachers largely determines the quality of the program. Teachers who are informed, intentional, and able to individualize their interactions help preschoolers and, just as importantly, parents of preschoolers. How do they do that?

Supporting Children

Providing Positive Caregiving. Good preschool teachers are sensitive, encouraging, and have frequent interactions with each child. More specifically, positive caregiving includes the following behaviors:

- *Showing a positive attitude*–being in good spirits, being helpful, smiling often.
- *Having positive physical contact*–hugging children, patting them on the back or holding hands, comforting children.
- *Responding to vocalizations*–commenting on what children say and answering questions.
- *Asking questions*–encouraging communication by asking questions at the appropriate level for the child.
- *Praising and encouraging children*–responding to success or positive actions with recognition and support, such as "You did it!"
- *Teaching*–encouraging the child to name objects or shapes, explaining the meaning of new words, using children's areas of interest to promote new information or ideas, and scaffolding learning to help a child reach a slightly higher level of understanding and skills.
- *Telling stories, singing songs, and reading*–children love stories and songs, which enrich their vocabularies, improve working memory, communicate values, add to world knowledge, and increase math and literacy skills.
- *Advancing behavior*–encouraging children to play with other children, practicing sharing, giving examples of good behavior, increasing compassion, and enforcing rule-following and logical consequences for problem behaviors.
- *Eliminating negative interactions*–being positive, not negative, in interactions with each child; taking a positive approach with each child, even when a child is "in trouble"; and interacting with and not ignoring children (NICHD ECCRN, 2006, p. 10).

Increasing School Readiness Skills. Good preschool programs help children learn their letters and numbers, grasp basic concepts in science and social studies, and start to love reading, music, movement, and art. By implementing high-quality curriculum and adapting it to individual needs, professionals help children learn to pay attention, ask questions and explore answers, uncover new ideas and interests, and generally start to see themselves as interesting people and interested learners. Preschool professionals open the door to children's learning and love of learning.

Focusing on the Whole Child. School readiness includes but is more than academic skills. While experts agree that skills in mathematics, language and literacy, and attention levels are the strongest indicators of later academic achievement, experts also emphatically note that domains of learning are closely intertwined in the early years: Children's social and emotional skills and their positive approaches to learning (Hyson, 2008) provide a secure base for academic competence. Children learn best when all their needs are met. Good preschool teachers help children become interested, engaged, self-controlled, connected to other people, and mentally stimulated. Then they are able to learn the academic content needed for kindergarten.

Balancing Instruction and Play. Readers of this book who are already familiar with early childhood education may know that children learn best with developmentally appropriate approaches that allow them to learn through play. On the other hand, some teachers take the idea of free play too far, allowing children to spend all their time in free play without providing the helpful teacher input that takes a child to the next level of learning. The false dichotomy of learning *or* playing is outdated. Good early childhood educators balance teacher-initiated instruction and child-initiated learning through play (Epstein, 2014); in particular, they use children's play to increase their knowledge, provide specific content knowledge, and build on what a given child finds meaningful and interesting.

Recognizing and Responding to Problems. For reasons beyond a teacher's control, some children will have problems in the program. Some children are exceedingly shy, unused to interacting with peers, not able to communicate well, show emerging signs of developmental delays or special needs, or bring challenging and noncompliant behaviors to the classroom (see Chapter 8). How well the preschool teacher recognizes and responds to these issues, including knowing when to collaborate with psychologists or other specialists, makes a difference to the child and the family.

Creating a Buffer. Creating a safe, warm environment is especially important for those who may not experience positive caregiving at home. If parents are too stressed, busy, ill, or unsure how to interact with their young child, interacting with a caring, knowledgeable adult in preschool can help a child experience the responsive interactions needed to develop properly. Preschool professionals, while not expected to overcome family problems, can serve as a buffer against hardships at home (see Chapter 6).

Supporting Parents

Including and Respecting All Families. One of the first things teachers do to make a difference, in addition to observing and getting to know the child very well, is getting to know the family very well. Teachers learn about families from different cultures and make each family member feel comfortable and valued in the program. Warm communication that acknowledges and respects all family structures–families with two fathers, foster parents, and others–is especially important. Good preschool teachers communicate with parents frequently–daily or weekly–about their children's activities, problems, and successes. Remembering that parents know children better than anyone, teachers also seek information from families about areas of concern and perceived changes to inform their goals, assessments, and instruction.

Providing Information. Simultaneously, teachers bolster children's well-being by giving information to the parents. Some information is general, regarding developmental milestones and appropriate expectations for preschool-age children; and some information is specific to the child. For example, assessment results are shared on a regular basis with parents, keeping parents informed about children's progress and next steps.

Connecting Families to One Another. Many parents of preschoolers have at least two jobs: parenting and paid employment. They can be tired, stressed, and unsure of their parenting skills, especially when things go awry–when a child goes through a difficult phase, when a family is in crisis or faces a change, or when a child has ongoing special needs. These families are often the ones who are most isolated because of their difficulties. Teachers can play a critical role by connecting parents, all of whom have at least one common bond: children of the same age. This contribution is sometimes overlooked by even the best teachers, who may focus more on their own interactions with children and parents than on linking families to one another.

PROFESSIONAL PROFILE

Jim Clay, Director, School for Friends, Washington, DC

Jim's work has been especially busy and varied lately. He visits each class daily, giving teachers written compliments, suggestions, and questions. Because the year's just begun, Jim has also met with each teacher to set annual professional goals. At the regular staff meeting, topics ranged from NAEYC accreditation criteria to library volunteers to playground duties. Besides interacting with teachers, Jim provided an individualized tour to a prospective parent who lives in Africa and won't be able to attend any open houses. The school also held its autumn back-to-school night, where Jim welcomed parents and shared his vision for the year. Later in the week, Jim welcomed a college student who's observing at School for Friends. In between, Jim traveled to Philadelphia for a Friends Council on Education meeting. He also traveled to New York City to facilitate a meeting of the alumni association of which he's president, staying in contact with the school through email and phone calls. Board committee discussions and other administrative work were woven throughout, with about an hour each day spent preparing to reapply for a contract with the city to care for low-income children within the School for Friends program.

Before becoming a preschool director, Jim was a classroom teacher of 2- to 4-year-olds. He has a master's degree in Early Childhood Leadership.

Professionals Are Lifelong Learners

Knowing how to interact with each child, how to involve the family, and when to call in help from administrators or specialists requires continual renewal as a professional. Becoming informed, intentional, and able to individualize teaching requires regular professional development to seek out updated information and ideas. Regardless of their prior education and training, all good preschool teachers look for opportunities to get new training, which also helps them stay connected to other professionals.

CONCLUDING THOUGHTS:
THE ROLE OF EARLY CHILDHOOD PROFESSIONALS
IN SHAPING GOOD PRESCHOOL POLICIES

Like Bree's family, millions of Americans need care for their preschool child while parents are at work. And also like Bree's family, millions want their children to have a wonderful, stimulating preschool experience that gives them all the skills they need to get ready for kindergarten and beyond. But how do parents know which program is not only safe, but also a good environment for their child? If they find one they like, can they get in, and can they afford it? The preschool years can be stressful for parents.

The preschool years, when children are exuberant and on the cusp of great discovery and delight, should be a delightful time for parents as well, not a time of stress and anxiety. We hope that our leaders will take advantage of the clear findings from education, economics, psychology, social work, and other fields, and invest to create the outstanding child care and education system that children and families deserve. Investing in the early childhood education system would allow us to prepare and keep excellent teachers who love working with young children, keep class sizes small, provide sufficient hours of coverage, and make preschool affordable for every family. These are the types of changes that would reduce families' *and* professionals' stress levels and protect children's well-being.

As policymakers grapple with questions about how to strengthen the early care and education system, early childhood professionals can influence the answers. As a current or future early childhood educator, you are probably more informed than most policymakers about what would work best in your area, which kinds of families have which needs, and what kinds of services programs should provide—as well as what kind of support professionals need to work effectively with preschoolers. Sharing your thoughts and expertise with the decisionmakers (such as members of Congress, state education officials, program directors, principals, philanthropists, and members of county or city councils) is another important responsibility. Policymakers often need, and want, professional input about how to improve access to and the quality of preschool programs. Your involvement in this process is one more thing for which Bree, her family, and millions of parents will be grateful.

REFLECTION, DIALOGUE, AND ACTION

1. If you are an early childhood educator or have had any experience interning or volunteering in a program, consider your actions and strategies as compared to those presented in this chapter. What are three things you did or do well and three areas in which you could improve?

2. Do some Internet research to learn about an initiative either in your school district, state, or at the national level that would increase the number of children who could attend a preschool program. Share information with others about this initiative: who would benefit, who would fund the program, and what kinds of services would be included? Do you think it's a good idea and why or why not?

3. Think of an early childhood program you know about. Find out what is known about the quality of the program. Has it gone through NAEYC accreditation, QRIS evaluation, or other review, and what were the results? Can you find out if the program is taking steps to improve? Can you determine any barriers to quality improvement? Explain how you found this information.

INFORMATION TO EXPLORE AND SHARE

Office for Early Childhood Development of the Administration for Children and Families, U.S. Department of Health and Human Services

The ACF provides information on the federal government's activities and efforts to improve ECE, including through its Office for Early Childhood Development. It includes information on President Obama's initiative to provide pre-K for all children, what states are doing with grant money to improve early childhood programs, data on Head Start, statistics on young children, and more. www.acf.hhs.gov/programs/ecd

Office of Early Learning of the U.S. Department of Education

Aiming to improve outcomes from birth through third grade, the Office for Early Learning collaborates closely with ACF's early childhood office, jointly administering the Administration's Race to the Top Early Learning Challenge Grants. The Office coordinates early learning activities with other efforts across the Department of Education. An Early Learning email listserv is available at www.ed.gov/early-learning

National Association for the Education of Young Children

NAEYC works to improve early childhood program quality and runs a national, though voluntary, accreditation system. It evaluates early childhood settings to see if they meet quality standards, including knowledgeable and caring teachers, a safe and attractive environment, a developmentally appropriate curriculum, family involvement, and more. www.naeyc.org

National Institute for Early Education Research

NIEER conducts research on ECE efforts and communicates the results for journalists, policymakers, educators, and others. Its annual *State Preschool Yearbook* tracks funding, access, and policies of state-funded preschool programs. www.nieer.org

CHAPTER 4

The Early Years Matter for Children in Kindergarten Through 3rd Grade

© Sebastian Monk

CARLOS'S STORY

Carlos's family has recently moved into a new school district, where Carlos has just started 1st grade. Tonight Carlos's parents attended the school's "Back to School Night," where families could meet the new principal and visit their child's classroom. They were impressed by a story Carlos wrote and illustrated about a friendly robot and by a complex-looking math project in process on his desk.

At the coffee hour afterward, Carlos's parents talked together about their impressions. Last year Carlos attended a half-day kindergarten program at the local elementary school. In kindergarten he was often teased, perhaps because he is overweight as well as shy. He would often say that he didn't like school and wanted to stay home. But his parents liked the kindergarten teacher's emphasis on learning letters and numbers and starting to read—they want Carlos to be successful in school. Neither of them attended college, and they know that if Carlos gets a good start and good grades, he will have a successful future.

At Back to School Night at the new school, they had some very positive impressions, but they also heard some information that concerned them. On the positive side, the new principal seemed very energetic and eager to work together with teachers and families to create a real community in the new school. She said that they would be using an empty classroom to house a small local child care program and another room for an informal gathering place for parents. That sounded great. The principal also told the parents that the district has a continuing concern about bullying; she serves on a task force to develop ways to deal with the problems. Teachers are already using these new antibullying strategies, which seem to be working. All of this sounded good to Carlos's parents, especially because of the problems he encountered in kindergarten.

But when Ms. James, the 1st-grade teacher, talked with parents later in the evening, Carlos's mother and father were not sure that they liked what they heard. Ms. James shared a lot of ideas about "projects" that the children were doing, such as learning about the markets in the neighborhood. She also showed them areas in the classroom where the children play with blocks, pretend to shop at the market, and use pebbles to make patterns; she said that these activities would help them learn mathematics and improve their literacy skills. This seems like fun, but Carlos's parents wonder if all this playtime will really help Carlos become a better student. Everyone in the neighborhood talks about how difficult the new Common Core State Standards are; doesn't that mean there should be less play and more work in 1st grade? Yet, for the first time since he entered kindergarten, Carlos comes home smiling every afternoon. Children don't tease him, and he loves school. But is he learning enough? Carlos's parents have a lot to think about.

CHILDREN FROM AGE 5 TO 8: MOVING TOWARD COMPETENCE, COOPERATION, AND NEW CONNECTIONS WITH PEOPLE AND IDEAS

This chapter focuses on children from age 5 to 8. Within NAEYC's and the United Nations' definition of early childhood, these are indeed "young children," and the programs that they attend—usually kindergarten to 3rd grade (K–3)—are, in a very real sense, "early childhood education." This chapter will describe the characteristics of children in the early grades, the ways in which the quality of their K–3 education makes a difference in their development and learning, and some innovative efforts to improve children's experiences during this part of their early years. But first, as always, we should turn to the children themselves.

Like every child, Carlos is unique. However, he shares many characteristics with other children in his age group. Knowing about these characteristics can help his parents and his teachers make good decisions about the kinds of experiences he needs to help him learn and develop well.

In their publication on developmentally appropriate practice (Copple & Bredekamp, 2009), NAEYC emphasizes that "The early grades are a time for children to shine—they gain increasing mastery in every area of their development and learning. They explore, read, reason, problem solve, communicate through conversation and writing, and develop lasting friendships. They delight in their new intellectual prowess, social skills, and physical abilities" (Tomlinson, 2009, p. 257).

Between ages 5 to 8, children typically become:

- More physically skilled and engaging in more challenging physical activities.
- More interested in playing games with rules–though sometimes rigid in applying the "right way" to do things.
- Able to develop and sustain friendships and cooperative projects.
- More aware of their own skills and characteristics in comparison to those of other children.
- Motivated to master skills that their family, community, and culture regard as important–anything from riding a bike to performing well on tests.
- Eager for approval from adults other than their parents–teachers, coaches, recreation leaders.
- Better able to understand others' feelings and points of view.
- Able to think and solve problems in more flexible, logical ways–while still needing concrete experiences to help them make sense of the world.
- Better able to focus attention, make a plan, and use strategies to help remember things.
- Capable conversationalists, readers, and writers (Centers for Disease Control and Prevention, 2012; Tomlinson, 2009).

FROM KINDERGARTEN THROUGH THE PRIMARY GRADES: ARE THESE STILL THE EARLY YEARS AND WHY DO THESE YEARS MATTER?

Despite these changes in interests, knowledge, and skills, in many ways children aged 5 to 8 have the same basic needs that they had when they were younger. To continue on a positive trajectory, during these years children continue to need warm, nurturing relationships combined with many playful, "challenging but achievable" learning opportunities (Copple & Bredekamp, 2009), at home and in school.

But in contrast to younger children, almost every child from age 5 to 8 is in school.

Patterns of School Enrollment

Carlos is one of more than 34 million children attending public elementary schools (pre-K to grade 8) in the United States. Another 2.5 million children attend private elementary schools, including faith-based schools, and about 1.5 million–under 3% of all American children–are home-schooled (National Center for Education Statistics, 2010).

These are the numbers, but what are the requirements? All states require students to attend school beginning in 1st grade. Kindergarten is available in every state, but only 15 states require children to attend kindergarten, and 6 states do not require school districts to offer kindergarten even on a voluntary basis. Even so, 98% of children attend kindergarten, with 76% enrolled in full-day programs (Child Trends, 2013; Children's Defense Fund, 2013b).

Beyond Enrollment: The Quality of Children's Experiences in the Early Grades

What matters for 5- to 8-year-old children is not whether they attend school (because they almost all do), but what happens when they are there. Chapters 2 and 3 provided evidence that the quality of infant-toddler and preschool services can influence development and learning in kindergarten and in later years. Turning now to the quality of K–3 education, we will show that those experiences can also have a major impact on children's lives, both during the K–3 years and in the future.

We can see the effects of those experiences in many ways:

- The early education experiences of children 5 to 8 years old–not merely before K–3 but during K–3–influence their approaches to learning: their interest, persistence, flexibility, and engagement in learning tasks and attitudes about school. These attitudes and skills, in turn, influence later academic achievement and long-term engagement in learning (Hyson, 2008).
- What happens in K–3 influences children's social skills and emotional well-being. Positive experiences with friendships, guided by teachers who create caring communities of learners, build social competence. On the other hand, children who struggle with social skills and emotion regulation–and do not receive help at school for these problems–are also likely to have these problems continue, and to experience academic difficulties not only in the early grades but also later on (Payton et al., 2008).
- Even at the beginning of 1st grade, the achievement gap between middle-class children and those living in poverty, or having other risk factors, is striking. However, excellent teaching and challenging, interesting curricula can close that gap, building children's competence in areas such as reading and math, and putting those children on a path toward later academic success.

Despite his parents' concerns, it appears that Carlos is attending a high-quality school that is prepared to help all children make the most of these important years. Later in this chapter, we describe some innovative ways that educators across the country, like the leaders in Carlos's school, are taking on this challenge. But first, let's do a reality check of the typical quality of 1st-grade classrooms.

K–3 EDUCATION IS ALMOST UNIVERSAL—BUT IS IT UNIVERSALLY GOOD?

Just as with programs for younger children, education for children ages 5 to 8 has to be of good quality to make a positive impact on children's lives. Unfortunately, quality is often low, especially for children who need good programs the most.

One national study found that only 23% of more than 100 1st-grade classrooms provided high levels of both instructional and emotional support (Stuhlman & Pianta, 2009). *Instructional support* includes stimulating children's higher-level thinking, having rich discussions, asking lots of open-ended questions, and giving feedback that expands children's learning. *Emotional support* includes warmth and respect, responding to children's individual needs, and connecting with children's interests. In contrast to these practices, the majority of teachers relied on rote learning, one-size-fits-all lessons, and teacher-directed instruction.

These statistics should worry us, because children need both instructional and emotional supports to enjoy school and find success there. Better instructional support leads to better language, literacy, and math performance; better emotional support leads to better social skills (Hamre & Pianta, 2007).

In exploring further, the researchers discovered that the children who were the most at risk were the most likely to end up in a low-quality 1st-grade class. These children, including those who had not done well in preschool and children from working poor families, are the children who most need excellent educational experiences, not just in preschool and the early grades, but throughout their education.

EFFORTS TO ENHANCE THE POSITIVE IMPACT OF K–3 EDUCATION: THREE EXAMPLES

Many efforts are under way to improve children's experiences during these important years. With Carlos and his parents in mind, we outline three promising directions.

1. Strengthening Vertical Connections: The Pre-K–3rd Grade Movement

Because early childhood development is a continuous process from birth through age 8, it makes sense that early childhood services—including programs in preschool, kindergarten, and grades 1–3—ought to connect smoothly across these years. These kinds of connections create a consistent but evolving environment where later education builds seamlessly on what came earlier.

A promising, relatively new initiative is the Pre-K–3rd Grade movement, which advocates for a coordinated system of services across the years from preschool through 3rd grade. Carlos is in 1st grade now, but he spent the previous year in kindergarten, and before that he was in a child care program while his parents were working. As is often the case, there were no opportunities for his teachers to communicate across these settings. Furthermore, in Carlos's education and more generally, there is seldom a logical progression in curriculum from preschool to kindergarten and through grades 1–3. To some extent, teaching methods should change with children's increasing age and evolving developmental characteristics, but methods are often confusingly inconsistent or even contradictory across different programs. For example, Carlos's kindergarten used a didactic, narrowly academic teaching approach, while his 1st grade is much more holistic, project- and play-based.

The Pre-K–3rd Grade movement is a policy and practice initiative intended to bring these currently disconnected pieces together. The idea is that by extending the early childhood continuum downward to include pre-K while ensuring a developmentally appropriate approach upward through 3rd grade, adults will be able to shape better learning environments for young children at every step along the way.

**STRENGTHENING THE EARLY CHILDHOOD
PERSPECTIVE ON K–3 EDUCATION**

1. Pre-K–3rd Grade Movement: Strengthening Connections across Preschool, Kindergarten, and the Early Primary Grades

2. Emphasizing the Whole Child in K–3 and Beyond

3. Enhancing Learning through Developmentally Appropriate Curriculum and Assessment

PROFESSIONAL PROFILE

Sharon Ritchie, Director, FirstSchool, FPG Child Development Institute, Chapel Hill, NC

FirstSchool's goal is to help schools close the achievement and opportunity gap by strengthening and enriching the learning, development, and early school experiences of African American, Latino, and low-income children and their families. Sharon and her colleagues ground their work in lessons learned during partnerships with eight elementary schools that have worked hard to make sustainable changes in their professional culture, relationships with families and children, instructional practices, and curricular choices.

Implementing this vision during a typical week, Sharon spends her time figuring out how to present FirstSchool ideas to a variety of audiences—and then doing it. She frequently speaks at local, state, and national conferences; at state departments of education; and at national webinars. These large-scale presentations are complemented by "up close and personal" professional development days and follow-up coaching with FirstSchool's partners in school districts in Michigan and North Carolina. This week, Sharon is also talking to primary-grade teachers who are finding the Common Core State Standards very helpful in supporting their quality instructional practices. After interviewing the teachers, the team will observe their classrooms. Finally, Sharon and the FirstSchool team are currently developing an online resource library.

Over the past 35 years, Sharon Ritchie has been deeply involved in education as a teacher, program director, teacher educator, and researcher. She has played multiple roles in working with elementary schools and public and private early childhood programs at local, state, and national levels.

The Foundation for Child Development (FCD), with many partners, has provided support and advocacy for these activities. In FCD's view, a coordinated pre-K–3rd-grade system should include components such as:

1. Public funding for full-school-day education starting at age 3 (voluntary until kindergarten);
2. Well-coordinated educational strategies and a well-rounded curriculum (including social and emotional learning), with collaborative planning and professional development across the pre-K–3rd-grade years;
3. Leadership from principals, program directors, and other ECE administrators to promote a coherent pre-K–3rd-grade curriculum and well-coordinated services; and
4. Close engagement with families, to support learning at home as well as in early education programs and classrooms (Foundation for Child Development, 2010).

A number of states, including California, Georgia, Massachusetts, Minnesota, and New Jersey, are designing programs and policies to help move toward this kind of coordinated system, ensuring that in the future Carlos and other children will experience a smoother progression of learning. One model is the FirstSchool partnership, bringing together the best practices from early childhood, elementary, and special education to provide high-quality Pre-K–3rd grade learning opportunities for African American, Latino, and low-income children (FirstSchool, n.d.; Ritchie & Guttman, 2013).

2. Bringing the Whole Child into K–3 Education

The term *whole child* refers to educators' efforts to promote all aspects of children's development: physical, cognitive, social, and emotional, as well as academic. In the past, and to some degree today, people might believe that running around on a playground, building volcanoes in a sand pit, and learning about sharing and good listening skills are appropriate for preschool but as children get older–say, starting in kindergarten or 1st grade–they should "settle down and focus on academic skills," as Carlos's father might say.

However, many education leaders and child development researchers now advocate a renewed emphasis on *all* aspects of children's development in kindergarten and elementary schools and in teacher preparation (Pianta, Hitz, & West, 2010). Professional organizations like the Association for Supervision and Curriculum Development (ASCD) have taken up the challenge of advocating for a more holistic education.

Many examples could illustrate this movement; we describe just a few. Some promote improvements across entire schools, while other initiatives specifically aim to improve children's physical and social-emotional well-being.

School Climate Initiatives. Recent discussions of school climate are part of the whole-child conversation. According to the School Climate Research Center's report (Thapa, Cohen, Higgins-D'Allesandro, & Guffey, 2012), a positive school climate "includes norms, values, and expectations that support people feeling socially, emotionally and physically safe" (p. 4). Carlos's parents could tell from the new principal's speech that she intends to collaborate with others in creating this kind of climate. This is more than just a nice thing to do: Schools with a positive climate have less bullying, better relationships among both children and staff, and more engagement in learning.

The Comer School Development Program. A very intentional effort to implement a whole-child perspective within public elementary schools is the Comer School Development Program, also known as the Comer Model (Yale School of Medicine, 2013). Initiated by James Comer in 1968, and now implemented in over 1,000 schools in the United States and internationally, the program began in some of the worst-functioning elementary schools in New Haven, Connecticut. The key seemed to be putting first things first: Warm, supportive relationships with adults are the foundation of the Comer Model. As suggested in other chapters, research shows that children who have more positive, less conflicted relationships with their teachers have fewer learning and behavioral difficulties in later grades (Hamre & Pianta, 2001)–and once again, this is especially important for low-income and otherwise vulnerable children. In the Comer Model, teachers along with parents and community members do whatever it takes to improve children's social, emotional, and academic outcomes (Comer, Haynes, Joyner, & Ben-Avie, 1999). As a result, the program has virtually eliminated behavior problems and absenteeism in the schools in which it has been well-implemented.

The School of the 21st Century. Similar in many ways to the Comer Model, the School of the 21st Century approach taps the potential of public schools to address the needs not only of the whole child, but also of the whole family. The concept was developed by Edward Zigler, who was also one of the founders of Head Start in the 1960s. Public elementary schools that follow this model (there are now more than 1,300) may offer services such as parent support programs; early care and education; before- and after-school and school vacation programs for elementary school children; health and education services; professional development for child care providers; and information and referral services for families and children (School of the 21st Century, 2002).

The principal of Carlos's new school is trying to adopt some features of the School of the 21st Century approach. Many families who have not had positive school experiences in their own lives, like Carlos's parents, find this new model of school-as-community-center especially welcoming.

Obesity Prevention. So far, we have described K–3 innovations that aim to change the climate and organization of an entire school. There are also more specific interventions that give a new priority to children's health and social-emotional competence, going beyond, although still closely connected to, skills in reading and mathematics. One is a school-based response to childhood obesity.

Childhood obesity has more than doubled in the past 30 years. Carlos is not alone in being heavy for his age: In 2010, almost 18% of American children aged 6 to 11 were obese, according to the Centers for Disease Control and Prevention (2013b). Besides creating long-term health problems, obesity puts other aspects of children's development at risk. Classmates may not accept obese children to the same degree as others and are more likely to bully them than other children. And the children at highest risk of school failure—children in poverty and children (like Carlos) of ethnic minorities—are most likely to be obese, often because of poor nutrition.

Some elementary schools are now taking on the challenge of supporting healthy eating behaviors and exercise patterns as part of their whole-child responsibility, but in other schools, administrators have chosen to reduce gym classes and recess to have children spend more time at their desks. Although research shows the benefits of recess in increasing physical activity, only 20% of school districts in the United States have a wellness policy that requires recess. Worse yet, the children who are most at risk for obesity—children who live in urban areas, are poor, or are members of ethnic groups with high levels of obesity—are the least likely to attend a school that provides recess (Robert Wood Johnson Foundation, 2012). Knowledgeable school administrators recognize the link between physical health and both social-emotional well-being and academic achievement. Young children need to move to learn.

In addition to protecting children's physical exercise time, children need teachers who encourage and promote good health habits. One recent study linked up health professionals and elementary school teachers to incorporate healthy messages into the school curriculum. The project was effective in reducing weight among 7- to 9-year-olds who were obese (Johnston, Moreno, El-Mubasher et al., 2013). For overweight children like Carlos, such programs may make a great difference in their physical, social, emotional, *and* academic well-being.

Bullying in K–3. Bullying hurts, whether it is physical or verbal. Children who are bullied, as Carlos was in kindergarten, are more likely to feel sad and to want to stay home from school. Like being obese, being bullied negatively affects many aspects of children's development and learning. Often, it is not only the children being bullied who feel terrible. The children doing the bullying also feel bad and need help. Because bullying tends to increase over the elementary school years, it should be a high priority for intervention in the early grades, as schools take on responsibility for the development of the whole child (AERA, 2013).

School-based programs can help to prevent and intervene in bullying. A comprehensive research review showed that antibullying programs in schools can be effective in decreasing incidents of bullying, reducing the number of new victims of bullying, and lessening antisocial behavior. The most effective programs are comprehensive, intensive, and long-lasting (Farrington & Ttofi, 2009). Children's satisfaction with school increases as they feel safer and more accepted by peers. Programs that are especially effective include parent meetings as part of the intervention and attend to discipline practices in school. Principals and teachers can build bullying prevention into the curriculum through techniques such as classroom role-playing activities. The new principal at Carlos's school, and the task force to which she belongs, are beginning to incorporate quite a few of these ideas.

3. Enhancing Learning Through Developmentally Appropriate Curriculum and Assessment

Research on early development and learning shows that although children change as they get older, many teaching practices that are considered effective when children are 3 or 4 years old continue to be valuable at age 5, 6, 7, and 8–all part of the early years. These high-quality early childhood practices reflect a continuing emphasis on:

- reliance on concrete, physical ways of learning;
- learning by making connections between what children experience in their immediate environments and what they receive as new information beyond what they have already experienced;
- playful learning, including child-initiated investigations; and
- learning through interactions with others.

What to Teach and How to Teach from Kindergarten to 3rd Grade. Much more than in preschool programs, what is taught in public schools from kindergarten onward is strongly influenced by standards—written descriptions of what children in each grade should know and be able to do. Each state has such standards, but now there are also national-level standards in language/literacy and mathematics: The Common Core State Standards (National Governors Association Center for Best Practices and Council of Chief State School Officers, 2010).

These standards include very detailed expectations for children's learning, beginning in kindergarten and continuing through 12th grade. For example, one expectation is that by the end of 1st grade, Carlos and other children should be able to "Retell stories, including key details, and demonstrate understanding of their central message or lesson." In math, children should be able to "Organize, represent, and interpret

---

PROFESSIONAL PROFILE

Beatrice Wambui Muriithi, Teacher, Grades 3 and 4,
El-Shabazz Public School Academy, Lansing, Michigan

Beatrice Wambui Muriithi has been an elementary school teacher for 8 years, but she has recently transformed her practices. In the spring of 2011, FirstSchool representatives were invited to El-Shabazz. Beatrice had always thought of herself as an effective teacher. However, the FirstSchool collaboration—including classroom observations and data analysis—gave her new insight into children's learning needs and her own teaching. As Beatrice says, "There's nothing like data!"

Before, a week in Beatrice's class emphasized seat work and stickers for "good" behavior. Now a visitor would see Beatrice's students working in small groups every day, often in locations of their choosing. Rather than looking for external rewards, children evaluate their day by reflecting and writing about it. As disagreements occur, children talk things out in a Conflict Resolution Corner. Every day, students share personal experiences with Beatrice, and in turn she shares her life with them, including being the mother of a young daughter. Even when she needs to redirect a child with challenging behavior, her relationship and caring tone touch the child personally. Every week, Beatrice now gives the children responsibility for duties she formerly managed on her own. Finally, Beatrice now engages more deeply with families, encouraging them to text or call her evenings or weekends.

Beatrice Wambui Muriithi came to Michigan from Kenya to pursue a college education. She earned her associate's degree, a bachelor's degree in elementary education, and then a master's in reading literacy.

---

data with up to three categories." Both of these standards, and other standards in the Common Core, were developed to help teachers focus on the most important concepts and skills. The developers of these standards were especially concerned that children should gain greater depth of learning, and that they should gain competencies that, by the time they leave school, will make them ready for college and careers.

Some early childhood educators who teach in K–3 classrooms are concerned that these standards will not allow them to teach in ways that fit with how children ages 5 to 8 learn best. There should be little cause for concern, however: Standards tell educators *what* to teach but do not dictate *how* to teach. In fact, children will more fully master these competences, and be more engaged in learning, if they are taught in ways that are *active, individually and culturally meaningful, socially connected,* and *challenging but achievable*–all characteristics of what NAEYC calls "developmentally appropriate practice" for children from birth through age 8 (Copple & Bredekamp, 2009).

Using developmentally appropriate teaching strategies, for example, Carlos's 1st-grade teacher might involve the class in a storytelling project using traditional stories from the children's families. Class books might be made with these stories, and the children might retell the stories to their classmates. In math, the children could visit a local farmer's market and keep a record of how many stands sold which kinds of products. Afterward, Ms. James might help the class add up and compare the number of fruit stands, vegetable stands, and baked goods stands, making a graph to represent the results.

These kinds of practices are likely to help children master the Common Core content. At the same time, the practices will help increase children's enthusiasm for learning and strengthen their social competence as they collaborate with classmates (ASCD, 2012; Biggam & Hyson, 2013).

Assessing Children's Progress with the Goal of Improving Teaching and Learning. As Carlos's parents know, from kindergarten onward schools are focused on assessing children's learning. Is this emphasis on assessment a good thing or not? It depends. Too often, formal testing becomes the focus of everything, and teachers feel they have to spend all their time cramming for tests, the results of which influence the teacher's and the school's reputation and rewards. This is one of the concerns that many educators have about the Common Core: They worry that these standards may lead to a greater emphasis on inappropriate and even harmful testing.

Although it is realistic to be concerned about inappropriate testing, appropriate assessments—not only based on formal tests—are an important component of good programs, both to assess overall progress and to assess children's individual development and learning. States and school districts are working toward developing assessment systems that will help teachers track children's progress in relation to the Common Core, not just to evaluate how schools are doing, but also to improve teaching and learning for each child. As this work moves forward, it is important for teachers, school leaders, and advocates to push for developmentally appropriate assessment practices, as recommended in a joint position statement addressing these issues (NAEYC & NAECS/SDE, 2003). According to this position statement, assessment of young children must always be done for specific, beneficial purposes—the most important of which is to help improve teaching and promote children's learning, not to label children or restrict their access to later learning opportunities. Comprehensive developmental assessment, with information collected over time with varied, appropriate methods, can give teachers rich insight into each child's unique characteristics, strengths, and needs—thereby increasing the effectiveness of what teachers plan for Carlos and others.

Beyond the School Day: "Out-of-School-Time" Programs

Learning does not stop when children leave school for the day. Many children ages 5 to 8 attend out-of-school-time programs before school, after school, and on vacation. It is important for children to have some unscheduled time, but supervision is also important, and working families are often unable to provide all of it. Programs that help fill before- and after-school hours in enjoyable, productive ways make a positive contribution to children's development.

Quality after-school programs, operated in public school buildings, community centers, or other neighborhood settings, do more than keep school-age children safe while their parents work. Rather, they engage children in challenging physical activities; provide academic support; encourage exploration of individual interests; do projects that strengthen children's confidence, cooperation, and positive work habits; and more. By promoting key competencies and attitudes toward learning, such programs have been found to boost children's school attendance, grades, and engagement in learning. As with many other interventions, the benefits are often greatest for those children who are most at risk (NIOST, 2008; Rand Corporation, 2005).

In after-school programs as in other services for young children, the key word is *quality*. Caring, responsible adult leaders (often including college students) are essential, and they should be given enough training and support to help them meet the program's goals. Quality elements also include a clear program mission; a safe, emotionally supportive environment; family and community partnerships; and frequent program assessment to help guide improvements (Bodilly & Beckett, 2005). In addition, quality out-of-school-time programs closely connect with the schools, so that leaders can offer complementary learning opportunities that align with, strengthen, and enrich what children learn during the school day (NIOST, 2008).

EARLY CHILDHOOD PROFESSIONALS AND K–3 EDUCATION

Both teachers and principals are essential players in making children's school experiences a source of enjoyment and productive learning. An early-years perspective is as important for K–3 teaching as in infant-toddler or preschool education.

Preparing Teachers for K–3 Education

Carlos is fortunate to have been assigned to Ms. James's class this year. To meet the needs of children ages 5 to 8, children need teachers like Ms. James, who understand their special characteristics and are skilled in helping them learn in developmentally appropriate ways. In the past, elementary-school teacher preparation has often focused mainly on learning how to teach academic content, especially reading. Teacher education programs gave less attention to knowledge of child development and required few in-depth field experiences, which are important to gain competence in implementing effective practices for K–3 children. Typically, a state's elementary teacher license has qualified graduates to teach from kindergarten to grade 6 or, in some states, even to grade 8. Teacher education programs that have attempted to cover this wide span have often been unable to focus on the distinctive characteristics and learning needs of younger children, the 5- to 8-year-olds.

Consistent with the new directions described in this chapter, including the national pre-K–3rd grade movement, and influenced by a number of states that now offer specialized teacher licensure in pre-K–3rd or pre-K–4th, many teacher educators are rethinking their past practices. The Comer Model and FirstSchool organizations are among the groups that work with teacher education programs to support a more holistic and developmentally appropriate preparation of pre-K–3rd-grade teachers. On many college and university campuses, the result is a stronger emphasis on child development and on methods appropriate for the continuum of learning from preschool through the early primary grades.

Principals as Leaders of Learning Communities

Clearly, teachers like Ms. James have a significant part in making sure that early years approaches and values matter in K–3 just as much as they do in preschool. But equally important is the school principal. In a recent study, Branch, Hanushek, and Rivkin (2013) found that school principals have a substantial impact, with differences in children's achievement being correlated with differences in the quality of the principal. At their best, principals–like the new principal in Carlos's school–are instructional leaders, guiding and inspiring staff, influencing overall school climate, and making strong connections with children as well as with families and the community.

The National Association of Elementary School Principals (NAESP) has long been a supporter of a connected system of education that supports development across the early childhood years. NAESP asserts that the principal's leadership is a key to quality and has outlined standards for what excellent elementary principals should know and be able to do in this role (NAESP, 2008). Interestingly, the new edition of the NAESP standards has even more emphasis on the whole child, on expanding the idea of the "learning day" to include out-of-school programs, and on strengthening connections with families and the community: exactly the kind of directions discussed in this chapter.

CONCLUDING THOUGHTS:
AN EARLY CHILDHOOD VISION FOR CHILDREN FROM AGE 5 TO 8

The years from 5 to 8 are part of the early childhood period, and what happens in these years matters a great deal. Like all young children, those in Carlos's age group have a broad range of needs–not just high-quality instruction in reading and math, essential though that is, but also supports for their physical, social, and emotional health and development. This whole-child perspective is at least as important in kindergarten and the primary grades as it is before that. Academic success, including competencies related to new academic standards, will be far more likely if teachers spark children's interests, respect their cultures, and base learning on children's everyday experiences. Children ages 5 to 8 are moving into an expanded world, exposed to new knowledge and new relationships. Taken together, the new directions described in this chapter show that a comprehensive, developmentally appropriate early childhood perspective continues to matter throughout kindergarten, 1st, 2nd, and 3rd grades.

Currently, the scale of implementation of the innovations discussed in this chapter is small; compared to the overall number of K–3 classrooms in the country, only a relative few schools use the approaches we have described. State governments and school districts responsible for curricula, assessment, teaching methods, and teacher training requirements should consider implementing these promising strategies, especially in schools serving children who face multiple challenges, including the challenge of poverty. As a general rule, low-income children in K–3 classes do not require a curriculum and teaching practices that are completely different than what more affluent children need. Rather, they need similar approaches implemented even more effectively: developmentally appropriate, engaging, perhaps intensive instruction, provided by the most experienced, caring, and knowledgeable teachers.

With these strategies in place, the result is likely to be significant improvements in children's well-being, academic achievement, and attitudes toward school and learning, as well as enhanced family involvement.

For this to occur, however, new strategies for K–3 require effective implementation, evaluation, sufficient funding, and professional development to support teachers as they engage in the difficult change process. And finally, policymakers, teacher educators, principals, and teachers themselves have a responsibility to speak out for this kind of early childhood vision, a vision that will support success for Carlos and every other 5- to 8-year-old child.

REFLECTION, DIALOGUE, AND ACTION

1. Think back on your own school experiences from kindergarten through 3rd grade. What are the similarities and differences between those experiences and what is described in this chapter? Compare notes with others.

2. If possible, interview a K–3 teacher or an elementary school principal. Seek insights about the challenges and satisfactions of working with this age group. You might explore how the teacher and school address issues like obesity and bullying, or how the new Common Core State Standards affect what is taught and how.

3. With permission, visit a K–3 classroom. Consider the extent to which the curriculum and teacher-child interactions are consistent with the quality practices discussed in this chapter. If they are not, what might be the reasons?

INFORMATION TO EXPLORE AND SHARE

Association for Supervision and Curriculum Development, Whole Child Initiative

Launched in 2007, ASCD's Whole Child Initiative helps educators, families, community members, and policymakers move from a narrow focus on academic achievement to a broader vision of what children need to be truly successful in the 21st century. www.ascd.org/whole-child.aspx

Foundation for Child Development, Pre-K–3rd Education Initiative

The Foundation for Child Development has been a leader in the Pre-K–3rd movement, which attempts to transform how children ages 3 to 8 learn in schools. fcd-us.org/our-work/preK–3rd-education

National Association of Elementary School Principals

NAESP is a professional association of principals and other education leaders. It has been a strong supporter of early childhood services as a foundation for education, and is a partner with FCD and others in the national Pre-K–3rd initiative. www.naesp.org

National Institute on Out-of-School Time

NIOST aims to ensure that all children, youth, and families have access to high-quality opportunities when children are not in school. www.niost.org

United States Department of Health and Human Services: StopBullying

This government agency has created a comprehensive website with resources for children, families, educators, and community members. Includes "Prevention at School" resources and a "Get Help Now" section to address urgent situations. www.stopbullying.gov.

The Early Years Matter
for Children in Low-Income Families

© Ellen B. Senisi

ANNA'S STORY

"I want something to eat," croaked Anna's dad, Malcolm, in a Cookie Monster voice as he read to his young daughter in the waiting room of a food pantry in Sacramento. Dark-haired and sturdy, wearing a worn blue and red dress under her winter coat, Anna waited patiently with her dad to collect their bags of canned peas, corn flakes, ramen noodles, and instant oatmeal. Malcolm lost his job when the bottom dropped out of the economy in 2008, and the construction field along with it. He found a temporary job in 2010, and then again more recently. When he is not working, he cherishes his time with Anna and her baby brother, but he knows the stress of constant worry, unpaid bills, and job hunting makes him quick to lose his temper. When his fuse gets too short, sometimes he leaves for a few days so he will not do something he regrets.

At age 3½, Anna is a strong-willed, social child who delights (sometimes) in sharing with her baby brother, playing hide-and-seek, and coloring on old newspapers that she gets from her neighbor's front steps. Mainly, though, she watches *Dora the Explorer* and other shows on television while her mother, Ruby, fusses with the baby, who seems sick all the time, or does laundry. When the electricity is cut off because of unpaid bills, which happens every couple of months, the days without television seem very long indeed. Anna does not like those days. Everyone seems worried and unhappy then, and her mother is not as patient as she usually is. Even though Malcolm works long days and sometimes nights, he does not get benefits because he works as a contractor. This means Anna and her brother do not go to the doctor for checkups and immunizations (although Anna once went to the emergency room). Malcolm can make up to $2,000 a month, of which half goes to rent and the rest goes to utility bills, groceries, bus fares, and visits to the thrift shop for clothes and other necessities. But some months he makes little or nothing, so Anna's parents do their best to save ahead on rent payments. They almost got evicted once but were able to borrow money from Ruby's brother.

Anna loves going to the River City Food Bank with her dad because he usually takes one of the few books she owns, donated by the library, to read while they ride the bus up Stockton Avenue. Anna cannot wait until she's 4, because her mother told her she will go to preschool then—unless they have to move to another apartment that is too far from the Head Start center.

DESCRIBING LOW-INCOME CHILDREN IN AMERICA

America is one of the richest countries on earth, yet the United States has a higher percentage of children living in poverty than all but one of the world's developed countries. In a survey of child poverty in 35 countries, the U.S. ranked at the bottom of the pile behind Canada, Australia, New Zealand, Japan, and almost all of Europe. Only Romania had a higher percentage of children in poverty (UNICEF, 2012).

Defining Poor and Low-Income Families

There is an invisible line, the poverty line, that policymakers use to decide who is officially poor and who is not. It currently stands at an income of $22,350 per year for a family of four (United States Department of Health and Human Services, 2011). However, the National Center for Children in Poverty (NCCP, 2012a) tells us that in most parts of the country families actually need about two times that much, $44,700, to meet their basic needs. To "meet basic needs" means to be able to buy fresh fruit and vegetables on a regular basis; have meat or fish once a day; have adequate clothing and two pairs of shoes; have a dry home with hot water; and have access to good health care and education. NCCP, other research and advocacy organizations, and policymakers describe these families as low-income, which means not officially poor but living on the economic margins. These families still find it difficult or impossible to provide children with the basics, in part because subsidized services may only exist for families living under the poverty line. In this chapter, we use the term *low-income* to include both poor (under the poverty line) and near-poor (near the poverty line) families because they struggle with the same pressures and challenges.

Almost Half of Young Children in America Are Low-Income

The percentage of children in low-income families is one of the most revealing signs of a country's well-being, because it shows how well that country takes care of its most vulnerable, voiceless citizens. By that standard, the United States is not doing very well: Twenty-five percent of children under 6 live under the poverty line, and 48% (11 million children) live under or near the poverty line (NCCP, 2012a). Anna's story is relatively common. Anyone can be poor, and many families move in and out of poverty at some points during their lifetime, often because of changing national and state economic patterns. All ethnic groups are represented, but low-income families are especially likely to be Black (70% are low-income), American Indian (68%), or Hispanic (66%) (NCCP, 2012a).

THE STRENGTHS OF FAMILIES AND THE COSTS OF POVERTY

Low-income families have the steepest uphill climb to success and well-being, but they have the fewest tools to make the climb. Persevering requires strength and savvy. Nonetheless, it can be grueling, disappointing, and seemingly impossible at times. Families who have the fewest resources need the most support.

Resourcefulness, Perseverance, and Other Strengths

Living with too little money involves a host of difficult choices every day for parents. Should Anna's family try to sleep without air conditioning to save on electricity, even though it is 100 degrees in Sacramento's sweltering summer? Does the baby really need to see a doctor about that persistent cough? Should the parents prioritize buying healthy food or paying the phone bill this week? Is it a good investment to pay someone to watch the children so both parents can look for work? If they have the money, is there anyone in the neighborhood they trust enough to take good care of the children?

There is a stereotype that poor families lack the ability to manage their own lives, yet it takes exceptional planning, prioritizing skills, resourcefulness, and perseverance to make those difficult decisions wisely multiple times a day and to keep a family running on very little. As summarized in Orthner, Jones-Sanpei, and Williamson (2004), and in Child Trends' report (Valladares & Moore, 2009), low-income families have many strengths and are often amazing in their capacity to "make it" with so little.

Low-income parents must have or develop great self-reliance and resilience in order to get by. On a daily basis, they need to solve challenging problems and look for ways to make changes in their lives. For example, Anna's parents always make efforts to save money for next month, even though they make little money and have pressing needs, including hunger, utility bills, bus fares, clothing, and rent. They also ask for help when necessary, borrowing money in order to keep stability in the family's life.

Despite these difficulties, just as in other families, people in low-income families often love one another deeply and show it through warm, loving, emotionally consistent relationships—even in the face of individual anxieties and unmet needs. Anna's parents certainly show love and resourcefulness, even when things were difficult. Anna's father cherishes his time with his children, and is insightful enough to take time out instead of getting to the point where he might snap; and Ruby is usually patient with the children, regardless of the amount of stress she is under. Being low-income says nothing about the amount of time families may spend together or how much joy, humor, and love people give each other—it just may be while going to a food bank rather than a movie or an expensive museum. Like Anna's family, many low-income families are loving, forward-thinking, and hard-working, often under the most difficult of circumstances.

And Yet . . . The Personal Costs of Poverty

In spite of individual resilience and resourcefulness, situations can seem or be inescapable when there is no safety net—no extended family, friends with connections, or good public programs—to help a family during tough times. Poverty is one of the most stressful situations families have to live with. Like Anna's parents, most low-income parents have a limited education and lack the training or networks to find well-paid jobs. Many are recent immigrants who do not know where to go for help, are perhaps afraid to identify themselves as undocumented, and are unable to communicate with officials. Although, like Anna's dad, they may be hard-working, reliable employees, low-income parents frequently do not earn sufficient wages to support their families and do not receive the benefits, such as health insurance, life insurance, or paid leave, that other employees get, all of which help create better conditions for raising children.

People under stress are often not at their best and may make bad choices. Poverty is not the only source of stress—others are discussed in Chapter 6—but it is a major one. Stress may make those living in poverty irritable, easily angered, and unable to make good decisions at every turn. At times they may try to fill emptiness and numb disappointment and anxiety with alcohol, food, or distractions. Living with enduring stress and worry can also contribute to mental illnesses that often accompany stress, like depression, anxiety, and addictions. Stress is further compounded when one parent is trying to do it all; 64% of low-income children (compared with 28% of all children) live with a single parent (Federal Interagency Forum on Child and Family Statistics; National Center for Children in Poverty, 2012a). Money is not everything, but it does make life easier. With only one income it can be hard to afford the commodities and services that are good for children, such as books, educational toys, technology, recreational activities, having a birthday party—or getting high-quality early education.

Certainly, many low-income children grow up to be successful, happy adults. Yet a serious and chronic lack of money can create ripples throughout and forward into children's lives. When a family is uprooted because of an eviction or to avoid bill collectors, when children eat Cheetos and Oreos from a minimart for dinner because a well-stocked grocery store is not within walking distance, when a mother is anxious and depressed, or when there is fighting between two economically panicked parents, children's well-being takes a nosedive. When extended family or community and friendship networks evaporate in the trail behind a family that is always on the move or that is unable to engage in a community, life for parents and children can be isolated and rocky.

EARLY CARE AND EDUCATION PROTECTS AND SUPPORTS LOW-INCOME CHILDREN

Even more than most children, children living in low-income families can gain protection, stimulation, and support from a variety of early childhood services.

Protection Against Immediate Risks and Stressors

Programs add predictability and joy to children's day-to-day lives while strengthening their development, preparing them for later school success, and supporting their families. Anna is a little girl who craves being read to and doing artwork, who is social and likes being around other children but rarely has the opportunity, and who spends too much time in front of the television. Her parents, although loving, have limited resources of their own to keep Anna learning and growing to her potential. Anna would be delighted by the carefully planned, fun, engaging activities, friendly faces, and steady routine of a welcoming preschool program At the same time, Early Head Start or a home visiting program (described in Chapter 2) would enhance the development of Anna's baby brother. Anna's parents would welcome these programs' respect and support for their efforts.

Poverty Relates to Achievement Gaps Very Early. Research shows that the most vulnerable children—those who are the poorest and the most at risk of not developing well—benefit the most from high-quality early childhood programs. At age 4, poor children are about 18 months behind middle-class children developmentally (Klein & Knitzer, 2006). On average, poor children begin school knowing about half the number of vocabulary words as children from higher-income homes (Hart & Risley, 1995). And compared with children ages 3 to 6 living above the poverty line, poor children the same age are less likely to be able to count to 20 (67% versus 49%), write their name (64% versus 46%), or recognize all the letters of the alphabet (35% versus 21%) (Child Trends, 2010). Taken together, these differences add up to a substantial achievement gap as children begin kindergarten, as shown in Figure 5.1. Children from the lowest-income families start kindergarten with the lowest knowledge and skill levels, in contrast to those in higher-income families.

The gap exists not because low-income children are born less capable, but because they often have fewer learning opportunities, poorer health and nutrition, less stability, and a greater likelihood of living in a dangerous or inadequate environment. Anna is a curious, capable child with a supportive family, which may help her beat those discouraging odds. Going to a good preschool would do a great deal to boost her chances.

Figure 5.1. Achievement Gaps as Children Begin Kindergarten

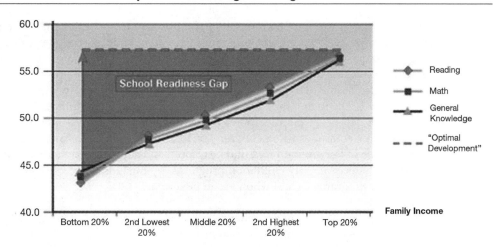

Source: U.S. Department of Education, National Center for Education Statistics, Early Childhood Longitudinal Study, Kindergarten Class of 1996–99, Fall 1998. In Barnett, Hustedt et al. (2004).

Low-Income Children Benefit from Holistic, Comprehensive Care and Education. Early childhood is a time when all children, especially those in low-income families, need support for *all* areas of their development. When children are healthy, rested, and well-fed, they can put their energy into playing and learning. As detailed in Chapters 2, 3, and 4, in a good early education program children from birth to 8 have a chance to immerse themselves in learning opportunities of all kinds. Depending on their ages, they may explore objects, look at books, play math games, learn how to hold a pencil, and gain other school-related skills they might not develop at home. They also get to play dress-up, practice language and negotiation skills, experiment with toys and materials, follow instructions, and concentrate for periods of time. These skills are equally as important for school readiness and school success as knowing letters and numbers.

For a child like Anna, who does not yet have all her immunizations and sometimes goes to bed hungry or filled up on junk food, it is especially important that a program be *comprehensive*. Comprehensive programs provide education services but they also address the child's holistic needs. It would have been great for Anna to be enrolled in Early Head Start, which would have provided such services to Anna and her family from infancy onward. But if Anna attends Head Start in the future, she will get nutritious meals and snacks; attention from a medical professional who will regularly track her health and nutrition; rest or sleep when she needs it; the chance to run and climb on playground equipment; *and* activities to build her skills in physical, emotional, social, and cognitive areas, including reading and math. At the same time, Head Start would help her parents get access to services they need—perhaps some suggestions about resume writing or information about health insurance—and encouragement to continue the positive things they already do, like reading to their children.

Protection Against Long-term Consequences of Poverty

It is not just in the here-and-now that children in low-income families benefit from high-quality early childhood programs. As young children become teenagers and young adults, they continue to live more accomplished, stable, and positive lives if they had participated consistently in a high-quality, comprehensive program when they were little (Yoshikawa et al., 2013). On the other hand, if low-income children miss out on such a program, they are at risk for experiencing more difficulties as they get older. The gap of 18 months found in the development of poor and better-off children at age 4 continues when children are 10 years old (Klein & Knitzer, 2006).

The Ounce of Prevention Fund (n.d.) explored and summarized many studies of the long-term effects of early childhood programs. It concluded that without participation in such programs a child who lives in poverty is:

- 25% more likely to drop out of school;
- 40% more likely to become a teen parent;
- 50% more likely to be placed in special education;
- 60% more likely to never attend college; and
- 70% more likely to be arrested for a violent crime.

In contrast to these discouraging statistics, low-income children who participate in good early childhood programs are likely to experience positive outcomes even after years and years have passed. Consider the Perry Preschool Project, discussed further below (Schweinhart, Montie, Xiang, et al., 2005). Children participating as teenagers were again more likely than nonparticipants to achieve well, not need special education, and graduate on time. In addition, at age 40, people who had participated in the program were more likely than nonparticipants to have a home and a savings account.

These findings do not mean that all poor children will end up on negative pathways toward the future if they do not attend a good early childhood program. Each person is different, and a person's own resilience, family support and other positive relationships, and other sources of strength can lead to a fine future even after the worst beginning.

Three Long-Term Studies That Demonstrate
the Positive Impact of Early Childhood Programs

The real-world issues that affect parents' decisions about early childhood services for their children make it challenging for researchers to conduct rigorous, long-term studies that can explain which programs really work for low-income children and why. Yet there are a few landmark studies, and they show significant, positive, and long-term impacts of early childhood education on the lives of children living in or near poverty:

- The Perry Preschool Project in Ypsilanti, Michigan, provided daily preschool for 123 poor children and weekly home visits to mothers for either 1 or 2 years. The intervention lasted from 1962–1967, and follow-up studies occurred until participants were 40 years old. Immediate gains in achievement test scores appeared at ages 4 and 5. Although gains seemed to fade out during middle childhood, well-being and success benefits reappeared in adulthood.

- The Abecedarian Project began in 1972 in North Carolina, and provided 5 years of early intervention starting when the 111 participants were infants, and followed participants' progress for 30 years. In adulthood, participants were more likely to graduate from college and be consistently employed and less likely to have early pregnancies or rely on public assistance.
- The Chicago Child Parent Centers project is a contemporary project that began in 1967 but continues to serve economically disadvantaged families as part of Chicago's public school system. One long-term study that started in the 1980s followed more than 1,000 participants until they were in their mid–20s. Participants showed higher achievement scores in elementary school and adulthood.

See Figure 5.2 for further details.

Figure 5.2. Prominent Evaluations Showing Long-Term Benefits of High-Quality, Comprehensive Preschool for Low-Income Children

The Perry Preschool Project*	**The Abecedarian Project[+]**	**The Chicago Child Parent Center Program[∞]**
• 123 participants born into poverty attended a half-day preschool program for 2 years. Parents experienced weekly home visits. • By 2nd grade, participants had significantly higher achievement scores and less need for special education services. • It reduced behavior problems (e.g., acting out, aggression) in elementary school. • By age 27, participants were more likely to have graduated from high school, earn more money, and own a home and a second car. They were less likely to be on welfare or have a criminal record. • At age 40, they were more likely to have a job, higher salary, home, and savings account. They were still less likely to have committed a crime or use drugs.	• 111 infants in poor families were assigned to an intervention or a control group. • Intervention-group children received an intensive ECE experience from infancy until they started kindergarten. They experienced full-day, full-year care using individualized educational games that emphasized cognitive and language skills. • They also received health care. • Participants scored 1.8 years higher in reading and 1.3 years higher in math, were more likely to go to college and find a skilled job, and were less like to have a child before turning age 18. They tended to smoke and use marijuana less. As adults, participants' health was substantially better.	• 1,000 children received half-day, center-based preschool promoting reading, math, and communication skills through classroom activities, field trips, and intensive parent involvement. • Health and nutrition services were provided. • Children received support through 1st grade, with reduced class sizes and teachers' aides in the classroom and enrichment activities. • Participants had higher achievement scores throughout elementary school. They were less likely to repeat grades or need special education services. • At age 20, participants were less likely than peers to have been arrested and were more likely to have graduated from high school.

Sources: * Belfield, Nores, Barnett, & Schweinhart, 2006; Schweinhart, Weikart, & Larner, 1986;
[+] Pungello, Campbell, & Barnett, 2006; Campbell et al., 2014;
[∞] Reynolds, 2000; Reynolds, Temple, Robertson, & Mann, 2001.

These studies and others show us what kind of difference comprehensive, high-quality early intervention can make in low-income children's lives. However, only a small number of children participated in these programs. Comprehensive and high-quality programs are not widely available for the average family, let alone families living in poverty, unless they find room in an Early Head Start, Head Start, or free pre-K program (see Chapters 2 and 3).

PROGRAM QUALITY FOR LOW-INCOME FAMILIES

Researchers curious about the types of early care and education choices *most* low-income parents have in the "real world" (as opposed to in ideal study conditions) must conduct observational studies that follow a large number of families over time. Researchers in the National Institutes of Child Health and Human Development (NICHD) Early Child Care Research Network designed a study that began in 1991, following over 1,300 then-pregnant women and their families over many years. As noted in Chapter 3, these researchers studied what choices the families made about early care and education for their children, and how those choices affected children as the years went by (Peth-Pierce, 2002). About one-third (35%) of the families lived in or near poverty.

Low-Income Families Tend to Use No Program or a Low-Quality Program

Preschool Quality. The NICHD researchers found that families consistently living in poverty were less likely than others to use any kind of early childhood services before school entry. Reasons for the lower rate of participation include not knowing about the value of early childhood services, not being close enough to a program to participate on a daily basis, not knowing where to get information about programs, not having the language skills to ask in the case of immigrant families, not finding space available in nearby programs, or, most frequently, not being able to afford services. When children in the study attended programs, whether at a neighbor's home, a licensed family child care program, or a child care center, it was all too common to find them in a place (a) that was not sufficiently safe and clean, and (b) did not have enough attractive, functional toys, books, and learning materials. Often there were too few adults in the room, and the adults were not always well trained for the challenging job of working with young children. In other words, these were low-quality kinds of programs.

Unfortunately, as noted in Chapter 2, the low quality of child care begins at the very beginning: 40% of infants and toddlers in care are in low-quality programs (Zero to Three, 2009b). More than half of the 12 million infants and toddlers in the United States live in low-income families, and these are the families who disproportionately attend low-quality programs. This is especially troublesome because at-risk babies and toddlers often receive care that is so low in quality that it may actually diminish children's inborn potential, leading to poorer outcomes across all domains of development.

K-3 Quality. By kindergarten age, cost is no longer a barrier for families to access education, but classroom quality continues to be a problem for most low-income families. As described in Chapter 4, in the United States much of a school's funding depends on the tax revenue within the local area. Therefore, wealthier areas have wealthier schools, and poorer areas have poorer schools. Biddle and Berliner (2002) noted multiple examples of these disparities: At the state level, a relatively wealthy state such as New Jersey has twice the educational resources as those available in a less wealthy state such as Utah. Disparities *within* a state can be even greater: For example, schools in affluent counties in Alaska and Vermont received about $15,000–$16,000 per child in 1998; schools in poorer counties received only $6,000–$7,000. Poorer schools tend to have less-qualified teachers, fewer resources for materials and activities, and less money for ongoing professional development or training for teachers. And better-qualified and better-supported teachers tend to have the most successful students, compared to underprepared teachers who have to figure things out on their own as they go along (Darling-Hammond & Post, 2000).

In summary, whether they are babies, toddlers, preschoolers, or school-agers, low-income young children often get the least, when they actually benefit the most from high-quality teachers and classrooms.

The Quality of a Program Impacts Child Outcomes

So we see that poor children get lower quality. How does that affect their development? In NICHD's study of early child care, when the researchers examined the effects of attending low-quality programs, they got worried (Vandell, Belsky, Burchinal, Vandergrift, Steinberg, & NICHD Early Child Care Research Network, 2012). Children who attended low-quality programs were likely to show more problem behaviors (such as hitting others, being disobedient, or frequent arguing), lower cognitive and language abilities, and lower school-readiness scores. As seen in other chapters, low-quality care is bad for any child, but it is especially bad for a child living in poverty, who is likely to face more hardships and have fewer learning opportunities at home than other children.

Other studies have found the same thing: Quality of early child care experiences influences many outcomes, including how well children do in elementary school (Peisner-Feinberg, Burchinal, Clifford, et al., 2001; Melhuish et al., 2008). The good news is that when low-income children have the opportunity to spend more hours in high-quality programs, they show greater academic benefits than children from better-off families (Desai, Chase-Lansdale, & Michael, 1989; Gormley, Gayer, Phillips, & Dawson, 2005). Anna and her dad, waiting at the food bank, hope they will get this opportunity.

Experiences in K–3 continue to have a critical impact on children's current well-being and long-term success. Children in low-income areas who attend underfunded and low-quality elementary schools show lower achievement levels than children in middle-income and affluent areas. The contrasts in achievement levels reflect the disparities in access to good schools and teachers with training and support.

Components of High-Quality Programs for Low-Income Families

Components of good programs for poor and near-poor children are similar to those that any high-quality program would have: warm, stimulating interactions between teachers and children, effective use of curricula, small groups and high adult-child ratios, mentoring and other supports for teachers–as well as some additional components. These components are equally important for children in K–3rd grade programs as for children in the preschool years. And as previously mentioned, good programs for low-income children are both holistic (promote growth in all domains of development) and comprehensive (provide for children's needs beyond in-class learning).

Nutrition and health services are foundational to children's ability to stay healthy and focused on learning, and should be included in programs serving low-income families. Connecting children to a regular medical provider, requiring and providing immunizations, and integrating comprehensive screenings (for diabetes, respiratory problems, measles, and so forth) have been shown to increase basic medical and dental health (Currie & Thomas, 1995).

In addition, a focus on parenting skills is helpful, especially one that models positive interactions and allows opportunities for parents to practice new skills and receive feedback. Parents have a special impact on children's psychological well-being and economic security, so program resources devoted to improving those aspects of family life are well spent in programs serving low-income families (Grindal, Bowne, Yoshikawa, Duncan, Magnuson, & Schindler, 2013). Programs that help parents as individuals–teaching parents to read, use a computer, or get a GED–are also likely to provide benefits to children. Studies evaluating the integration of these services into early childhood programs are under way (Ascend at the Aspen Institute, 2012).

Lastly, good programs intentionally commit to connecting parents with other parents. As shown in Chapters 2 and 3, these connections are important for all families; however, low-income, stressed-out parents can feel very isolated and vulnerable. They may appreciate help getting "plugged in" to their community, which can begin at the early childhood program. Parents can be excellent sources of support, friendship, and practical information for one another, strengthening low-income parents' sense of connection and empowerment. These connections can also help parents feel calmer and more in control, feelings that improve the emotional tone at home (Browne, 2009). Parents' connections with one another can also boost connections between children. Teachers can foster these family-to-family connections through simple social events in the program, such as inviting parents to view children's work in a classroom gallery, a group picnic, or sharing contact information (with parents' consent).

HEAD START, THE NATION'S EARLY CHILDHOOD PROGRAM

As already mentioned, early education programs can be provided by a neighbor, a house of worship, a private company, a nonprofit agency, or a school district. Only one program is provided by the United States government, however: Head Start (and the related Early Head Start programs, discussed in Chapter 2). President Lyndon Johnson initiated Head Start in 1964 as part of the administration's War on Poverty, and it has served more than 30 million poor children since.

The goal of Head Start is to promote low-income children's school readiness by enhancing their social and cognitive development. The program, which is free, is

---

PROFESSIONAL PROFILE

Donna Widmaier, Head Start Teacher, School District of Philadelphia, PA

Because it is early in the year, Donna has been meeting with parents and children to conduct initial screenings and to discuss health, nutrition, and parenting topics. During class time, Donna works individually, in small groups, and with the whole group, implementing a curriculum that blends academic and social-emotional development while addressing specific goals for children with disabilities. Donna spends time every week completing Work Sampling, an ongoing assessment that helps her track children's progress and adjust her teaching. Once the children have gone home, Donna develops weekly lesson plans based on long-range themes.

Donna interacts with families as they escort their children to and from school. She encourages parents to volunteer in her classroom, and she describes how she's supporting their child's learning. During some weeks, Donna's schedule may include home visits or parent conferences.

Donna meets frequently with her Teaching Assistant to discuss how they coordinate efforts to meet children's goals. Because Head Start focuses on all aspects of development, Donna also collaborates with support staff—an instructional specialist, social worker, nurse, special needs coordinator, and others. Finally, Donna has served as a Mentor Teacher for a Head Start learning community, helping everyone focus on improving teaching and children's learning.

Donna Widmaier began her teaching career as a kindergarten to 5th-grade teacher, and has worked in Head Start for 15 years. She has a bachelor's degree in elementary education, a master's in early childhood, and is a 2012 National Board Certified Teacher.

---

only available to families living below the poverty line. As a comprehensive service, Head Start teachers and administrators make sure they build personal relationships with families and provide nutritious meals for children and access to medical, dental, and mental health services.

Evaluating Head Start's Effectiveness: Concerns and Actions

To see if the program meets its goals, the government conducted a large, nationally representative impact study of 5,000 families, comparing results between Head Start participants and other children in poverty who did not participate in Head Start (United States Department of Health and Human Services, 2010). Initial results were promising: After 1 year in Head Start, children did show better school readiness skills than children who attended other programs or no program. Disappointingly, however, by 3rd grade almost all of the Head Start children's cognitive improvements seemed to fade out, and in other areas, like social-emotional development, health care, and parenting, the impact of Head Start compared to the impact of another program or no program were small to begin with.

The results of this research initially seemed discouraging, but there are several important things to note: (a) many children enrolled in the program, who were included as participants in the study, did not actually attend the program on a regular basis; (b) 60% of the "non-participants" in the control group actually attended another early childhood program (Puma et al., 2012); and (c) many Head Start programs were not high-quality programs, discussed further below.

Moreover, although positive effects seemed to fade out in middle childhood, there are clear long-term gains from participation in Head Start. Studies show effects on important societal outcomes such as high-school graduation, years of education completed, earnings, and reduced crime and teen pregnancy (cf. Yoshikawa et al., 2013).

The Quality of Head Start Needs to Be Better

As discussed in previous chapters, quality always matters. Although all Head Start programs should be high-quality, in reality the quality of centers varies tremendously. In one study, not even 1 in 20 participating 4-year-olds was enrolled in a center that observers rated as having excellent quality. Only half the children were in centers meeting the recommended criteria for number of children per teacher. Moreover, on average the instructional quality levels were well below where they should be (Moiduddin, Aikens, Tarullo, West, & Xue, 2012). In general, program quality varied but was often low.

In order for Head Start to do the job it is meant to do, which is to improve the well-being and success of low-income children, and in response to these findings, Head Start is systematically improving the quality across its centers by revising the program's performance standards, training, and technical assistance system (National Forum on Early Childhood Policy and Programs, 2010). Programs have to increase the number of teachers with a college degree and teachers have to enhance their curricula. The office of Head Start will not continue to fund those centers that do not show evidence of success.

Beyond Early Head Start and Head Start (and other early childhood programs), as seen in Chapter 4, kindergarten and primary-grade classrooms need to keep the momentum going. They need to provide the kind of engaging, challenging curriculum and interactions that can sustain early gains. Yes, Anna needs to be in a program such as Head Start, and her baby brother needs to be in a program such as Early Head Start, but they also need to go to a good elementary school to deepen their early progress. As described here and in Chapter 4, many kindergarten to 3rd-grade classrooms are of low quality, and these are most often classrooms that have more than their share of low-income children. It is difficult to sustain the gains of even the best Head Start interventions under these conditions.

WHO GETS TO GO? BROADENING ACCESS TO HIGH-QUALITY SERVICES FOR CHILDREN IN LOW-INCOME FAMILIES

Increasing quality is only the first step. Increasing access is equally critical: Most low-income families cannot find a space in a free program and cannot afford a space in other high-quality early childhood programs.

Head Start Is Free but Has Too Few Spaces

Although Head Start is free, money and space are available for only 51% of eligible 4-year-olds, 36% of eligible 3-year-olds, and less than 4% of eligible infants and toddlers. Long waiting lists of families wanting to enroll are not uncommon. However, investments in Head Start to serve additional children have been a recent White House priority; with this support, Head Start is working to make space for more families–families with infants and toddlers are especially in need.

There Are Increasing Numbers of Spaces in State-Funded Pre-K Programs

As of 2011–2012, 40 states and the District of Columbia offered some children spaces in free or subsidized pre-K programs. In a few rare states (Oklahoma and Florida, for example), pre-K is available to any family that would like to enroll a child, but in most of these states, the spaces are reserved for low-income families. This trend is encouraging and it is showing results: The availability of center-based programs for low-income preschoolers is on the rise (National Forum on Early Childhood Policy and Programs, 2010). There are also signs of increased political will to support the expansion of early care and education, including recent proposals to provide pre-K for all low- and moderate-income 4-year-olds in America (Barnett, 2013). If there is continued commitment and follow-through to support large-scale public early childhood

---

PROFESSIONAL PROFILE

Cathy Grace, Director, Early Childhood Education,
Gilmore Early Learning Initiative, Amory, Mississippi,
Consultant, Early Childhood Policy, Children's Defense Fund, Washington, DC

Cathy works in two worlds, directing an early childhood program serving low-income children in Mississippi and serving as the early childhood policy consultant to the Children's Defense Fund. Her days often blur the reality of working directly with children and families in poverty and reviewing and developing policies to support low-income children more generally. As a local program director she often works with parents to ensure their children receive services to which they are entitled and provides guidance to teachers on instructional strategies and curriculum. As a consultant to the Children's Defense Fund she participates in conference calls and meetings to formulate policies that increase access for low-income children to a high-quality early childhood system. It can be challenging to combine the role of child advocate/educator in a local community with that of a child advocate in a national organization where statistics need to tell the story. However, Cathy feels that her daily experience of living these two perspectives helps her focus more closely on the child and the stories behind each statistic. The result is a more pragmatic problem-solving approach in both worlds.

Cathy has been a classroom teacher, university ECE program director, Mississippi Department of Education's early childhood coordinator, local family support program founder, and advisor to state legislators, governors, and policymakers.

programs, the future looks very hopeful indeed for families like Anna's—the ones who most benefit from good early childhood programs.

Barriers to Overcome

The country is not yet providing universal access, however. Low-income families may not be able to find an Early Head Start, Head Start, free pre-K, or other afford- able program near them, or they may be unaware of the places that do exist. Low- income, marginalized families may be reluctant to get involved in any program or worry that they do not belong there because of their culture or home language. And ironically, living just above the poverty line actually puts children more at risk for not attending an early childhood program than living under it. Officially poor children qualify for free programs like Early Head Start, Head Start, and pre-K. Near-poor children, who have barely more resources than poor children, do not. At the mo- ment, there are not enough affordable programs to serve the half of the population that is poor or near-poor. However, Anna's family may have more options in the future, whether they are able to stay in their current home or have to move yet again.

CONCLUDING THOUGHTS: LOW-INCOME FAMILIES DESERVE BETTER ACCESS AND BETTER-QUALITY PROGRAMS

Low-income children need the most and get the least. Compared with children from middle-income families, through no fault of their own, low-income children are less likely to live in environments that promote their development, less likely to go to an early childhood education program as a toddler or as a preschooler, more likely to go to a low-quality program when they do participate, and more likely to attend a low-quality elementary school.

This differential access by family income is a big part of the reason behind the continued disparities between the rich and poor in the United States. As already em- phasized, the difference in access is important because going to a high-quality early childhood program for a year or more matters more for low-income children than for other children (OECD, 2011; Yoshikawa et al., 2013).

Certainly early childhood education is not a magic bullet that can stop the effects of poverty in their tracks. It *is,* however, a way of slowing down the impacts of pov- erty and helping children find their way onto a track that leads to greater well-being, achievement, and success. There are two basic improvements the early childhood system needs to make to help more low-income children get on a better track.

First, the system needs to ensure that any family under or near the poverty line— half of all children under age 6 in America live in one of these families—can enroll their infant or young child in an early childhood program. Second, the system needs to ensure that the quality of the program is good and worth families' money and time.

Given the low rate of enrollment among low-income families compared to other families, and given the high likelihood of low-income children attending a program of questionable quality, making these two fixes will require a commitment from stake- holders and society. It will also require a financial investment—but there is almost no better investment policymakers can make in terms of both personal benefits and economic returns. The most conservative estimates done with the most rigorous analyses show that providing high-quality early childhood services to low-income families leads to at least $7 saved for every $1 spent (Yoshikawa et al., 2013).

We need to ensure that we find ways to make the investment. Every child deserves the chance to grow and stay healthy; be full of curiosity, wonder, and confidence; and find delight in life. If we succeed in giving every child the chance to participate in good early childhood services and attend good schools, Anna and her brother can grow up with a love of reading, a good supply of colorful crayons, and a full stomach, hungry only for the chance to learn and play.

REFLECTION, DIALOGUE, AND ACTION

1. Have your ideas about young children living in low-income families changed as a result of reading and discussing this chapter? If so, in what ways?

2. If possible, identify an early childhood professional in your community who works with children in low-income families. Interview this person about his or her work, and share your insights with others. Or, if this is the focus of your own work, describe your work to others.

3. On the basis of this chapter, what might you say to someone who says that there is no point working in programs such as Head Start because the problems are too great to even begin to address?

4. Search Research Connections, www.researchconnections.org, for recent "Fact Sheets and Briefs" using the search term "early childhood programs children in poverty." Look at the short descriptions of some of these reports, download a few, read, and share.

INFORMATION TO EXPLORE AND SHARE

National Center for Children in Poverty

NCCP is the nation's leading public policy center dedicated to promoting the economic security, health, and well-being of America's low-income families and children. Want a profile of how your state is doing in addressing poverty among young children? Want free publications to download? These and more are available here. www.nccp.org

Office of Head Start

Learn all about Head Start services, the history of Head Start, and Head Start research. Sign up for a free e-subscription to receive updates from Head Start's Early Learning and Knowledge Center. www.acf.hhs.gov/programs/ohs

Children's Defense Fund

CDF is a nonprofit organization that advocates for the needs of children, especially poor and minority children. CDF works to influence federal and state legislation and funding for services including health, quality early education, and a strong foundation for the future. www.childrensdefense.org

CHAPTER 6

The Early Years Matter
for Children Who Experience
Violence and Stress

© Anita Patterson Peppers

Charlotte and Tanya's Story

Charlotte was only 3 years old when Eddy, her mother's boyfriend, started coming into her room at night. Charlotte's sister, Tanya, older by 2 years, used to be visited that way; now it was Charlotte's turn. One time, the girls' mother Jeannette came into the room and found Eddy lying on top of her daughter, rubbing his body over hers. She started locking the doors to the girls' rooms at night, but Eddy would just break the locks when he felt like it. Then Jeannette started giving the girls brooms to protect themselves. But she never kicked Eddy out of their apartment or their lives. The abuse went on for 6 more years, until Eddy moved away. After that, Jeannette still lived in the house but was never very present in her children's lives. Charlotte's older sister, Tanya, did most of the cooking and caretaking; she was the one who gave hugs when they were needed.

In 2nd grade, Charlotte had a wonderful teacher named Ms. Julie. Ms. Julie didn't know what was happening at home for her sweet student, but she worried about Charlotte, who was quieter and more tired than other children. Ms. Julie was observant and kind, and most important, stayed involved in Charlotte's life. Ms. Julie kept an eye on her throughout school. With that help, Charlotte got through academically and graduated from high school. She became a licensed practical nurse.

Now 23, Charlotte is married and has a 4-year-old son, Benjamin. She has rough patches, but nothing she feels she can't overcome. She adores her son and cherishes her family life. Every couple of months, she calls her former teacher Ms. Julie for a pizza night.

Charlotte worries a lot about her older sister, Tanya, though. Tanya has a son, Osborne, who is about the same age as Benjamin. Tanya struggles more than Charlotte. She is often overcome by the challenges of balancing single parenting and her job as a motel clerk. There are days when she just cannot seem to get out of bed, and her son, Osborne, is left to find the cornflakes on his own. At other times she gets so angry with Osborne that she screams and strikes out at him. She tells Charlotte that she has recurring nightmares about Eddy breaking into her room. Some days she has panic attacks that make her feel unable to breathe. Charlotte tries to help on the bad days by taking care of Osborne or bringing over dinner. Sometimes Charlotte thinks that perhaps all Tanya's mothering skills were used up on her when they were children. She wonders if some of Tanya's problems are partly her fault.

THE KINDS OF VIOLENCE AND STRESS YOUNG CHILDREN EXPERIENCE

"How serious can a 5-year-old's problems be?" a parent asks. The myth is that early childhood is a carefree time, a period in life to splash in rain puddles and get wide-eyed over grasshoppers and fireworks. This is what every parent and teacher wants for their children, joy and wonder—the absence of fear and stress. Yet fear and stress are chronic problems for many young children, affecting their development and opportunities to learn and enjoy life in the moment and into the future.

This chapter outlines some of the types of stress children may experience, as well as what teachers can do to counteract the serious problems that may be happening outside the early childhood program. Early childhood teachers are in a unique position to support families going through hard times for at least three reasons: The earlier children receive intervention, the better they fare; teachers often represent a safe, nonstigmatized resource person for parents; and early childhood teachers know how to recognize and build on people's strengths, deterring problems before they begin—or before they overwhelm.

Types of Stress

Some stress can actually be positive: Children need new and mildly challenging situations to gain resilience and resourcefulness. Examples of these kinds of stressors are things like joining a new class, getting booster shots, or staying with friends for a weekend when parents need to travel. These experiences are manageable and have the potential for benefits—and they certainly do not cause children harm.

Harmful stress is needing to hide from your mother's boyfriend, not eating dinner, having nowhere to sleep, not getting a bath for 10 days, or ducking bullets.

Some of the terrible experiences that children have are the fault of the adults in their lives who are supposed to love and protect them, some are the fault of weak or absent laws that fail to provide good care for families needing help, some are the fault of nature or life in a complex world, and some are no one's fault.

Young children have parents who are alcoholics and drug addicts; families split up because of divorce, deportation, or incarceration; caregivers have mental illnesses; parents abuse each other; children lose their homes to tornadoes, earthquakes, fires, and eviction; they lose loved ones to cancer and accidents. Children themselves get cancer and get hurt in accidents. They get shuttled between foster care homes and get lost in the child welfare system that is supposed to help them. They go to school hungry and go to bed hungry. Shooters come into schools, theaters, and malls; and children are told to stay below the windowsills when they watch television. Children are abused by their parents and neglected by them, a condition collectively called *maltreatment*–the issue of particular focus in this chapter.

Characteristics and Numbers of Children Affected by Trauma and Stress

Children of all socioeconomic and ethnic backgrounds experience stress, abuse, neglect, and traumatic experiences, although children living in poverty are especially at risk. While children of all ages experience violence and stress, children under age 4–like Charlotte when her maltreatment began–are the most vulnerable to abuse. The younger the child, the greater the risk for severe injury and death from abuse (NAEYC, 1996). Children with problem behaviors or special needs may be especially in danger of maltreatment, as well as children of parents living in highly stressful conditions, such as living with poverty, unemployment, mental health problems, or addiction (U.S. Department for Health and Human Services, n.d.).

Every day in America, over 1,800 children are abused or neglected and 4 of them die from it; 7 children die from guns; over 800 children experience physical punishment at school; over 2,700 babies are born into poverty and over 1,200 children are born without health insurance; and 24 children die by accident (Children's Defense Fund, 2013a). A 5-year-old's problems can be very serious indeed.

The list of violent or stressful experiences children encounter is long, even in a country as supposedly safe and advanced as the United States. Child protection policies related to abuse and neglect are not particularly effective in protecting children and families from maltreatment, especially infants and toddlers, which may be one reason that thousands of children come in contact with the child welfare system every year–and there are thousands more not counted because they never receive help (Jordan, Szrom, Colvard, Cooper, & DeVooght, 2013).

What happens in children's development as a result of violence and high levels of stress depends on several factors, including the duration of the stress, how trusted adults explain and manage the problem, children's own temperament and strengths, and what sources of support children have beyond their families. The number of stressors families have to manage is another factor determining long-term outcomes. It seems children may be somewhat equipped to handle one difficult situation but not multiple difficult situations at once–a common occurrence called *cumulative risk factors*.

The Problem of Cumulative Stress

One bad event can trigger new problems, especially when families have few resources–financial or social–to begin with. A child who has had one adverse experience is 80% more likely to experience another (CSSP, n.d.), and the more risk factors a family has, the less likely it is to be able to get help. Children are not able to–and should never be expected to–advocate for the help they need for themselves, so it is usually only when an adult speaks up that children get help. Speaking up is therefore an important role for early childhood professionals.

Consider these two scenarios, in which one stressful situation triggers others in a downward spiral:

- A father is "downsized" by his employer, the family loses his income, and the family slides into poverty–a major source of stress. The father starts becoming depressed and drinking more. To hide what is happening, the family stops talking to neighbors. The mother starts taking overtime hours to make extra money, leaving the children to miss her and eat more junk food instead of meals. The children are left to fend for themselves more and more, neglected both physically and emotionally.
- A family who has just lost a home in a tornado in Oklahoma has to move to Texas, where they do not know anyone except the sister they will stay with. The apartment is too small, which makes everyone tense. Eventually, the fighting becomes unbearable and the family moves out. With nowhere to go and too ashamed to stay in a shelter, they stay in their car, parking at public parks or on dark streets to sleep at night. With no address, the children cannot enroll in school.

As these examples show, when stressors pile on top of one another or continue on and on, children may experience a serious condition known as *toxic stress*.

CONSEQUENCES OF TOXIC STRESS ON YOUNG CHILDREN

When we feel threatened, our bodies react physiologically. We have an increased heart rate, higher blood pressure, and a flood of stress hormones such as adrenaline and cortisol. Prolonged, frequent, or intense adverse experiences make the stress toxic, or poisonous to children's growth and development. When children are young, like Charlotte and Tanya were when their abuse began, chronic stress is especially damaging because excessive cortisol disrupts developing brain circuitry and damages learning and memory, among other things. Simultaneously, deprivation–like the neglect Charlotte and Tanya experienced from their mother–also affects brain development because this development depends on responsive, dependable adult interactions. For example, research shows that, over time, young children raised in understaffed orphanages where adults cannot respond to infants' needs develop serious cognitive deficits and atypical patterns of social behavior (Shonkoff, 2012).

Some of the immediate and long-term consequences from violence, neglect, and toxic stress include cognitive delays, attachment disorders, low self-esteem, poor social skills, loss of insight and empathy, extreme sensitivity to threat, physical health problems extending into adulthood, post-traumatic stress disorder, depression, and anxiety (Jordan, Szrom, Colvard, Cooper, & DeVooght, 2013; Sidorowicz & Hair, 2009; Shonkoff, 2012). Charlotte and, particularly, Tanya experienced several of these consequences, and Osborne is at risk as well.

HOW EARLY CHILDHOOD PROGRAMS CAN REDUCE THE CONSEQUENCES OF VIOLENCE AND STRESS

Even for children who have experienced toxic stress, early intervention and the care of loving, responsive adults can improve a child's brain development, sense of resilience, positive outlook, and opportunities for healthy development. Children are remarkably good at finding ways to heal when they have help.

Early childhood programs of all kinds can make a huge impact on children's and families' well-being. For example, a study of children in early childhood programs in high-poverty areas of Chicago showed that children attending preschool were 52% less likely to experience maltreatment by age 17 than children not enrolled in a preschool (Reynolds & Robertson, 2003). In another study, children who experienced difficult early years, and would therefore be expected to be more aggressive, showed fewer behavior problems and less aggression both in kindergarten and as teenagers if they had attended high-quality early childhood education programs. In contrast, those young children living with stress who did not go to high-quality ECE programs were 70% more likely to be arrested for violent crimes by age 18 (FPG-UNC Smart Start Evaluation Team, 1999). These studies show that early intervention can slow down or perhaps stop repeating cycles of violence.

Teachers Connect Families with Specialized Professionals Who Can Help

More than half of American children—12.5 million out of 20.5 million children under age 5—participate in some type of out-of-home care before kindergarten (Laughlin, 2013), and 98% of children enroll in kindergarten by age 5. Although disadvantaged children are less likely to be enrolled very early in care and education programs than their middle-class peers, by kindergarten disadvantaged and advantaged children are enrolled at almost equal rates. In addition, violence and stress affect children from all family backgrounds, not only low-income families. Therefore, early childhood education programs—from preschool through the early grades—make a good first point of connection between professionals and troubled families.

Because, by kindergarten at least, school is an almost-universal experience, a teacher may represent a safe and knowledgeable person from whom families may get information and support. Some parents do not know who else to ask for help or want to avoid the stigma of seeing a mental health professional. A teacher can be a "safe" resource person who can be consulted with no stigma attached. Thus, teachers play a critical support role as trained professionals and caring individuals—not by providing therapy to family members, but by recognizing warning signs and connecting families to other specialized professionals.

Teachers Identify Warning Signs

One of the most important influences on children's well-being is a relationship with at least one concerned, caring, knowledgeable adult. In Charlotte's case, Ms. Julie intuited that something was not right in Charlotte's family, though she had no reason to think that Charlotte experienced sexual abuse. Following her observations that Charlotte seemed more fearful, withdrawn, and tired than other children, Ms. Julie made herself available as someone Charlotte could trust, talk to, ask advice of, and get practical help from. She provided stability and love.

Teachers are often key people in children's lives, but they are not meant to be surrogate parents or therapists. Often when teachers sense "red flags"–signs of concern such as sudden acting out, withdrawal, lack of appetite, or excessive crying–their role is to confer with program leaders and parents to link the family to an appropriate specialized professional. Psychologists and other mental health and social workers play a key role in providing necessary diagnostic and therapeutic services for young children and their parents.

Teachers Are Mandated Reporters

Like all professionals who work with children, early childhood teachers are mandated to report when they see signs of abuse and neglect (Child Welfare Information

---

PROFESSIONAL PROFILE

Lacy Carter, Licensed Marriage and Family Therapist (LMFT),
Private Practice, Sacramento, California

As a therapist, Lacy partners with children and families to nurture healthy development. One child she currently sees is a 6-year-old referred for tantrums and aggression through the school district. His treatment begins with standardized assessment measures and person-centered techniques to help develop comfort in the therapeutic relationship. He will benefit from Parent-Child Interaction Therapy (PCIT), which involves his parents and will reshape aggressive and disruptive patterns. Lacy may also provide individual child therapy or take part in Individual Education Plan (IEP) meetings with district staff.

Lacy also serves families with open Child Protective Services (CPS) cases as a group therapy facilitator for Seeking Safety, a 12-week program to develop safe parenting practices. As a CPS social worker, Lacy partners with community agencies, family courts, foster agencies, and families. As a new case develops, Lacy meets with a 4-year-old girl removed from her home while multiple abuse allegations are investigated. Lacy works to address the girl's fears and questions while helping her feel safe. She needs therapy for symptoms of PTSD, anxiety, depression, and disrupted attachment. Lacy meets with the child and her parents regularly to support their progress and supervise weekly visits.

Lacy Carter was formerly a county social worker and outpatient therapist. She began her career providing counseling in elementary schools. She is certified in PCIT, a model for children aged 2–7, and Trauma-Focused Cognitive Behavioral Therapy. She has a Master's in Counselor Education.

Gateway, 2012). In situations where the child is in danger, or suffers from a lack of appropriate hygiene, nutrition, supervision, or attention, the early childhood teacher is legally required to report the situation to authorities. For example, if Ms. Julie had had definite suspicions that Charlotte was being sexually abused or neglected, she would have been obligated to report her concerns.

Reporting a family to child protective services can be a painful experience because it may mean separating the child from the family. But it may also mean protecting the child from suffering or even saving a child's life. The goal of the reporting is to ensure children stay safe and cared for. Think what a difference this might have made in the lives of Charlotte and Tanya.

HOW EARLY CHILDHOOD TEACHERS CARE
FOR STRESSED CHILDREN AND ADULTS

Beyond their role as mandated reporters, teachers can help children who experience violence or stress by providing support to the child both directly and by empowering parents.

Direct Support to Children

Stressed and even traumatized children benefit from early care and education for a number of reasons, including how teachers engage directly with individual children.

Interacting Warmly and Creating Safe, Encouraging Environments. Specifically, good teachers of stressed children:

- Engage with children in warm, responsive, and dependable ways.
- Create safe, predictable environments with rules and routines.
- Encourage children to communicate and express themselves in appropriate ways.
- Help children explore, inquire, master activities, and be autonomous.

Although these practices are important for all children, intensifying the use of caring teaching strategies can help put stressed children's brain development; social and emotional skills; approaches to people, institutions, and learning; and concepts of right and wrong back on a positive developmental path.

Providing a Safe, Welcoming, and Predictable Environment. As discussed in Chapter 3, teachers who create a safe, healthy, joyful atmosphere provide a buffer for all children. This kind of buffer is especially important for children who are maltreated or at high risk for maltreatment. Being welcomed into a classroom by a teacher who cares how the child is doing, who is attentive to the child's mood changes or physical well-being, and who provides interesting, fun activities to participate in can make a world of difference to a child who goes home where emptiness, chaos, or stress are evident. Tanya's son, Osborne, would benefit a great deal from a place like this, for example. Again, early childhood programs and teachers cannot replace what children need from their families, and teachers must report potentially dangerous situations, but these services and interactions can reduce the impact of a troubled home life.

Teaching Good Social Skills. One of the most important roles of good early childhood teachers is to teach children the social and emotional skills they may not have been able to learn at home because of maltreatment or other stressful conditions. Teachers can help children learn positive social skills by helping children build friendships, regulate emotions, and develop social problem-solving skills. Children who are constantly reliving a trauma or who act out inappropriate behaviors can seem deviant, scary, or just plain weird to other children. As good role models, teachers show children how to manage their feelings in order to stay within the bounds of what other children normally feel comfortable with. Early childhood programs are safe places for children because teachers define which behaviors are okay and which are not, and they apply logical and consistent consequences—which minimizes children's defiant, aggressive, or otherwise negative behaviors related to the stress in their lives (Myles & Simpson, 1998). Chapter 8 provides further insight into how to understand, prevent, and address young children's challenging behavior, whatever its source.

Building Resilience in Young Children Living with Stress. Imagine a rubber band being stretched by two hands, then let go on one side: It will bounce back to its initial shape. That is resilience, the ability to bounce back. Being able to bounce back is a skill that naturally comes easier to some people than others. For example, Charlotte seems to have been more resilient than Tanya in the face of the same abusive environment. However, resilience *can* be taught to all children (Duncan, Bowden, & Smith, 2005). Resilience gives children and adults the ability to adapt and recover from stressful situations in ways that help them cope better in the present and protect themselves from similar situations in the future (Masten, 2013).

Experts are quick to point out that being resilient does not mean being invulnerable. Children experiencing toxic stress usually feel very scared, sad, vulnerable, and anxious. These emotions should not be discounted or overlooked, but rather acknowledged and validated as normal reactions to terrible situations. However, teachers can simultaneously help children build the language, attitudes, beliefs, and skills that create resilience.

In the International Resilience Project (Bernard Van Leer Foundation, 1995), researchers identified several factors that contribute to children's resilience, such as (this is not the complete list):

- Having trusting relationships and role models.
- Having structure and rules to follow.
- Having encouragement to be independent and responsible, while also receiving help.
- Believing one is lovable and loving.
- Being proud of oneself.
- Being able to communicate.
- Having good problem-solving skills.
- Being able to gauge the temperament of oneself and others and manage feelings and impulses.

Children may inherently be resilient in some areas of development and not others. Being sensitive and aware of the context and children's ages and needs, good teachers decide which areas of resilience to focus on for individual children in the program.

Indirect Support to Children: Improving Parenting Skills

Teachers not only help children directly, but they also help their families; this may be the most powerful way to impact the stressful or damaging aspects of young children's lives. Teachers link stressed and at-risk parents with other professionals, as already mentioned; give them knowledge about child development in general and feedback about their own child in specific, at the relevant time; and connect them with other families.

Parents whose children go to an early childhood program often find that the influence of a caring, supportive, and nonjudgmental professional can go a long way toward calming a charged atmosphere at home. A survey by the Center for the Study of Social Policy (CSSP) explored processes in 39 family child care programs around the country that were nominated for doing an exemplary job of connecting with families. Participating families were from all types of income levels and backgrounds. Results showed that parents perceived themselves to be more nurturing, patient and child-centered as a result of their interactions with program staff (Browne, 2009). A parent's improved self-perception is potentially an important factor in reducing child maltreatment. In this study, families felt the program helped them improve their functioning in the following ways, by:

- Using more positive reinforcement.
- Using less spanking and generally being less harsh or punitive.
- Yelling less and using a less angry tone of voice and volume.
- Talking to their children more, asking them more questions, and listening more.
- Giving their children more developmentally appropriate choices about, say, what to wear, which fruit to eat for breakfast, or what game to play.
- Providing healthier meals.
- Being more likely to create and follow a daily routine.
- Having more realistic expectations of their children.
- Being more aware of themselves as role models.
- Being more aware of how to set and enforce limits.
- Providing more consistency in, for example, enforcing rules, sticking with routines, and reactions to misbehavior.
- Feeling calmer and more confident as a parent. (pp. 53–54)

This kind of responsive, consistent, warm parenting helps children feel calmer, more secure, happier, and more confident, too–and thus less likely to misbehave. When children misbehave less often, parents are less likely to lose their cool and do something that could harm a child.

What is it specifically that teachers do to help parents get to that place of warm, positive parenting? Recent research shows that the most effective approaches include teacher modeling of parenting skills to parents, along with opportunities for parents to practice new skills and receive feedback. Workshops and group classes where parents are passive recipients of information may be less effective (Grindal et al., 2013). Although large-scale integration of successful parenting interventions is not yet a common occurrence within preschool systems, Strengthening Families is an approach that has proven successful in diminishing maltreatment of children.

THE *STRENGTHENING FAMILIES* APPROACH
TO PREVENTING ABUSE AND NEGLECT

Discussing interventions for every type of dangerous environment and toxic stress that families and young children experience is beyond the scope of this chapter. Here we consider child maltreatment (abuse and neglect) as one example, referring back to the hypothetical case of Charlotte and Tanya. The Center for the Study of Social Policy's (2007) *Strengthening Families Through Early Care and Education* approach shows how early childhood programs can strengthen families' protective factors to reduce the risk of child maltreatment.

In an in-depth study of 21 exemplary center-based programs, CSSP researchers found that those centers used a number of strategies that a large body of previous research suggests are likely to prevent child abuse and neglect:

1. *Connecting families to one another.* Family loneliness is closely connected to child neglect. Early childhood programs can facilitate friendships and mutual support among families. Having connections with other families who have children the same age, and probably live somewhat close to each other, can provide a buffer against loneliness and isolation.

2. *Enhancing parenting skills.* Teachers strengthen parenting skills by helping parents at just the time they most need information and support. Early childhood professionals can guide parents in understanding how to manage children's behavior in positive ways; what to expect from children and what is in the expected range of behavior for various stages; how to use effective disciplining techniques; and how to support children to play, learn, and grow in healthy ways.

3. *Helping during crises.* For families in crisis, program staff can provide a lifeline of concrete support and logistical help. It could be that a program keeps the child extra hours so the parents can go to counseling sessions; an administrator refers a new widow to a local grief support group she knows about; or a teacher organizes a collection of warm clothes as winter approaches.

4. *Integrating families into the community.* Linking families to services and opportunities can broaden a family's support network and strengthen the family's assets. Teachers can link parents with local resources and services such as food banks, community programs, after-school or summer programs, job fairs, counselors, hospitals and health specialists, faith-based programs, libraries, public pools, addiction services, and English-language classes.

5. *Strengthening children's social skills.* Children who respond well to others (as Charlotte did when she was young) have a better chance of overcoming

the odds than children who are aggressive, out of control, or unable to reach out to or respond well to other people. Helping parents develop their children's social skills–suggesting a playdate between two children, for example, or teaching a child to look at a person to show they are listening– is another way teachers can work with families.

6. *Responding to red flags.* By being observant, teachers can respond to early warning signs of abuse or neglect. Careful observers watch how families interact, how children react to parents and other adults, how children's bodies move or seem unusually sensitive, whether children's moods change drastically, and listen to how children talk or avoid talking about topics. Charlotte's teacher Miss Julie did that. Although her relationship with Charlotte was not enough to prevent the abuse that her teacher was unaware of, it built Charlotte's resilience then and for the future.

7. *Being encouraging and kind to parents.* A teacher's or other staff person's word of encouragement can soften the heart of any parent, no matter how stressed. Parents, who often receive little recognition for the relentless, sometimes exhausting work of parenting, can be energized by a teacher's welcoming smile and nonjudgmental listening. Talking about how a parent's choices positively impacted a child's day can boost parents' self-esteem and motivation. For example, if a teacher mentions how the change in nightly bedtimes has made a difference for Annika's energy level, or how Oscar has talked about his new paint set every day this week, this communication can tell parents that their actions truly matter and remind them that no one in the world is more important, powerful, or special to their child than they are.

Since 2007, at least 30 states have adapted the Strengthening Families approach for some programs in their state, an encouraging statistic (CSSP, 2012). However, nonparticipating states and programs, even otherwise high-quality ones, may not be aware of how important it is to implement these kinds of strategies. Using excellent teaching practices with children is always central to the role of an early childhood professional. However, for families who are disorganized, dysfunctional, in crisis, or under stress, teachers may best protect children by reaching out to parents in ways that go beyond the classroom.

OTHER PROGRAMS FOR CHILDREN LIVING WITH VIOLENCE OR STRESS

The Strengthening Families approach is intended to be integrated into mainstream early childhood education programs, with the notion that all families can benefit from the strategies suggested. Other early childhood programs address the needs of specific types of families experiencing specific types of stressful situations.

Programs Aimed at Prevention

Like the Strengthening Families approach, the following two programs aim to prevent problems before they occur, recognizing that children who cause stress to

PROFESSIONAL PROFILE

Nilofer Ahsan, Senior Associate, Center for the Study of Social Policy, Washington, DC

Nilofer leads the Strengthening Families Initiative nationally. In more than 40 states Strengthening Families is being used as a research-informed framework to help early childhood professionals and others learn how to support parents in building those protective factors shown to be associated with lower rates of abuse and neglect and optimal child development. A typical week will find Nilofer in the field helping practitioners integrate Strengthening Families into their work. Her work might take her to Los Angeles, which is using its tobacco funds to fund a focus on early childhood in 14 communities; to Philadelphia, where the city is adopting Strengthening Families as a framework for its child welfare services; or to a leadership team meeting in one of the many states that is using Strengthening Families as a framework across all its child- and family-serving systems. When not on planes, trains, and automobiles, Nilofer might be developing new tools for practitioners who implement Strengthening Families on the ground, talking with federal government partners about how Strengthening Families can connect with and support federal priorities, or working with partners from the many national organizations that are bringing this initiative to their constituencies.

Nilofer Ahsan has spent more than 20 years building stronger systems to support children and families. Before joining CSSP she was the Director of Knowledge and Policy at the Family Resource Coalition. Nilofer has a master's degree in public policy from the University of Chicago.

families—babies who won't stop crying and children with special needs—are especially vulnerable to maltreatment.

The Fussy Baby Network. Because babies are small, need constant care, and sometimes seem to cry nonstop, they may be in danger of maltreatment (U.S. Department for Health and Human Services, n.d.). The Fussy Baby Network, provided through the Erikson Institute, aims to support the parents of these infants. Staff also support early childhood teachers who may have these babies in their centers. Telephone "warmline" support, home visits, and other services are available for adults who have questions about infants' development; are concerned about a baby's crying, sleeping, or feeding habits; think a baby has colic; or feel exhausted and overwhelmed and need to talk to someone. Services are free or available on a sliding scale fee, and resources are provided in English and Spanish (Erikson Institute, 2013).

The Devereux Center for Resilient Children. The Devereux program works in at least 11 states to promote the social and emotional well-being of all children by building resilience, using a strengths-based approach and strong partnerships between families, teachers, and others who work with young children. The Center's resources include DVDs with video examples that can be used in professional development, assessment tools, and positive behavioral interventions for school staff (Devereux Foundation, 2012).

Programs Providing Intervention

The following two programs are designed for families or children already dealing with a crisis or stressful experiences.

Parents and Children Together (PACT). This is an intervention program in Baltimore, Maryland, that specializes in serving children who are experiencing or have experienced homelessness, through its Therapeutic Nursery and Family Roots programs. The program serves children under age 3 and their families under the auspices of Early Head Start, with the aim of enhancing parent-child bonds and mental health while increasing stability in their lives (Kennedy Krieger Institute, 2005).

Lefika La Phosido—the Art Therapy Centre. This is a nonprofit art therapy program in South Africa that began in 1993 as a way to help children suffering from abuse, poverty, HIV/AIDS, and violence in the community. It works to engage children who have experienced traumatic experiences through art, which is a creative and healing outlet for young children, inexpensive to implement, and not bound by cultural or language barriers. Services include counseling, crisis intervention, and professional development and training. Providers collaborate with education specialists, psychosocial professionals, and arts and culture experts (Art Therapy Centre, 2013).

CONCLUDING THOUGHTS: PREVENTION IS BETTER THAN INTERVENTION

In spite of our well-intentioned hopes that every child has a carefree childhood, one only has to turn on the news to know that many children go through terrible experiences before they can even talk. Children are shot at, ignored, underfed, hit, scorned, sexually abused, and deprived of safe shelter, places to play, and stable, loving relationships. Childhood can be hard.

Instead of trying to treat children for these experiences after they happen, our preferred solution is to prevent toxic stress and harm from happening in the first place. By building on a family's and a child's strengths, teachers can sometimes stop or slow down the snowball effect of cumulative stressors.

Most early childhood professionals already realize that their greatest asset in improving the lives of young children is the family. Even families with severe problems come to the table with strengths, and good early childhood teachers try to build on those strengths.

Research from multiple studies identifies several factors that can protect families (Horton, 2003). When parents are resilient, connected to others in the community, knowledgeable about child development, and have concrete help to get through tough times, families have some protection against stress. And when children have good social and emotional skills, they are less at risk of harm.

Unlike many other professionals, early childhood teachers have a special opportunity to strengthen these protective factors, because such a wide array of families use early childhood programs, whether they know they need help or not.

Incorporating a strengths-based approach into every program takes intentional awareness and commitment on the part of professionals. However, it is a worthwhile commitment with big dividends for individuals and society. Not only should we intentionally incorporate strengths-based prevention strategies into our programs, but we should implement voluntary home visiting programs, described in Chapter 2, for most or all parents. The families early childhood professionals most need to reach are often the very families who are too ashamed, disorganized, and overwhelmed to enroll in early childhood programs. Wide-scale home visiting programs are a missing link in the system.

In Charlotte's case, Ms. Julie was incredibly important in her ongoing support to Charlotte. However, if Ms. Julie had been able to forge connections with Charlotte's mother as well, or if a home visitor had noticed the locks on the children's bedroom door, the family might have gotten help. Charlotte's mother did not know how to get out of a bad situation, but she loved her daughters and wanted to do better by them. Early childhood professionals, whether working with infants or 3rd-graders, at a center or doing home visits, have a unique opportunity to touch the lives of children at risk.

REFLECTION, DIALOGUE, AND ACTION

1. Think back to a time when you observed an adult mistreating a child in public, such as at a grocery store, mall, or ball game. Or, if a child was maltreated in your family or a friend's, reflect on a scene you remember. What specifically was the adult doing that seemed wrong to you? How did the child react? What feelings did you experience? Write down your responses, as well as how you might handle the same situation if the family were participants in an early childhood program at which you worked. (If the child or the adult pictured was you, please consider seeing a counselor, if you have not already done so.)

2. Go to the Child Welfare Information Gateway link on page 86 or another site to find out the laws and regulations specific to mandatory reporting of maltreatment in your state. Write down the conditions requiring a report, the agency or person you would need to contact, whether you can report anonymously, and the steps that would take place after you make the call.

3. Imagine you have received a huge grant, meaning you have funds to start an early childhood program of your own, with you as the founder and director. What special population of children at risk of maltreatment or trauma would you want to provide services for—foster care children, homeless families, teenage parents, children living in violent neighborhoods, children of alcoholics or addicts, a group discussed in the chapter, or some other group? How would you structure the program, what services would you provide, and how you entice families to enroll in your program? Write down your thoughts or discuss the ideas with a partner.

INFORMATION TO EXPLORE AND SHARE

Child Welfare Information Gateway

The Information Gateway is a service of the Children's Bureau of the United States Administration for Children and Families. It connects professionals and the general public with information and tools related to child abuse and neglect, strengthening families, and child welfare. The website includes state requirements for mandated reporters, how to report suspected cases of abuse or get help with a personal situation, a hotline number for speaking with a counselor, and resources for early childhood professionals to share with families. www.childwelfare.gov

Fight Crime: Invest in Kids

Fight Crime: Invest in Kids is an anticrime organization that focuses on investing in early childhood as a way to prevent violence, based on data showing that good early experiences protect children. The organization is made up of thousands of violence survivors, as well as sheriffs, prosecutors, and early childhood proponents. It presents statistics and legislative efforts related to investments in good preschools as a way to reduce the impact of violence, reduce incarcerations, and save states millions of dollars. www.fightcrime.org

Strengthening Families: A Protective Factors Framework

Strengthening Families is an approach to working with children and families that builds five research-based protective factors with families—both at-risk and other families—to prevent child abuse and neglect and promote optimal child development. The program is an initiative of the Center for the Study of Social Policy. The website explains the approach, the protective factors, and federal partners, and provides resources on child maltreatment. www.cssp.org/reform/strengthening-families.

CHAPTER 7

The Early Years Matter for Children with Disabilities

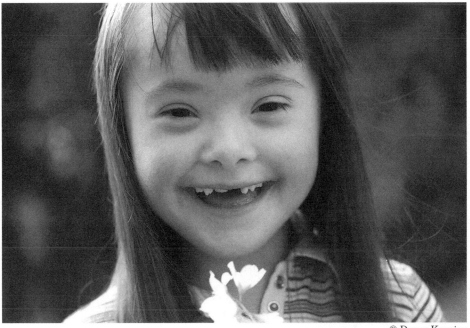

© Denys Kuvaiev

Today is Friday, and it's going to be a busy day for 1st-grader Melanie. She has been out of school for the last week with a bad cold and has missed being with her friends. Melanie's big sister Grace helps her get ready for the bus. Sometimes Melanie forgets to bring something, like her eyeglasses, but she is getting better at remembering, with Grace's helpful although sometimes annoying reminders.

On the bus, Melanie sits with Jacob, who is in her class and lives down the street. When they get to school, Melanie's teacher, Mrs. Bonilla, greets her and gets her started on some of the work she missed when she was out sick. A lot of activities at school are difficult for Melanie, especially reading. But she works hard at it and gets extra help from her teacher and from Ms. Anderson, who also works in Melanie's class.

At lunch, Melanie sits with her friends and then goes out to the playground with them for recess. After school comes soccer practice. This is Melanie's 2nd year on the team, and she loves it. She likes to wear her team shirt to school. Today she hopes she will score a goal; she is not as speedy as the other kids on her team, but she tries. Stopping at the store with her mother on the way back from soccer practice, Melanie sees Miss Julie, who was her favorite preschool teacher. Melanie gives Miss Julie a big hug and tells her about soccer. Miss Julie tells Melanie and her mom that she cannot believe all the new things that Melanie is learning this year, and how much she has grown since preschool. Miss Julie also tells Melanie that her birthday is coming up (she remembers that she and Melanie have almost the same birthday). When they get home, Melanie's mom and sister help Melanie make a card for Miss Julie.

It's been a great day.

CHILDREN WITH DISABILITIES

The Child as More Than a Disability

Melanie is a child with a disability. She has Down syndrome, a developmental disability caused by the presence of an extra chromosome, resulting in difficulties in intellectual development and language and communication delays, as well as other physical and health challenges (Pueschel, 2002). You may wonder why there was no mention of her disability in "Melanie's Story." Certainly Melanie's disability is significant, and it has affected many aspects of her life: her difficulties with reading, her frequent respiratory infections, and her need for glasses.

But, like other young children with disabilities, Melanie is much more than her disability. Despite her academic struggles and physical differences, many of Melanie's characteristics are like those of typically developing children. She's affectionate, generous, usually joyful, and eager to make friends. These are also characteristics that she shares with most other children with Down syndrome. Melanie also has a unique personality and interests, just like every other child. She has her own offbeat sense of humor, can be quietly stubborn at times, loves stuffed animals of all kinds, and will do anything for chocolate ice cream.

In speaking of disabilities, advocates always recommend what is called *person-first* or *people-first* language. We say that Melanie is *a child with a disability;* specifically, *a child with Down syndrome.* In the past, Melanie might have been called a "Down syndrome child," a "disabled child," or "a mentally retarded child." (Incidentally, until October 2010, the Individuals with Disabilities Education Act used the term "mental retardation"; now that Rosa's Law is in effect, the preferred term is "intellectual disability" [National Dissemination Center for Children with Disabilities, 2011]). These language issues are not just a matter of word order. Person-first language reminds us that *all* children are first and foremost children. The disability is part of who Melanie is, but it does not define her.

Prevalence and Causes of Disabilities in Young Children

Many young children have disabilities, with the prevalence of specific disabilities varying by country. In the United States, the Centers for Disease Control and

Prevention (CDC) estimates that as many as 1 in 6 children (aged 3 to 17) have some kind of developmental disability, and approximately 13% of infants have significant developmental delays (Rosenberg, Zhang, & Robinson, 2008). Based on large studies in the United States, most children's disabilities are developmental (including intellectual), emotional, or behavioral in nature, with the most common developmental disabilities in children age 3 and up including speech problems, learning disabilities, Attention Deficit Hyperactivity Disorder (ADHD), and autism spectrum disorder. Children over age 6 are twice as likely to be identified as having disabilities as younger children, in part because the demands of school make some problems, such as specific learning disabilities, more apparent (Currie & Kahn, 2012). Precisely comparable data are not available for children under age 3, but in 2011, over 336,000 infants and toddlers and their families received early intervention services through Part C of the Individuals with Disabilities Education Act (IDEA), generally because of developmental delays or specific conditions such as Down syndrome or low birth weight.

In this chapter, we use the term *disability* as a kind of shorthand, to include both developmental disabilities and developmental delays. Children with disabilities are those with chronic difficulties in physical, intellectual, and/or social areas, usually persisting throughout life. A child with Down syndrome such as Melanie or a child with autism are in this category. Children who are developmentally delayed develop on a slower timetable than most children, although the delay can sometimes be overcome. A child who is late in learning to sit or walk or a child who has almost no words at age 3 might be considered to have developmental delays. Sometimes it is only after time and intervention that specialists can determine whether early problems indicate a disability or a delay. Although they would not be identified as having disabilities, much of this chapter is also relevant to young children who have chronic health conditions such as diabetes or epilepsy.

Different disabilities have quite different causes, and in some cases the causes may not yet be understood. Melanie's disability, Down syndrome, is a genetic condition, and a relatively common one: Approximately 1 out of every 700 babies in America is born with Down syndrome (Centers for Disease Control and Prevention, 2013c). In addition to genetic conditions, other disabilities may be caused by problems before birth, such as heavy alcohol use in pregnant women (frequently causing fetal alcohol syndrome, with intellectual and social disabilities). Still other disabilities result from problems during the birth process itself, such as a lack of oxygen to the baby's brain (often a cause of cerebral palsy). We still do not have a clear understanding of the complex causes of disabilities such as autism.

YESTERDAY AND TODAY: CHANGING ATTITUDES AND RECOGNIZING RIGHTS

Great and positive changes have occurred in attitudes about, and the legal rights of, people with disabilities. Years ago, children and adults with disabilities were often hidden away from society, and had no right to an education—a situation that continues today in many developing countries. In the United States before 1975, there would probably have been no place in 1st grade for a child with Melanie's diagnosis: Only 1 in 5 children with disabilities attended public school (United States Department of Education, Office of Special Education and Rehabilitative Services, n.d.).

WHAT IS EARLY INTERVENTION?

In the case of disabilities, *intervention* means any treatment provided by a specialist or team of specialists to help a person with specific challenges. These specialists may include psychologists, pediatricians, other health professionals, occupational therapists, speech and language pathologists, and social workers; and family members are almost always critical to interventions. Treatments may focus on physical, intellectual, social, and emotional areas of development. While the term *intervention* can apply to treatment for someone of any age, *early intervention* is a specialized term that refers to experiences and opportunities provided to children with developmental disabilities from birth to age 3.

Passionate advocates, many of them parents of children with disabilities, and a growing body of research led to a series of landmark laws. Beginning in 1975, with the Education for All Handicapped Children Act, and then in 1987, with IDEA, most recently revised and reauthorized in 2004, government legislation has protected the rights of those with disabilities. Many of the services and supports that Melanie and her family have received since her birth have been made possible through this legislation. Services in the important early years–for Melanie and for other children and families–can make an enormous difference in their development and learning.

Two areas of research illustrate this point: research on the value of early intervention for children birth through age 2, and research on the value of providing what is called *inclusive early childhood education.*

PROGRAMS FOR YOUNG CHILDREN WITH DISABILITIES: EARLY INTERVENTION AND INCLUSION

Earlier Is Better: The Value of Early Intervention from Birth to Age 3

The earlier children are identified as having, or having a risk of, disabilities and developmental delays, the greater the chance that interventions will make a significant difference in their development (National Research Council and Institute of Medicine, 2000). Early intervention can have positive impacts across many areas of development–physical health, language, cognition, and social-emotional well-being. Melanie's parents enrolled her in early intervention services in her first few months of life, and they have certainly seen these benefits. Indeed, children who have these services in the first 3 years of life are less likely to continue to need special education when they are older–a plus for them, their families, and society (Hebbeler et al., 2007).

Care and Education in Natural Environments: The Value of Inclusion and Specialized Instruction

From the time she entered preschool, Melanie has participated in an inclusive early childhood program. Most children with disabilities benefit tremendously from

EARLY CHILDHOOD INCLUSION

The term *inclusion* refers to the practice of bringing children with disabilities together with typically developing children. In the past, children with a disability would perhaps receive special services alone with a therapist, or maybe in a class with other children with various disabilities. But the segregation of children by disability often slowed their development. Now, the law (IDEA) requires that children of *all* abilities should learn together in the "least restrictive environment," which usually means in an early childhood program or other setting in which typically developing children participate.

participating in interventions provided within natural environments or the least restrictive environment, which often means within an early childhood program for typically developing children, as well as at home or in community settings. Inclusion not only meets legal requirements, but also reflects our values and beliefs about the rights of all children, as a DEC/NAEYC (2009) joint position statement on inclusion emphasizes.

Melanie's story illustrates that, in most ways, what children with disabilities need in their early childhood programs is the same as what all children need: warm relationships, an engaging curriculum, teaching practices that support continuous development, and careful assessment of progress.

Moreover, children with a disability usually do better when they spend time with typically developing children, and typically developing children become more empathic people when they play and learn with children with disabilities (Center to Mobilize Early Childhood Knowledge, 2013; National Professional Development Center on Inclusion [NPDCI], 2011; Odom, Buysse, & Soukakou, 2011).

However, the benefits of inclusion do not magically appear just from placing children with disabilities in inclusive classrooms or community environments. As part of inclusive education, young children with disabilities need specialized instruction from their teacher or a trained paraprofessional who can tailor the early childhood program's content to the child's unique needs and abilities. For example, Melanie is likely to need special instruction and different teaching strategies that are sometimes embedded in activities in which all the children participate but are sometimes more intensive and targeted to her specific learning goals.

Research, early childhood values, and legal guidelines suggest that in most situations, most children with disabilities will be best served within inclusive settings. However, it is important to emphasize that IDEA does not require every child with a disability to be in an inclusive program. Children who will not benefit from a particular environment may receive intervention, care, and education in a specialized setting. To think through this decision together, a team assesses each child's strengths and needs and considers what kinds of environments may best meet that child's needs.

PROVIDING ACCESS TO EARLY CHILDHOOD SERVICES

Melanie and other children with disabilities need and are entitled to services starting at birth or whenever they are identified as being eligible for these services. Each state has its own specific guidelines, but some elements are similar everywhere. The following sections describe these elements, which are both legally mandated and consistent with research, professional values, and best practices in child assessment and family involvement for everyone, not just children with disabilities.

The Process of Identifying Children Who Need Services

As a component of the IDEA law, states must have a Child Find system to identify, locate, and evaluate all children who need early intervention (ages 0–3) or special education (ages 3–21) services. In some situations, such as Melanie's, the disability is quickly identified at or even before birth. Or parents may begin to notice some issues that cause concern, for example, when their child does not seem to hear noises at home, or if their child is struggling in school much more than her or his classmates. Health care providers are on the alert for possible developmental challenges and regularly conduct screening assessments during checkups. However, parents typically lack detailed knowledge of normative early development, and health care providers lack the day-to-day interactions in natural environments that early childhood educators have. Therefore, early childhood educators can play an especially important role in identifying concerns about a child's development (National Dissemination Center for Children with Disabilities, 2013).

Awareness of a possible problem is only the first step in identifying issues that need more in-depth evaluation (Meisels & Atkins-Burnett, 2005). Child care teachers or health care providers can help parents connect with Child Find and request an evaluation by a team of professionals. Early childhood teachers who work in public school programs are part of a different system and need to communicate with their school's special education staff to determine what the next steps may be. Consistent with the early childhood field's belief in family engagement, a school professional can request an evaluation only if the child's family agrees and is involved. Importantly, decisions about whether a child has a disability are never made on the basis of one assessment. Instead, information from many people and many sources, including specialists' firsthand observation, is taken into account. Like other aspects of the process, this assessment approach is consistent with research on developmentally appropriate assessment for all children, with and without disabilities (e.g., NAEYC & NAECS/SDE, 2003).

Even with this system in place, many young children who could benefit from services do not receive them. The problem is especially acute for infants and toddlers: Some states, though legally required to provide special interventions for children diagnosed with a disability, are not required to provide any special services for young children who are at risk for disabilities (that is, children whose development is of concern but who do not have a formal diagnosis). In those states, at-risk children who would benefit greatly from these services are not eligible. And across the country, infants under age 1 are much less likely to receive services than older children, despite the importance of the "window of opportunity" to promote positive development in the first 3 years of life. Further, vulnerable populations such as immigrant families, who may not be aware of their rights or do not know how to become connected with service providers, are less likely than others to receive intervention services for their children. And as Chapter 9 will show, these barriers affect children in immigrant families whether the children have disabilities or not.

When a Child Is Eligible for Services: What Next?

The goal of evaluation is not just to determine whether a child has a disability. Rather, it is a step in the important process of identifying the child's individual educational needs to decide what kinds of services will best support the child's development. This process began very early in Melanie's life and has continued regularly, with many updates and discussions.

For Melanie and other children, states must not only provide specialists to conduct formal evaluations and diagnoses of a disability, but also provide services to help each child and family once a diagnosis has been made.

The next step is to develop a plan: Depending on the age of the child, this is called either an Individual Family Service Plan (IFSP, for children under 3 and their families) or an Individual Education Plan (IEP, for children 3 and older). In both cases, the plan is developed by a team that includes the family. For the IFSP, other team members usually include those conducting the evaluations, those who will provide intervention services, and other family members if requested by parents. For the IEP, other team members include key school or early childhood program staff such as regular and special education teachers, and others with special knowledge of the child. Together, the team agrees on the most important outcomes, or desired results, for the child. In all cases, the planned outcomes should be meaningful to the family, fitting in with what they want for their child. So, for example, if participation in soccer is important to Melanie and her parents, a goal may be to improve Melanie's physical strength and coordination, with physical therapy as a possible strategy. New outcomes can be added any time additions are desired or needed (National Dissemination Center for Children with Disabilities, n.d.). Once again it is important to remember that, although this process is more detailed and has more formal legal requirements, it is consistent with good early childhood practices for *all* children—learn as much about the child as possible, develop plans to support that child's positive development, implement the plans, assess regularly to see if the plans are effective, and make changes as needed.

IMPLEMENTING INTERVENTION AND EDUCATION SERVICES: MELANIE FROM BIRTH TO AGE 6

The essential elements of developmentally appropriate practices (Copple & Bredekamp, 2009) apply to all children, with and without disabilities, yet children with disabilities also need and have the right to special services. The fact that Melanie's disability was diagnosed at birth meant that she received those services from the beginning. Let's see how services were implemented across Melanie's first 6 years. Other children may have different disabilities and therefore different needs, but the general process is likely to be the same.

From Birth to Age 3

When Melanie was a baby and a toddler, her day-to-day experiences were pretty similar to those of other children. However, special help was available and necessary for her development. For example, like many children with Down syndrome, Melanie has low muscle tone (her big sister affectionately called her "Floppy Bear"), so her parents got ideas for exercises from a physical therapist. Melanie was also late to start talking; her parents worked with a speech and language therapist to create enjoyable ways to stimulate Melanie's language development throughout the day. Like other children her age, Melanie went with her family to shop, visit the playground, and see friends, including a playgroup of other children with Down syndrome and their parents.

The Preschool Years

When Melanie turned 3, the school district's special education system started providing services. At that time, Melanie began attending a local, inclusive preschool. The changing goals for Melanie's development, outlined in her IEP, continued to depend on her family's input and the results of assessments of her progress. In general, her family was pleased with their partnership with the program. The staff in the preschool collaborated with an early childhood special education consultant who helped them decide how to embed Melanie's IEP goals in their everyday curriculum.

PROFESSIONAL PROFILE

Cindy McCann, Early Childhood Special Education Teacher,
Los Angeles Unified School District, Los Angeles, California

For Cindy McCann, a typical week is filled with exhilaration and exhaustion. As the special education teacher within a large, inclusive child care center, Cindy is involved with all of the center's children and staff, serving as a resource on special needs and participating as a regular member of the teaching team. The center builds all its activities around the state of California's Learning Foundations while differentiating activities to meet children's diverse needs. Every day, the staff records highlights for the overall assessment system—the Desired Results Profile (DRP)—and the Individualized Education Program (IEP) for those children who have disabilities. Besides these informal daily meetings, Cindy participates in weekly meetings to create schedules and lesson plans, while discussing strategies to support individual children's progress. Cindy also conducts IEP meetings with families and other staff, observes and consults with teachers about individual children, works closely with specialists, and helps modify the curriculum and teaching strategies for children with and without IEPs. Cindy meets regularly with families whose children have disabilities to discuss their progress and supports their transition from child care to kindergarten.

A former kindergarten and 2nd-grade teacher, Cindy McCann's volunteer experience in an after-school program for children with special needs changed her life. With a master's degree in early childhood special education, she has now worked in that field for 22 years. She is especially interested in the inclusion of children with autism in early childhood programs.

Elementary School and Beyond

Now Melanie is in elementary school. Her IEP again is regularly revised to reflect new goals, and her teachers as well as other specialists, such as the school psychologist and speech therapist, continue to plan and implement her school experiences. As key members of the team, Melanie's parents continue to discuss how to help Melanie make progress, especially in some challenging areas of the academic curriculum.

From kindergarten on, a big issue for Melanie and many other children with disabilities is ensuring what is called *access to the general curriculum*, especially the literacy and mathematics outcomes expected by the new Common Core State Standards. While the Common Core applies to all students, a range of supports and accommodations must be provided to those who have disabilities (National Dissemination Center for Children with Disabilities, 2012).

Beyond the academic issues, as Melanie gets older her family has become concerned about her social integration. Right now, Melanie has friends at school–thanks in part to her teachers' active promotion of friendships (Guralnick, Connor, & Johnson, 2011)–and she participates in activities such as the community soccer league. Thinking ahead, her parents wonder if she will become rejected or even bullied as she gets older. Because Melanie has been served by inclusive programs for years, the chances are less likely that this will happen, and yet it is a concern.

The school district will continue to support Melanie's parents and provide special services to Melanie until she turns 21.

FAMILIES: CHALLENGES, RESOURCES, AND REWARDS

The Challenges

Having a child diagnosed with a disability is a challenging and potentially devastating experience. Initially, families like Melanie's often go through something like a grieving process, in which they must create a new set of hopes and dreams for the child they have, not the child they expected to have. The practical tasks of caring for a child with a physical, intellectual, or emotional disability can be daunting and scary. Even though many services may be available, families must gain access to these services through systems that often are hard to negotiate unless families are knowledgeable advocates for their child–an unfamiliar and challenging role for any family. It is no wonder that many families experience high levels of stress, fatigue, marital strain, and lack of social support (Reichman, Corman, & Noonan, 2008). Within this process, often forgotten are the brothers and sisters of children who have disabilities, who may feel resentful or neglected. Having a disability is truly a family affair.

Resources That Can Help

The early intervention and early childhood special education systems (EI/ECSE) recognize that families are the center of their children's lives and that they are able to support their child in everyday ways. What families of children with disabilities need, like all families, is practical help in how to do this.

Even if children with disabilities are enrolled in an inclusive program, they usually spend most of their time at home with their families. If there is close collaboration with their child's teachers and specialists, families can learn how to embed a child's therapy or other intervention into everyday routines, instead of just relying on a specialist to "deliver" the therapy during scheduled appointments (McWilliam, 2010a). When families assume this role, everyone benefits: The family is empowered to help their child, and the child is able to practice skills throughout the day.

Many resources are available to give families practical help and to guide early childhood professionals about how to partner with families in strengths-based, culturally competent ways (McWilliam, 2010b). Resources are also available for the brothers and sisters of children with disabilities. For example, the national Sibling Support Project has online resources and a network of community workshops or *sibshops*. Depending on the disability, specialized organizations such as the National Down Syndrome Society can also provide information and support.

The Rewards of Having a Child with a Disability in the Family—and in an Early Childhood Program

Despite the challenges, and with the help of the resources noted here, the rewards of having a child with a disability are great. Yes, Melanie's family was initially sad and overwhelmed by her diagnosis, and there are still days that find everyone, including Melanie, discouraged or frustrated. But the joys outweigh the difficulties: Melanie's parents and her sister Grace love her deeply, laugh with her, play with her, and are building positive family memories piece by unforgettable piece. Early childhood professionals can contribute to this joy, sharing funny stories, tales of progress, and special moments with parents and other family members.

DEIRDRE, MOTHER OF A CHILD WITH DOWN SYNDROME

"I was so sure I was the parent who was not going to be able to deal with a child who was in any way different. . . . I had this baby everyone thought was a disaster, and my journey has been to find all the things that are amazing about her. . . . All the surprises [since she was born] have been good ones. She's one of the nicest, kindest, most thoughtful, sensitive people that I've ever met." (Solomon, 2012, p. 192)

PROFESSIONALS SERVING CHILDREN WITH DISABILITIES AND THEIR FAMILIES

Children with disabilities can thrive with the support of high-quality, family-centered early childhood services. But for this to happen, well-prepared professionals are essential.

For All Teachers: Creating Knowledge, Skill, and Comfort in Working with Children Who Have Disabilities

Because so many children with disabilities are in inclusive programs, the "regular" or "general" early childhood educator is at the center of early intervention and early childhood special education services. More than one future teacher has probably thought, "I really don't want to work with children with disabilities. I wouldn't know what to do and I don't have the patience to deal with it." And the reality is that it *can* be incredibly hard, usually because teachers either have insufficient knowledge and skill or—too often—insufficient resources and professional support.

With those realities in mind, NAEYC's standards (2009) for early childhood teacher preparation programs emphasize that *all* teachers need basic competence in early childhood intervention and early childhood special education. NAEYC also expects that students who prepare for careers in early childhood education should have field experiences with diverse children and families, including those with disabilities and developmental delays. This kind of preparation is not enough to prepare a graduate to be a specialist, but it can build the confidence and competence professionals need to teach in an inclusive setting. Knowledge and comfort with children with disabilities are important for all early childhood professionals, given the IDEA law and the field's emphasis on including all children in all programs.

Blended Teacher Preparation

One way to ensure future teachers' competence to work with children who have disabilities is to embed the competencies in a regular, or general, early childhood teacher education program. Another very promising approach is what is called

---

PROFESSIONAL PROFILE

Rosa Milagros Santos, Professor, Special Education,
University of Illinois, Urbana-Champaign, Illinois

Rosa Milagros Santos, called Amy (Ah-mee) by family and friends, has no typical week—each is filled with variety. When she's not travelling for conferences or meetings, Amy mentors her many doctoral students, an important, rewarding, yet challenging responsibility. Since 2008, Amy has collaborated with her colleague Brent McBride on a research project studying fathers' involvement in the lives of young children with disabilities. Amy, Brent, and their team of students meet every week. Because of research commitments, in the last few years Amy has taught only one course per semester. She dedicates at least a day a week to preparing, teaching, and holding office hours for those students, and another day-into-evening to reading their papers and projects. Away from the bustle of her main office, she values a quiet spot where she can write and edit the *Young Exceptional Children* journal. Finally, Amy wants people to know that activities like walking with friends, reading to her daughter, and family dinners are essential to re-energizing—for more meetings, teaching, and writing!

Amy Santos began her career as a teacher in an inclusive toddler classroom and later at a school for children and adults with disabilities. Following graduate school, Amy coordinated the Early Childhood Research Institute on Culturally and Linguistically Appropriate Services at the University of Illinois. In 2000, she joined the faculty at the University of Illinois, where she is now a full professor. She has a Ph.D. in special education.

blended or *unified* professional preparation. In blended programs, future teachers receive preparation that meets both NAEYC standards (for general teacher preparation) and the standards of the Division for Early Childhood (DEC) of the Council for Exceptional Children (CEC), along with CEC's core standards for all special educators. Teachers prepared this way will be in a better position to meet the needs of all children—those who are typically developing as well as those with a range of disabilities.

Specialization in Early Intervention/Early Childhood Special Education

For those who want to specialize in working with children who have disabilities, whether in an inclusive setting or a specialized program, a degree in early intervention/early childhood special education is the usual pathway. Some students gain this degree as undergraduates, while others add a master's degree following a general early childhood undergraduate degree. DEC has standards for what graduates of these specialized programs should know and be able to do.

Development of Competence in a Related Field

Some people may decide to work with children with disabilities as members of nonteaching professions. For example, pediatric medicine and nursing, child psychology, school psychology, physical and occupational therapy, speech and language therapy, family services—individuals in these and other specialized fields may be part of a multidisciplinary support team.

The Importance of Teams in Early Intervention and Early Childhood Special Education

For young children with disabilities, it is especially important that professionals work in teams. Children's complex needs often require services from many specialists. But to function as an effective team requires coordination and communication, so that the focus is on the whole child and not just on one aspect of the child's development. Influenced by innovations in health services, the concept of *interprofessional collaboration* (Anderson, 2013) is emerging in early childhood special education as a model to improve the quality of professional preparation and, ultimately, the quality of services for children and their families.

Gaps in Preservice and Ongoing Professional Development

Despite the promising teacher preparation options just described, and despite what is emphasized in NAEYC's standards, national surveys show that many students who enroll in early childhood degree programs do not have adequate opportunities to learn about and work with young children with disabilities and their families (Chang, Early, & Winton, 2005). And professionals in various fields still tend to operate separately; physical therapists, for example, receive little training in how to provide services within inclusive or natural environments (Bruder & Dunst, 2005).

The early childhood field is also beginning to recognize that even the best teacher preparation is not enough to ensure that teachers *implement* high-quality practices. The relatively new field of *implementation science* (Halle, Metz, & Martinez-Beck, 2013) emphasizes that merely informing professionals about the research is insufficient. A strong system of administrative and ongoing professional supports needs to be in place. Even motivated, talented teachers may leave the early childhood field if they feel overwhelmed in the classroom. Additionally, early childhood professionals who have opportunities to observe, use, and receive feedback about evidence-based practices with children with disabilities are more effective than those who merely read about using them. Many resources can help, for example, coaching and consultation, web-based videos of excellent practice, and online communities where teachers may share experiences and practical tips (Odom, 2009).

CONCLUDING THOUGHTS:
GIVING TO AND LEARNING FROM CHILDREN WITH DISABILITIES

Melanie and all children who have disabilities have the right to a joyful, productive life, integrated into their communities and with their contributions warmly welcomed. But achieving that goal means overcoming significant obstacles. The obstacles are not so much about the children as about the lack of resources to help them reach their potential. Well-planned, individualized services are expensive–they require highly skilled personnel, technical support from multiple parties, and ongoing services–but they are necessary to the well-being of the child and the community. The United States continues to invest relatively little in early intervention and early childhood special education, failing to take advantage of opportunities to change the trajectory of early development (Zero to Three, 2009a). Children with disabilities and their families deserve the attention and resources they need to flourish, an outcome that is good for individuals and good for society.

One more thought: Although this chapter has shown how children with disabilities benefit from being part of a wider early childhood community, that wider community also has much to learn from the services and practices originally developed for children with disabilities. Family-focused services, collaborative goal-setting and ongoing assessment, the concept of differentiated instruction, intentional teaching, and scaffolded interventions for children who are struggling as learners are all practices that emerged largely from work with children with disabilities. As shown in other chapters of this book, many of these practices are now mainstream. All early childhood professionals, settings, and families benefit from them.

Likewise, children learn from one another whatever their abilities or disabilities, and typically developing children deserve the chance to witness and learn from the often-amazing strengths that children with disabilities have to share. A child like Melanie has much to give her peers. Years from now, typically developing children who have worked and played with children who have disabilities may reflect those children's strengths in their own adult characteristics: in an accepting perspective on life, humility, perseverance in the face of obstacles, wisdom in relationships, patience, or joy in accomplishment. Together, we're better.

REFLECTION, DIALOGUE, AND ACTION

1. If you have a disability or have a family member with a disability, or if you currently work with children who have disabilities, consider your experiences in light of what is discussed in this chapter. How similar are your experiences? If they have been different, why might that be?

2. Do you know someone who has a child with a disability? If so, try to have a conversation about their experiences. Share your insights with others in your class or work setting.

3. On the basis of this chapter, what might you say to the parents of a child who has just been diagnosed with a significant developmental disability? If possible, role play this discussion.

INFORMATION TO EXPLORE AND SHARE

The Division for Early Childhood of the Council for Exceptional Children

The Division for Early Childhood promotes policies and advances evidence-based practices that support families and enhance the development of children who have or are at risk for developmental delays and disabilities. Resources include publications, including *DEC Recommended Practices*, and special interest groups, including a student forum. www.dec-sped.org/

Head Start Center for Inclusion

This site offers information, training materials, videos (including "15 minute in-services") and other resources for teachers, disabilities coordinators, trainers, other professionals and families. depts.washington.edu/hscenter

National Professional Development Center on Inclusion

The Center works with states to ensure that early childhood teachers are prepared to educate and care for young children with disabilities in settings with their typically developing peers. Includes resources for faculty members, teachers, and others to support inclusion, including online videos. npdci.fpg.unc.edu/

CHAPTER 8

The Early Years Matter for Children with Challenging Behavior

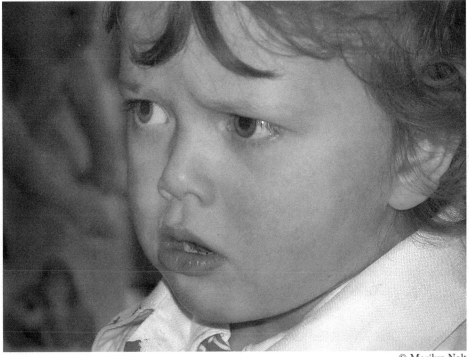

© Marilyn Nolt

MIKEY'S STORY

Mikey's child care teachers, Mr. Sandy and Ms. Alma, are at their wits' end. Mikey, a red-haired 2½-year-old, has been at the Shady Hollow Center for 6 months. At first he was just a playful, energetic little guy who tested classroom rules often—not unusual for a toddler. Compared with others in his class, Mikey has been late learning to talk, but he has always been curious and excited about learning.

Now, however, Mikey has become Monster Mike, in the eyes of both teachers and classmates. Over the last couple of months his behavior has become much harder to deal with. He grabs toys from other children and almost seems to enjoy making them cry. He either can't or won't sit still during group activities. Instead, he usually gets up and runs around the room—or even into the hall—until one of the teachers catches up with him and carries him back, kicking and yelling. At cleanup time, rather than helping, he dumps things on the floor or hides under one of the tables. On the playground, he hits other children, and has even hit his teachers. Major meltdowns happen almost every day.

It seems the teachers spend all their time reprimanding Mikey: "Mikey, *noooo!*" is a constant refrain. The other children avoid his company; some children seem scared of him. Parents are complaining. The teachers have not talked to his parents about the problems, but they've seen his mother yell at him often. At a recent staff meeting there was discussion about whether they ought to ask the family to find another child care center for Mikey. Miss Alma, a new teacher, has started to hate coming to work because of the stress Mikey creates. The whole situation isn't good for anyone right now.

THE NATURE OF CHALLENGING BEHAVIOR

Mikey's behavior certainly is challenging—to him, his teachers, and no doubt his parents. "A challenging behavior is any repeated pattern of behavior that interferes with learning or engagement in social interactions" (McCabe & Frede, 2007, p. 1). Challenging behavior may also create safety problems, harming the child or others around the child. With children under age 5, the most frequently seen challenging behaviors look a lot like Mikey's: physical or verbal aggression, disruptive or defiant behavior (refusing to do what is asked), and frequent tantrums.

Of course, lots of 2-year-olds act up—this age is called the "terrible twos" for a reason—and temperamentally, some children seem to be born feistier than others. Some children do go through a phase when, like Mikey, they constantly push their parents' and teachers' buttons. But many children *do not* just grow out of these behavior problems as they get older. Those children are this chapter's concern.

Children with Challenging Behavior

Because definitions vary, researchers estimate that between 10% and 30% of young children have persistent challenging behavior (Perry, Holland, Darling-Kuria, & Nadiv, 2011). Whatever the exact percentage, it's a lot. Any child may develop behavior problems, but some children are statistically more at risk for developing these problems than others. According to McCabe and Frede's review (2009), some of these risk factors include:

- Prenatal drug or alcohol exposure.
- Living in poverty.
- Having a developmental disability, especially a disability such as autism, which affects social and emotional functioning (see Chapter 7).
- Harsh, punitive parenting (as Mikey's teachers may be noticing).
- Communication difficulties because of being a late talker (as in Mikey's case).
- Long hours in center-based child care programs.

This last factor needs a bit of explanation. As discussed in Chapter 3, some research suggested that the more hours children spend in child care centers, the more likely they were to develop disobedient, aggressive behavior (Belsky, 2002). Differences were not large, and most children did not develop these problems. However, later research showed that teachers in some of these programs paid too little attention to helping children develop social skills. When this oversight was corrected, the increases in challenging behavior disappeared (McCabe & Frede, 2007). In one large study in Canada, looking at the effects of child care on 2- and 3-year-old children from high-risk families, those who were not enrolled in child care showed more aggressive behavior than children who were enrolled (Borge, Rutter, Côté, & Tremblay, 2004).

Thus, although there is a risk that lots of time in child care centers, especially centers that do not promote social-emotional competence, can contribute to later patterns of challenging behavior, the opposite can also happen. High-quality early childhood programs can serve as a protective factor for those children who might otherwise develop serious behavior problems (McCabe & Frede, 2007).

Finally, Mikey is an example of a well-documented statistic: Across the board, boys are more likely to have challenging behavior than girls (McCabe & Frede, 2007).

WHY ATTENTION TO CHILDREN WITH CHALLENGING BEHAVIOR IS NECESSARY IN THE EARLY YEARS

Both in the short run and over the long term, children who engage in severe, persistent challenging behavior are likely to have significant difficulties with relationships as well as with academic success. In the sections that follow, we discuss some of these difficulties based on research summaries from the Technical Assistance Center on Social Emotional Intervention (TACSEI, 2004).

Difficult Relationships with Teachers and Other Children

As discussed in many chapters, warm relationships with teachers are critically important for young children. Yet these relationships can be hard to achieve when teachers are frustrated by a child's continuing aggression or defiance. Children with challenging behavior often have negative relationships with their teachers and are constantly in conflict over issues large and small. Conflicted teacher-child relationships in early childhood predict less positive behavioral and academic outcomes throughout later schooling (Hamre & Pianta, 2001). Mikey's negative relationships with Mr. Sandy and Ms. Alma suggest he may be at risk for future problems.

Teachers are not the only ones who have problems with children like Mikey: Children with challenging behaviors are not usually welcomed by other children, either. Classmates may avoid these children or actively reject them as friends. This lack of close peer relationships, in turn, may cause difficulties with forming social relationships in later years.

Expulsion or Suspension from Preschool

Mikey is not the only child whose teachers might ask the family to withdraw from the program. Expulsion is three times more likely for preschoolers than for older children—a shocking statistic for many people—and challenging behavior is the most common reason (Gilliam, 2005). Of great concern is a recent report on the high rate of preschool disciplinary suspensions, with African American boys especially at risk (U.S. Department of Education Office for Civil Rights, 2014). Furthermore, the number of young children expelled for problem behavior seems to be on the rise (Perry, Holland, Darling-Kuria, & Nadiv, 2011), perhaps because teachers and administrators feel pressure to concentrate on boosting academic skills and test scores rather than promoting social and emotional competence. Children like Mikey, many educators find, "interfere" with their success.

Experiencing Later Failure and Dropping Out

As children get older, a pattern of severe, persistent challenging behavior predicts difficulties in academic performance as well as in social competence. Preschool children's social and behavioral competence (or lack of competence) actually predicts their 1st-grade academic skills better than does their preschool intellectual ability. And in the longer run, children with challenging behaviors are at increased risk for dropping out of school, with devastating long-term effects.

Developing Long-Term Patterns of Antisocial Behavior

When a child has serious and untreated behavior problems in the early years–especially high levels of aggression and defiance–there is a troubling likelihood that the child will later develop delinquent and even antisocial behavior. Antisocial behaviors are major clinical disorders that are highly correlated with criminal activity and arrest rates.

THE GOOD NEWS: EARLY CARE AND EDUCATION PROGRAMS CAN HELP CHILDREN FEEL BETTER AND ACT BETTER

This evidence makes it clear that adults should not just wait and hope for the best when young children like Mikey show chronic negative patterns of behavior, or when behavior problems emerge in kindergarten and the primary grades. Once again, the early years matter, and fortunately we know much more than we used to about practical, evidence-based ways of both preventing and addressing challenging behaviors in young children (Kaiser & Rasminsky, 2012).

When early care and education programs implement a well-planned set of strategies, good things can happen for Mikey and other children with challenging behavior. Using the right strategies, teachers can prevent many behavior difficulties before they even begin. If they create or strengthen a well-structured, developmentally appropriate environment, teachers who thought that *most* of their children had behavior problems often find that the number is reduced to just a few. And intentional interventions, often involving teams of teachers and other specialists, can help those few children by teaching them new social-emotional skills and rebuilding their relationships with teachers and classmates. At the same time, families can become partners with teachers in addressing challenging behavior helpfully and consistently. As summarized in TACSEI's (2004) review of research, high-quality intervention that occurs early can have the following positive effects:

PROFESSIONAL PROFILE

Mary Louise Hemmeter, Professor, Early Childhood Special Education,
Vanderbilt University, Nashville, Tennessee

Besides serving as a faculty member in early childhood special education, Mary Louise Hemmeter is the Co-Faculty Director of the Susan Gray School (SGS) for Children, which serves children ages 1–5, with and without disabilities. A typical week combines responsibilities from both positions—leading a seminar for master's degree students enrolled in a practicum in the Susan Gray School; working with coaches on the Teaching Pyramid Research Project; meeting with SGS staff about individualized behavior support plans for children who have challenging behavior; observing a new child and offering suggestions about how teachers can support his transition into group care for the first time; and having a reading group meeting with doctoral students to discuss their research projects. Several times a month, Mary Louise travels to other states (and sometimes other countries) to provide training on strategies for supporting children with challenging behavior. In addition, her travels allow her to work directly with faculty collaborators on federally funded grants related to supporting children with disabilities and challenging behavior in early childhood programs.

With a master's in early childhood special education and a Ph.D. in education and human development, Mary Louise Hemmeter has been a faculty member at the University of Kentucky, the University of Illinois, and Vanderbilt University. One of her most rewarding professional experiences was leading the Center on the Social and Emotional Foundations for Early Learning, where she and her colleagues developed the Pyramid Model for Promoting Social Emotional Competence in Infants and Young Children.

- Reduce children's aggressive, disruptive behavior;
- Improve their relationships with other children;
- Improve their self-regulation and overall emotional health; and
- Increase academic success.

These benefits may sound like "pie in the sky," and of course they will not happen for every child and under every condition. But success can happen more often than one might think. Let's see how.

HOW TEACHERS CAN PREVENT AND INTERVENE WITH CHALLENGING BEHAVIORS: THE TEACHING PYRAMID

The Teaching Pyramid is a widely used model of prevention and intervention developed by the Center on the Social and Emotional Foundations of Early Learning (CSEFEL).

The Teaching Pyramid is not intended to be a quick fix for Mikey or other individual children with challenging behavior (Hemmeter, Ostrosky, & Corso, 2012). Instead, it is a comprehensive set of strategies ranging from those that are (a) meant for *all children* in a group; (b) targeted just to *some children*, and (c) intended for only a *very few children* whose behavior issues persist even when all the other strategies are in place. Practitioners find this mix both practical and powerful.

Figure 8.1 illustrates the progression of teacher strategies in the Teaching Pyramid. It begins with the first two levels, which together are the foundation for *preventing* challenging behaviors.

The Foundation for All Children:
Positive Relationships and Supportive Environments

As Benjamin Franklin's proverb says, "An ounce of prevention is worth a pound of cure." Teachers and researchers agree that most challenging behaviors can be prevented by putting in place the essentials of high-quality, developmentally appropriate early childhood environments (Copple & Bredekamp, 2009). Many of these essentials have been described in other chapters. Some of the most important for prevention are:

- Creating positive adult-child relationships—these are like money in the bank. Warm, one-on-one interactions build closeness and trust (Vick Whittaker & Jones Harden, 2010) and reduce the likelihood of behavior problems in young children.

Figure 8.1. The Teaching Pyramid

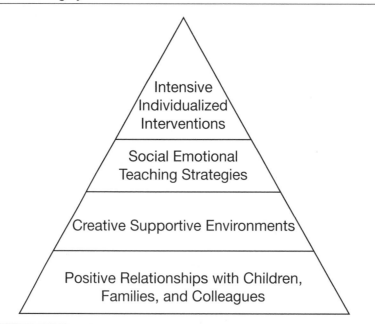

Source: Fox, Dunlap, Hemmeter, Joseph, & Strain, 2003. Reprinted by permission of the Center for the Social and Emotional Foundations of Early Learning.

- Establishing a positive classroom climate—what NAEYC calls a "caring community of learners"—in which all children are expected to respect and care about one another (Copple & Bredekamp, 2009). Teachers may use classroom jobs, group projects, buddies, and other ways to make everyone feel valued.
- Setting predictable schedules and routines. It is comforting for children to know what to expect. For very young children or children with problems of self-regulation, picture schedules or other concrete reminders are great. Schedules should minimize waiting time and organize transitions like cleanup (always a problem time for Mikey) in easy-to-follow patterns.
- Developing classroom rules. Especially for children age 3 and older, a small number of simple, well-understood classroom rules make expectations clear. (Younger children's need for predictability can be met through routines and rituals around feeding, napping, and other caregiving activities.)
- Choosing and structuring activities that can allow all children to participate at their own level and that reflect their interests and developmental characteristics. Young children love to be active and to have a small number of interesting, engaging choices within a predictable framework. Mikey's child care program seemed to have too many choices and too little intentional teacher involvement in children's activities. The issues are not very different for older children; many 5- to 8-year-olds spend countless hours sitting at desks filling out worksheets that are boring or frustrating or both. No wonder the children act out. The kind of developmentally appropriate curriculum and teaching practices described in Chapter 4 would immediately reduce these challenging behaviors in K–3 classrooms, allowing teachers more time to teach and requiring less time on classroom management.

Especially Important for Some Children: Intentional Teaching of Social-Emotional Skills

Looking at the Teaching Pyramid (Figure 8.1), even though the first two levels provide a foundation for prevention, quite a few children need—and all may benefit from—intentional teaching of specific social-emotional skills, level 3 in the pyramid. Some of this teaching occurs in everyday situations. For example:

- Intentionally acknowledging children's appropriate behavior. Mikey gets plenty of attention for his inappropriate behavior and not enough attention at the times when he behaves constructively and is simply a lively, funny little boy.
- Intentionally modeling or demonstrating appropriate ways of dealing with conflict or frustration. Especially with very young children, teachers can supply appropriate language: "Mikey, you can say 'May I please have that truck?'" or "Tell him 'No! I don't like you to do that.'"
- Using puppets, books, and games to teach and practice specific skills, such as being able to recognize and name feelings or figure out different ways of dealing with conflicts. As Greene (2008) reminds us, most children misbehave because they do not have certain social and emotional skills. Just as early childhood teachers intentionally teach children foundational literacy and math skills, teachers can and should teach foundational social-emotional skills.

• Implementing a social skills curriculum. Such a curriculum does not take the place of all the other strategies described here (and these are only examples), but it can give teachers an evidence-based framework to improve children's social competence. Figure 8.2 lists examples of a few social skills curricula that have considerable evidence of effectiveness (at least in the short term) in reducing aggression and other problem behavior and increasing children's social and emotional competence. Most have adaptations for younger and older children and have parent components as well.

Intensive, Individualized Interventions for a Few Children

Finally, at the top level of the Teaching Pyramid are a set of intensive individualized interventions for those children who continue to have severe problem behavior despite programs' good implementation of the more broadly applied strategies previously described.

One such intervention is called Positive Behavior Support or PBS (Fox, Dunlap, & Powell, 2002; McCabe & Frede, 2007), which was initially developed for older children but, with adaptation, is now implemented in many preschool classrooms. The PBS process begins with what is called a *functional assessment.* A group of professionals that might include the classroom teachers, specialists or therapists, and administrators make up a team to systematically observe the child and try to identify the purposes or functions of the challenging behavior.

Figure 8.2. Sample Social Skills Curricula for Preschool Children

Curriculum	Selected Features	Source
The Incredible Years	Workshops help teachers learn how to use positive management strategies and encourage children's social competence.	www.incredibleyears.com
Promoting Alternative Thinking Strategies (PATHS)	Weekly lessons teach children social skills, anger management (the Turtle Technique), and social problem solving.	www.revention.psu.edu/projects/Preschool_PATHS.html
Second Step	Teachers use photo cards, puppets, and other activities organized around weekly themes to build self-regulation and emotional competence.	www.cfchildren.org/second-step.aspx
Positive Behavior Support	Intended for children with serious, very persistent challenging behavior; begins by team assessment of the functions of the behavior; then a focused individual plan is implemented and assessed.	www.challengingbehavior.org/explore/presentation_docs/10.08_pbs_goes_to_preschool.pdf

Source: Adapted from Fox, Dunlap, & Powell, 2002; McCabe & Frede, 2007; Raver, Jones, Li-Grining, Metzger, Champion, & Sardin 2008.

Consider Mikey as an example. By observing, his team might discover that he uses highly aggressive strategies to try to connect with other children; to Mikey, a negative response is better than no response. On the basis of those findings, the team develops a behavior support plan, including changes to the environment that make the behavior less likely to occur. Perhaps one of the teachers stays with Mikey during times that seem to trigger the aggressive interactions. They also teach Mikey new skills that can replace the problem behavior. Families are involved every step of the way. Other children's challenging behavior may serve different functions: Maybe one child is always overtired and is trying to get some downtime away from his classmates. Another child may have language difficulties and uses challenging behavior as her way of communicating with others.

It is important to emphasize that PBS and similar interventions are not a punishment. They focus on the positive, on developing new skills, and on responding to a child's individual needs. Positive Behavior Support appears to be very effective—again, for those small number of children whose behavior problems warrant this kind of intensive intervention (McCabe & Frede, 2007). And finally, for children with clinical diagnoses such as autism spectrum disorder or oppositional defiant disorder, individual therapy may be a valuable support in close coordination with classroom-based interventions.

ENGAGING AND SUPPORTING FAMILIES

It is not easy to be the parent of a child with challenging behavior. Like Mikey's teachers, Mikey's parents most likely feel frustrated, angry, hurt, and at times inadequate in the face of his behavior. Perhaps they have tried various ways to deal with these problems, as the teachers have, with little success.

In spite of the value of partnering with families, teacher-parent partnerships do not always occur. In studying 20 children who had to leave their child care centers because of challenging behavior, researchers found that often there had not been a collaborative relationship between the center and the family (Perry et al., 2011). Maybe, like Mikey's teachers, the staff avoided communicating with the family because they did not know how to discuss the problems tactfully, did not want to offend the parents, or thought that the parents would blame them. In turn, families may have been thinking the same thing.

In spite of everyone's reluctance to talk about a child's challenging behavior, teachers need to start an honest conversation with parents—sprinkled with a good dose of kindness and avoidance of blame. Well before the conversation about the problems occurs, it is important to develop positive connections through friendly, casual chats when parents are dropping off or picking up their child, emphasizing what's going well. These exchanges can also help teachers get to know the child and the family situation better, which may help teachers better understand what the family is experiencing. Maybe Mikey has a new baby sister; or maybe a grandparent has been ill, and he picks up on the stress. These kinds of insights will help the teachers be more effective in addressing the challenging behaviors that make life difficult for everyone.

Teachers who use one of the social skills curricula described earlier in this chapter may already know about the parent components of these curricula. Many curricula have materials for parent workshops or provide other kinds of family support resources. With consistent messages and strategies being used at home and in the early childhood program, the curriculum's impact is likely to multiply.

Another resource to help programs support families is the Backpack Connection Series developed by the Technical Assistance Center on Social and Emotional Interventions (TACSEI, 2011). These free, online handouts, which can go home in children's backpacks, help teachers and parents/caregivers work together to promote social-emotional skills and reduce challenging behavior. Each Backpack Connection handout contains information about the social-emotional skills that their child is learning at school and gives parents specific ideas on how to use a specific strategy or skill at home—for example, "How to Help Your Child Recognize and Understand Frustration" and "How to Help Your Child Have a Successful Morning."

Challenging behaviors can start very early, as happened with Mikey, and teachers can be a crucial link in providing or obtaining help with these issues. But of course, many infants and toddlers do not participate in any out-of-home care. In these cases, it is helpful when other early childhood professionals—home visitors, parenting coaches, pediatricians, or nurses—are on the lookout for signs that children are behaving in unusual ways, especially in ways that cause stress for the people around them. Often there are certain routines or times of the day, such as bathtime or bedtime, which are especially difficult for everyone. As defiance and tantrums escalate, home visitors can give practical suggestions for parents to try, always keeping cultural preferences in mind and conveying respect for parents' choices (Powell, Dunlap, & Fox, 2006). (Helpful as home visitors may be, however, the reality—as discussed in Chapter 2—is that most American families do not have access to home visiting programs.)

EARLY CHILDHOOD PROFESSIONALS AND CHILDREN'S CHALLENGING BEHAVIOR

Helping Children with Challenging Behaviors Stay in Early Childhood Programs

Certainly a small number of children need and are likely to benefit from individual therapy or a therapeutic program. However, most children who have challenging behavior, including those with disabilities, do better if they stay in early childhood programs rather than being removed from programs and receiving treatment only in a clinical setting. This principle means that early childhood teachers are usually at the front line when it comes to addressing challenging behavior. In addition to other duties, teachers are responsible for creating a supportive environment, implementing social skills curricula to meet children's needs, and being part of teams that design positive behavior support interventions when necessary—a huge range of responsibilities.

Support for Teachers

Mikey's teachers are not alone in their feelings of frustration and helplessness. Because up to 30% of young children persistently show challenging behaviors (Perry et al., 2011), almost every early childhood educator will regularly teach and care for children with behavior problems. In fact, teachers say that addressing challenging behavior is their #1 training need. They also say that challenging behavior in the classroom is their greatest source of job dissatisfaction (Fox & Smith, 2007). It is hard to be happy at work when children's behavior is interfering with your ability to teach effectively and to enjoy your job. Teachers like Mr. Sandy and Ms. Alma want to enjoy all the children–that is why they entered the profession–so it's discouraging to feel that some children may not even like you . . . and vice versa.

College-level teacher preparation does not always help future teachers. A national survey of higher education faculty found that preparation to address challenging behavior was often inadequate (Hemmeter, Santos, & Ostrosky, 2008). Fortunately, though, new resources are being developed to support faculty and other professional development providers. For example, colleges can incorporate the six reproducible Positive Behavior Support modules into existing courses, giving students strategies to apply when addressing persistent challenging behaviors in their classrooms (Hanline, Wetherby, Woods, Fox, & Lentini, 2004).

PROFESSIONAL PROFILE

Stephen O'Connor, Early Childhood Mental Health Specialist, DC Department of Behavioral Health, Washington, DC

Stephen's work with his department's Healthy Futures program brings him into many early childhood education centers to help promote social and emotional development. In the program's "embedded model," Stephen stays connected with six centers where he develops a continuing relationship with children and staff. In weekly classroom visits to observe teacher-child interactions and the teaching of socioemotional skills, he often finds himself drawn into toddlers' activities—enjoying the experience for itself while also informally demonstrating how to promote child-led, reflective play. Classroom observations may lead to discussions of child assessment data, team planning, and skill-building workshops for teachers. Workshop topics often respond to what teachers themselves say they need, to help children gain social and emotional competence.

Besides connecting with teachers and children, working with families is a priority in Stephen's work. A typical week may find him attending an evening PTA meeting to talk about the Healthy Futures program. Afterward, parents—including families in multiethnic communities—usually share with Stephen their questions and concerns about children's behavior. These conversations and individual meetings with parents are often followed by classroom observations and meetings with teachers, in order to plan how to address issues such as parent-reported difficulties with transitioning into child care or parents' worries about tantrums and defiant behavior.

Stephen O'Connor is a Licensed Marriage and Family Therapist (LMFT). Before becoming involved in early childhood, Stephen taught high school English and history. After becoming a therapist, he worked with teenagers and their families and directed a program for homeless young adults.

For teachers already working in early childhood programs, help is increasingly available. The free, online resources identified in this chapter give teachers good ideas about how to deal with the challenges of children like Mikey. Several early childhood social skills curricula, like The Incredible Years, have a teacher-training component in addition to resources that teachers can use in their classrooms.

A number of states have developed partnerships with the Center on the Social and Emotional Foundations of Early Learning. The Center helps states make strategic plans to enhance support for young children's social-emotional competence. For example, the state of Maryland intends to incorporate the CSEFEL Teaching Pyramid approach into its 12,000 licensed child care centers and other early education settings. Although funding continues to be an issue, pilot and demonstration projects have been implemented, classroom coaches and professional development providers are being trained, and multiple partners are coordinating efforts to prevent and address challenging behaviors from preschool through the elementary grades.

Early Childhood Mental Health Consultants

Mental health consultants, trained as family therapists, school counselors, and psychologists, can play a very helpful role in addressing challenging behavior, and more states and communities are including early childhood mental health consultation as part of their planning (Perry, Allen, Brennan, & Bradley, 2010). At the program level, Gilliam (2005) found that when ECE programs regularly involved a mental health consultant, they expelled significantly fewer children than programs that did not have this support. With expertise in young children's mental health, these professionals can partner with classroom teachers, administrators, and families to gain better understanding of an individual child's behavior difficulties and to help plan effective interventions.

CONCLUDING THOUGHTS:
TURNING TODAY'S CHALLENGES INTO TOMORROW'S SUCCESSES

Children's challenging behavior is *the* issue that causes early childhood educators the most distress, a fact that may have some readers nodding in agreement. Yet teachers are not the only ones who feel distressed by behavior problems: Children like Mikey can feel out of control, scared, and alienated from both adults and children. These feelings, in turn, affect children's overall self-image as bad or worthless, having an impact on the way children approach people and learning tasks for years to come. Parents also struggle with anxiety, guilt, and feelings of failure and frustration when their children have persistent behavioral difficulties. Challenging behavior is like a heavy rock thrown into a pond—the ripples spread as far as one can see, creating broad, long-term difficulties.

It is sometimes tempting to oversimplify the causes of these behaviors and to focus on the behavior alone, rather than on their complex or perhaps traumatic underpinnings. Conditions described in other chapters can contribute to challenging behavior. These may include the stark poverty discussed in Chapter 5, toxic stress from abuse and neglect as portrayed in Chapter 6, a variety of disabilities described in Chapter 7, the stresses of immigration and refugee status in Chapter 9, and the war, hunger, and multiple challenges experienced by children in developing countries, the focus of Chapter 10. What seems to be "bad behavior" for its own sake may be, in its own way, an adaptive response: a young child's effort to take control of scary situations and to manage anxiety, fear, anger, and grief.

Understanding the roots of challenging behavior is only the first step in addressing it. This chapter has shown that with lots of support, early childhood professionals can be catalysts for change. Unstructured program environments can be made more organized and structured, benefiting all children, not only those whose behaviors are challenging. Small-group learning; interesting, relevant activities; and warm personal relationships—all the features of quality early childhood programs—can help children work on academic skills without falling apart in frustration. Social skills curricula give all children better tools to make friends and be a friend. Teachers can intentionally provide struggling children with different ways to deal with angry feelings. Teams of professionals and parents can work together to help children, even those with significant behavioral difficulties, to function more effectively in school and community settings.

We know how serious the long-term consequences may be for young children who persistently challenge, disrupt, act out, and bother or intimidate others. The very good news is that, once again, the early years matter: We have ways to prevent these negative future developments if everyone begins early and works together.

Part of the process of prevention and transformation involves recognizing that on the flip side of challenging behaviors may be notable strengths. Like other children with challenging behavior, Mikey has many admirable qualities: a strong will, abundant energy, insatiable curiosity, assertiveness, and persistence. The same stubbornness that drives his teachers crazy can be reframed and transformed into focused dedication to an important goal. With the benefit of caring, insightful teachers and parents who recognize children's potential and guide their social and emotional development, young children who seem like "problems" can grow up to be adults admired for their strength, passion, single-mindedness, and energy—skills invaluable in any future leader.

REFLECTION, DIALOGUE, AND ACTION

1. Spend some time talking to either a parent or a teacher who has a child with challenging behavior. What are the frustrations? What kind of support is available or should be available?

2. If you are especially interested in the role of mental health consultants in early childhood programs, follow up the information in this chapter to learn more about this emerging professional role.

3. Learn more about one or two of the social skills curricula described here. Websites have extensive information, and Research Connections (www.researchconnections.org) may have information about evaluations of the curricula. If possible, talk with teachers or directors who have used the curricula.

4. If you are currently teaching, try to implement one of the recommendations from the first two levels of the Teaching Pyramid. Give it enough time, and see if the changes make a difference in preventing challenging behavior in your class.

INFORMATION TO EXPLORE AND SHARE

Center for Early Childhood Mental Health Consultation

Based at Georgetown University and supported by the Office of Head Start, CECMHC provides resources for Head Start staff, families, consultants and others dealing with challenging behavior and other social and emotional issues—including stress and relaxation tips for teachers! www.ecmhc.org

Center on the Social and Emotional Foundations of Early Learning

CSEFEL is a national resource center funded by the Office of Head Start and Child Care Bureau. Find "What Works Briefs," teacher training kits, scripted stories to help children learn social skills, and more. csefel.vanderbilt.edu

Devereux Center for Resilient Children

The Devereux Center aims to promote the social and emotional well-being of all children, using a strengths-based approach and strong partnerships between families, teachers, and others who work with young children. The Center's resources include DVDs with video examples that can be used in professional development. www.centerforresilientchildren.org

Technical Assistance Center on Social Emotional Intervention

Funded by the United States Office of Special Education Programs, TACSEI has special emphasis on challenging behaviors among young children who have, or are at risk for, disabilities and developmental delays. Free resources include articles, workshop outlines, videos, booklets, and more. www.challengingbehavior.org

CHAPTER 9

The Early Years Matter
for Children in Immigrant Families

© Jenkedco

EDVARDO'S STORY

For as long as Edvardo can remember, he has been in the blueberry fields. His mother, Liliana, tells him exciting stories about how she sneaked Edvardo under her shawl when he was a baby to keep him with her in the fields. She does not say that she took him only because she had no one else to watch him, or that she worried about the intense heat under those blue North Carolina skies. Last year, when he was 3, Edvardo even "helped" pick the blueberries, staining his plump little fingers blue and getting stuck in the mud. He got uncomfortably hot and thirsty, and his mother worried about exposure to pesticides, but she did not have much choice. The trailer—where they still live—costs $60 a month, and the 2-hour van ride to and from the fields is $7 a day. She distracted Edvardo and herself from her worries while they picked blueberries by telling funny stories about her girlhood in Mexico.

But this year, Edvardo and his mother are delighted to have a rare spot in a Head Start program that is specifically geared toward migrant and seasonal workers. The program is open 12 hours a day, 6 days a week, so Liliana doesn't feel anxious when the farm owner asks the workers to keep picking, and she can work Saturdays if there is no rain. The program is free, which is more than a huge help; it is what allows her to use the program. Best of all, she feels relief, joy, and peace knowing that her funny, talkative little boy is in a safe place with people who not only take great care of him and feed him family-style meals three times a day, but also teach him things that will help him next year in kindergarten. Liliana smiles when she talks about the stories he tells from school—about how he built a volcano with Juan and played tag with David. His curiosity and language skills seem to be blooming.

A woman from the program came out to their home a month into the program to talk about Edvardo and what goals Liliana had for him. Before this, Liliana had not articulated her goals even to herself, beyond making sure Edvardo was safe, fed, and happy. But now she is sure that she wants him to learn how to use those little fingers to hold a pencil properly (instead of just picking blueberries), to write his name, to start learning English, and to wait his turn more patiently. Besides help with Edvardo's schooling, Liliana also now has information on where to get affordable help about one of Edvardo's teeth that looks gray, and about his frequent ear infections. Her days are hard and the rundown trailer is not much of a home, but she is passionately glad that Edvardo will never experience the violence of a life in drug gangs that killed his father. She feels hopeful about the year and their future and loves sharing "school" stories with Juan's mother on the van.

CHILDREN IN IMMIGRANT FAMILIES IN AMERICA: COUNTRIES OF ORIGIN AND NUMBERS OF CHILDREN

America is a nation of immigrant families, some of whom came in the 1700s and some of whom arrived yesterday. So what does it mean to be an immigrant child? It means being 1 of 17 million children living with a parent who was born in Bolivia, Ghana, Vietnam, Iraq, Poland, or another country but who now lives in America–in a family that probably speaks "the home language" at home, eats foods from their home country whenever possible but perhaps also loves mac n' cheese and hot dogs with ketchup, and likely celebrates Cinco de Mayo or another holiday from home, while also being enchanted by fireworks on the Fourth of July. Of that 17 million, 15 million were born in the United States and are called second-generation immigrants. The other 2 million were born in another country and are called first-generation immigrants (Britz & Batalova, 2013).

The History of Immigration to America Has Shaped the Nation

America has historically been a land of immigrants, with the very first European settlers, mainly Spanish and English, seeking to escape religious, political, and economic oppression in their home countries–not unlike current immigrants. After America became a sovereign nation and created a Naturalization Act in 1790, there have been three seminal waves of immigrants: the forced migration of Africans as slaves; Europeans escaping famine, revolution, and industrialization; and South and Central Americans coming during and after World War II (from 1942 to 1964), when Congress asked for immigrants because of a shortage in laborers (Waggoner, 2013).

Then and now, people have come to America to seek freedom, to have better economic prospects than in their home country, to escape persecution, to be with family, and to escape violence, as in Liliana and Edvardo's case. The laws and values resulting from these waves of migration shape American identity; by law or belief, Americans say slavery is illegal; schools must be integrated and available to every child; every adult has the right to vote; everyone has the right to freedom of religion, speech, and political beliefs; and hard work merits success, not family background. The country is deeply divided, however, on how to set immigration policy and what to do about undocumented individuals who already live in the United States. This divide contributes to children in immigrant families not receiving important early childhood services.

Where Immigrant Families Come from Today

Of the 75 million children now living in the United States, one-quarter are children of immigrants. Although the children may have been born in the United States, they are considered immigrants for the purposes of this chapter if their parents were born in another country, because the family heritage, home life, and experiences in America emerge in part from having emigrated. Children of immigrants in the United States come from all over the world, but most new immigrants are from South and Central America: 2.3 million are from Mexican families (39% of all immigrant children under 6), 1.4 million are from Latin America and the Caribbean (25%), another 1.4 million are from Asia (23%), over 400,000 are from Europe and Canada (7%), and over 300,000 are from Africa and the Middle East (6%) (Capps, Fix, Ost, Reardon-Anderson, & Passel, 2005).

IMMIGRANT FAMILIES HAVE COMMON EXPERIENCES AND UNIQUE STORIES

There are endless varieties of backgrounds and experiences that make each family's story unique, starting from country of origin. In Asia, it is often middle-class families who choose to migrate, while in Latin America, and Mexico in particular, it is usually families with low levels of income and education who migrate. According to the U.S. Census, 36% of Mexican immigrants have less than a high school education compared to 17% of all immigrants (Greico, 2004).

In spite of the unique nature of each family's story, immigrant families also share many common experiences. They are more likely to be poor than non-immigrant families; almost one-third (31%) of poor children in the United States live in immigrant families (Britz & Batalova, 2013). They also are more likely to include parents who have not graduated from high school (26% compared to 8%) or are not proficient in English (61%) (Fortuny, Capps, Simms, & Chaudry, 2009). Although there are many exceptions, these challenging experiences mean that many immigrant children do less well in many aspects of child development and school achievement than children of non-immigrant parents.

DIVERSITY IN THE DEVELOPMENT OF IMMIGRANT CHILDREN

Many factors influence young immigrant children's development: parents' education levels, income levels, reasons for leaving the home country, experiences upon arrival in the United States, certainty or uncertainty of deportation, ability to understand and speak English, and more. The diversity in families' stories directly relates to the diversity we see in child outcomes. On the one hand, some children are at the top of their class; but on the other hand, there are disproportionately high numbers of dropouts among immigrant children.

The variations in the achievements of Asian immigrant children reflect the complexity of immigrant experiences. In general, children of Asian immigrants tend to be high academic achievers and have at times been referred to as "a model minority" (Ng, Lee, & Pak, 2007; Suarez-Orozco, Suarez-Orozco, & Todorova, 2008). However, not all Asian children do well in school. Moreover, even if they do perform well, many Asian immigrant children feel sad or feel that they do not fit in (Qin, Way, & Mukherjee, 2008). Children who excel in academics may not have such positive outcomes in the emotional domains.

Whatever their ethnicity, children in immigrant families on average have difficulty achieving at the same level of education as non-immigrant children. Because of life circumstances, children of Latin American immigrants often seem to have particular challenges. Studying preschoolers like Edvardo, researchers found that although both immigrant and non-immigrant children made gains from enrollment in preschool, immigrant children still had weaker cognitive and language performance than non-immigrant children (De Feyter & Winsler, 2009).

Yet, like Edvardo, other Latino immigrant children have strengths to note and admire: De Feyter and Winsler (2009) found that the immigrant children showed *better* social-emotional competence than non-immigrant children of the same age. Teachers rated the Latino immigrant children higher than the non-immigrant children on initiative, self-control, and closeness with adults, qualities that Liliana values and has encouraged in her son.

CHALLENGES FOR AND STRENGTHS OF IMMIGRANT FAMILIES

Liliana tries to protect her young son from knowing too much about her own struggles, but she certainly experiences them: fear and anxiety at being able to provide a home and food, loneliness without her family, culture shock moving from Mexico to North Carolina, language barriers as she tries to learn English, and, before Head Start, not knowing where to get help, to name just a few. These types of challenges are the norm for immigrant parents.

Immigrant parents also may hold very different beliefs about children's behavior than their new neighbors, or even their young children's teachers, who may not be from the families' country of origin. Liliana felt fortunate to be welcomed by a program intentionally adapted for her culture and circumstance, but other immigrant families may not be so lucky. For example, many Asian parents teach children the importance of quietness as a sign of respectful attention and being a hard worker. But in the United States, people often think that silence shows a lack of intelligence or assertiveness and perhaps indifference. Both parents and children may initially be confused by the new code of conduct that is expected but never quite explained. Parents can sometimes experience a sense of grief as they realize dearly held beliefs and cultural patterns could be lost as they and their children adapt to the American value system. Many immigrant parents want their children to know and be proud of their country of heritage–as well as be part of their new country.

In spite of the challenges, it is important to recognize the assets these families bring to the table, and the critical one is family. First of all, children of immigrant parents are more likely than children of non-immigrant parents to live in two-parent households, which is a protective factor for children's well-being. Immigrant families' households also tend to include more extended-family adults, not just parents (Fortuny et al., 2009), meaning that a working parent may have an extra pair of hands available to help care for a young child. Family bonds are a key strength of many immigrant families, as they have been in the past.

Nonetheless, "it takes a village to raise a child," as the saying goes, not just one family. Early childhood programs can be an important part of a child's "village," especially for immigrant families–but many children of immigrants never participate in an early childhood program.

ACCESS TO EARLY CHILDHOOD PROGRAMS BY IMMIGRANT FAMILIES

In spite of the many ways that good early childhood education programs can actively support immigrant families, many immigrant children never enroll; in contrast with 29% of non-immigrant children, 43% of immigrant children never participate in a program, whether at a Head Start, a child care center, or a friend's home-based program (Fortuny et al., 2009).

Why is it that immigrant children are staying at home, when early childhood programs can contribute so much to children's and families' well-being? Here are some of the obstacles affecting immigrant (and ethnic minority and low-income) parents' decisions to enroll a child in an early childhood education program (California Tomorrow, 2004, p. 10):

- Language barriers between parents and service providers.
- Cultural beliefs about child development and health and mental health care, and how they align with or differ from those of a potential early childhood program.
- Reliance on informal information networks within an immigrant community that may be misinformed about options and eligibility requirements.
- Services that do not recognize the key role in childrearing played by extended family networks in many immigrant communities.
- Family support approaches that misguidedly seek to change healthy family behaviors, such as those related to diet or parenting skills.
- Hours of service that do not meet working parents' needs, especially for those working multiple jobs or unusual shift hours.
- Difficulty getting the child to the program–services are too far or in an unfamiliar area, lack of a car or gas money, and there are language and cost barriers impeding the use of public transportation.

- Lack of knowledge about availability of services, financial assistance, and eligibility requirements; for example, many immigrant parents do not know their child is eligible for Head Start and that the program is free (Matthews & Ewen, 2006).
- Fear that trying to enroll a child in a program could jeopardize a family in which a parent is in the United States without documentation.
- Unaffordable fees–usually the biggest factor for immigrant parents as well as many others (Takanishi, 2004).

These barriers represent lost opportunities for children and the country, in the eyes of both teachers and economists.

THE VALUE OF EARLY CHILDHOOD PROGRAM PARTICIPATION FOR IMMIGRANT CHILDREN, FAMILIES, AND COMMUNITIES

When immigrant families can overcome the barriers and enroll in early childhood education programs, good things tend to happen.

PROFESSIONAL PROFILE

Donald Hernandez, Professor of Sociology, Hunter College, New York, Senior Advisor, Foundation for Child Development

In multiple ways, Donald Hernandez's work supports research and public policies related to immigrant children and families. A recent week began with an advisory meeting in Washington, DC for the United States Administration on Children and Families. The meeting focused on identifying the kinds of questions to ask on government surveys to assess the needs of immigrant and language-minority children, especially those in low-income families. Several days were spent preparing for and teaching a class on Children and Public Policy, emphasizing research from neuroscience, psychology, sociology, and anthropology on the benefits of dual-language curricula that foster bilingualism and biculturalism. Later in the week, Don met with officials of the Foundation for Child Development to evaluate and make decisions about whether to fund various proposals for research on the effect of Pre-K–3rd-Grade programs for children in immigrant families. Finally, another day was spent developing statistical indicators of the health, education, and economic well-being of the 25% of young children who have immigrant parents, compared to those with United States-born parents.

Donald Hernandez earned his Ph.D. in Sociology; among his professional positions, he was Chief of Marriage and Family Statistics at the United States Census Bureau for 20 years, and Director of a Study on the Health and Adjustment of Immigrant Children and Families at the National Academy of Sciences/Institute of Medicine. He also has been a sociology professor at the University of South Carolina and the University at Albany, SUNY.

Children Gain School Readiness Skills

Early childhood programs almost always seem to have particularly powerful benefits for disadvantaged or at-risk children. Children in immigrant families are no exception. Studies show that early childhood education improves school readiness skills for this group of children in particular (Gormley, Gayer, Phillips, & Dawson, 2004; Rumberger & Tran, 2006). In some areas of development, such as language ability, early education has an even larger effect on immigrant children's gains than on other children's gains (Magnuson, Lahaie, & Waldfogel, 2006). In Tulsa, Oklahoma, pre-K participation led to even larger effects for Hispanic children from Spanish-speaking homes than from English-speaking homes, and researchers found similar results from the Head Start Impact Study (cf. Yoshikawa et al., 2013). School readiness at kindergarten or 1st grade is an important foundation for children's long-term achievement levels and future well-being.

Parents Have Time to Work and Ease of Mind

Most immigrant families are among the working poor, especially when they are from Mexico and Central America. The emphasis in this case is on *working*: 91% of immigrant children live with a working parent or caregiver (Fortuny et al., 2009). Not only are most immigrant parents working, but they also work long hours. Among low-income families in the United States, immigrant parents work more hours than non-immigrant parents. It can be hard to put together a full week of work, every week, for 52 weeks a year from temporary, part-time, or odd-shift jobs, but many immigrant parents find ways to do so. Sometimes multiple jobs are necessary because employers pay immigrants less than the minimum wage, taking advantage of uncertainty about laws and fears of deportation that could follow complaints.

Combining working and commuting hours, shift work, and multiple jobs, many immigrant parents need extended hours of child care, as provided by Edvardo's Head Start program. The hours are important, as they allow Liliana to keep her job, support the family, and contribute to the economic growth of the county and the country.

Beyond the hours of coverage, parents need the peace of mind that a good child care or education program brings. Parents can take care of other business knowing their child is well cared for, having fun, and learning. Even more than parents in other families, perhaps, immigrant parents count on the education system to help children have a strong start in life this new country.

Communities Have an Engaged and Educated Work Force

Liliana's boss would probably enthusiastically support good early care and education opportunities in his community as much as Liliana does. Immigrants have provided the country a hard-working pool of labor and leadership since its founding, and that continues to be true; today's immigrant children make up America's future work force. It is in everyone's interest to have citizens who are educated, healthy, and productive members of society, all of which are long-term results of high-quality early childhood programs. Today's young children will become America's entrepreneurs, scientists, academics, politicians, teachers, taxi drivers, farmers, restaurant workers, attorneys, business owners, and parents.

Next, we look at what it is that teachers and administrators do in early childhood education programs to contribute to immigrant children's well-being, education, achievement levels, and success in life.

HOW EARLY CHILDHOOD PROGRAMS AND TEACHERS CONTRIBUTE TO GOOD OUTCOMES FOR IMMIGRANT CHILDREN

What is the magic that happens in good early childhood programs? Are there secret keys that unlock positive development for immigrant children? Many of the general principles of high-quality early childhood programs apply to immigrant children in particular. What follow are some specific keys that good teachers use to open doors for immigrant families and their children.

Doing Background Research on Program Participants

Since 1.9 million immigrant children go to preschool or kindergarten programs at some point, and millions more enroll in the early primary grades, most early childhood teachers will teach immigrant children, perhaps from dozens of countries. Teachers who do not know much about a family's home country can easily find information on the Internet or at the library to discover ways to connect what the child learns in class to what the child might remember from the birth country or hear about at home. Internet translation programs can show how to write basic signs or labels to welcome and orient parents and children in their native language. Taking real interest in the background of a child and family, and reflecting their native culture in program elements, are among the highest forms of care.

Creating a Welcoming Place

Physically, a classroom environment that is safe, welcoming, and laid out to encourage children's interactions and explorations will help immigrant children understand how they can be active participants in their learning, even if they do not yet speak English. Teachers can put up simple signs in the child's home language, learn and share simple songs or rhymes from the home country, and invite parents to bring in favorite snacks from their home country or lead the class in a game or dance from the home country. Having all children in the class create an "All About Me and My Family" poster with photos or cutouts from magazines can allow immigrant children to share both some of their family heritage (like traditional clothes they may wear) and characteristics that make each child a unique individual (like being allergic to bees and having 11 cousins).

Reaching Out to Parents and Other Family Members

Teachers agree that reaching out to families–immigrant or not–and together establishing common goals for the child throughout a family's program experience are important. Doing so can be challenging when teachers and parents do not share the same language and culture. But simply being aware and making the effort goes a long way. Good teachers keep in mind that immigrant parents sometimes feel intimidated by school settings, may be unsure of culturally "appropriate" rules of etiquette, and often view the teacher as a person of great authority. Therefore, culturally sensitive teachers do not wait for parents to approach them; instead, they respectfully reach out to the parents, as Edvardo's teacher did so skillfully to Liliana. They also find out who else may be important to welcome from the child's extended family.

Engaging Children in Projects

When children become curious about a topic, whether it is Thanksgiving, jungles, or bicycles, they start to formulate good questions, problem-solve, test theories, use technology to answer questions, and engage in teamwork (Jones & Shue, 2013). Teachers' engagement with the topic of interest is important for all children, but has special value for those in immigrant families. Teachers take advantage of children's curiosity to design special projects related to their experiences and interests, which encourages communication skills and conceptual development. Some teachers find that putting children in pairs—immigrant with non-immigrant children, for example—can promote turn-taking, thinking strategies, language skills and role-playing in a non-threatening situation (Alanis, 2013).

Using Appropriate Assessment Strategies

In all areas of development for immigrant children, whether in mathematics, reading, social development, or general knowledge, assessments need to be developmentally and culturally appropriate and used to improve instruction for the child. Certainly this is important for all children, but there are special considerations when assessing immigrant children who are dual language learners (DLL). Depending on a child's age of exposure to English, assessments may underestimate dual language learners' knowledge and abilities; DLL children rarely show their full potential when assessed only in English. And equally as important as language ability is culture; a first-generation immigrant recently arrived from Peru may have a sophisticated vocabulary and skills related to sewing and weaving but may not yet know about chalk, water colors, glitter, glue, or other art activities in the early childhood education program. Children need time to become familiar with their new environment. Staff should consider the case of each immigrant child individually to be sure that the program is using appropriate assessment strategies, which may well require the use of both English and the home language (Espinosa, 2013).

Approaching Sensitive Topics with Delicacy

Especially if they are refugees, many children have experienced, and may still be experiencing, uncertain, painful, and possibly traumatic situations. Edvardo's father died violently, and despite his mother's best efforts, the shadow remains in Edvardo's life as well as in hers. Besides memories of the past, current challenges could include transient housing, separation from loved ones, food insufficiency, and often-overwhelming feelings of sadness, tiredness, and stress. It can be easy to overlook the quiet child or pigeonhole the badly behaved child as a trouble-maker, especially when one's hands are already so full with the many responsibilities of teaching. But through communication with the family and observations of the child, teachers can learn more about what has happened or is happening in the child's personal life. Looking at relevant books, drawing, role-playing, and using puppets or dolls can help children process difficult issues related to their immigration experiences.

Encouraging Children to Master Both Their Home Language and English

The fact that some immigrant children have to learn two languages–the home language and English–is only partly a barrier; it is also a gift. Being bilingual, as Edvardo and many other children are or will become, is a lifelong skill that should be admired and promoted–not only for immigrant children, but for all children. Bilingualism shows intelligence and social sophistication and improves cognitive skills. This is a critical but sometimes complicated issue for children in immigrant families, so it is worth further discussion.

DUAL LANGUAGE LEARNING

All young children are language learners. Many immigrant children are dual language learners (DLLs), learning two (or more) languages at once. There are a number of myths related to dual language development that cognitive neuroscience and psycholinguistic research contradict. The myths usually emerge from what seems like common sense. For example, there is a myth that learning two languages will confuse young children and delay their acquisition of English. Another myth says that total immersion in English is the best way for young dual language learners to learn English. Although these ideas seem logical, the research shows that they are both false. Children's cognitive skills *and* English-language skills benefit from learning English while continuing to master the home language.

Improving Skills in the Home Language While Learning English Has Multiple Benefits

Children actually do better in cognitive and language development, including English, when they solidify learning in their home language rather than trying to replace it immediately with English (Ball, 2011; Patrinos & Velez, 2009; Posel & Casale, 2011). It is not an either-or situation: Promoting learning within a child's home language should not come at the expense of learning English, nor should learning English come at the expense of further mastery of the home language. Linda Espinosa (2013), Karen Nemeth (2012), and others cite several reasons teachers should support children's fluency in their home language while simultaneously scaffolding the development of English skills:

1. *It supports cognitive development.* From 7 months of age to the grandparent years, dual language learning strengthens mental abilities. It improves working memory, inhibitory control, mental flexibility, and attention to relevant cues, all of which are the biological foundation for school readiness (Bialystok, 2008). Compared with children who speak only one language, DLL children also show better problem-solving and creative skills (Genesee, 2008). Also, children can easily transfer early literacy skills from one language for another, especially once they have grasped the concept that words are made up of written symbols (Espinosa, 2010). Later in life, bilingualism may even serve a protective function against developing Alzheimer's (Craik, Bialystok, & Freedman, 2010). Completely dropping the home language in favor of English puts conceptual and academic development at risk. Espinosa (2013) writes: "For young children who are actively processing and have not yet mastered the fundamentals of their first language, completely shifting to a new, unfamiliar language during the early childhood years may negatively impact the ongoing development of their home language, as well as academic achievement in the long run" (p. 9).

2. *It increases self-esteem.* Nemeth (2012) writes, "Children's language is as much a part of them as their name, their home, their family traditions, and their connections to their parents and siblings" (p. 9). It is important for teachers to encourage children to feel good about their home language and the identity it carries, while also promoting English. Children should be proud to be able to speak multiple languages.

3. *It strengthens family ties.* Children need to be able to continue to talk about what happened during their day and communicate at increasingly sophisticated levels with the people at home who love them most. Conversations about increasingly complex topics in the home language are important for linguistic development and parent-child relationships—and do not detract from gains in English-language skills.

4. *It improves social interactions.* Sometimes a child who only speaks the home language can feel isolated. Teachers can take advantage of children's natural skills at adapting their language for others who do not easily understand them and create ways to increase interactions for non-English-speaking children. Even if communication is not sophisticated, it is far better for children to interact than be left out. As DLL children in English-only classrooms gain basic English skills, they will begin to have more fulfilling interactions. Social interactions will improve language skills, and language skills improve social interactions in a virtuous cycle.

5. *Learning two languages improves English-language skills for DLL children.* For the highest achievement in English in 3rd grade (and beyond), DLL children should experience systematic, deliberate exposure to English during the earlier years, combined with ongoing opportunities to learn concepts in the home language. By the time they reached junior high and high school, DLLs who had opportunities to strengthen both languages in an early childhood program consistently outperformed those who had attended an English-only ECE program (Collier & Thomas, 2009).

How Early Childhood Professionals Can Support Immigrant Children Who Are Dual Language Learners

Children who start speaking two different languages at home from birth—say, speaking French with the mother and English with the father—tend to learn both languages in the same way at the same time. But children like Edvardo, for whom English is introduced after about age 3, learn the second language through a somewhat different path, which is based on their learning of the first language. By building on what children already know, teachers play a key role in helping children learn English while strengthening the home language. Below are just a few examples of what professionals do to support DLLs.

Provide Dual Language Programs. When there are many children in a program who speak the same home language and there are bilingual staff, as in Edvardo's program, a dual language program is ideal. Children learn academic content, social-emotional skills, and language skills with correct and increasingly sophisticated language, both in the home language and English. These types of programs welcome both DLL and English-only children and keep the children together. Teachers do not switch between languages, nor do they translate into the

---

PROFESSIONAL PROFILE

Michele Dandrea and Anna Yu, Co-Teachers, Acorn Center for
Early Education and Care, Boston Chinatown Neighborhood Center, Boston, MA

The Acorn Center, where Michele and Anna co-teach a combined pre-K and kindergarten class, functions as an extended family for the children and their parents, many of whom are immigrants. Most of the children in their class are dual Chinese/English language learners, so Michele and Anna, her Chinese-speaking teaching partner, pay special attention to cultural connections and language development. However, most of the hours in each day and week are spent simply running a lively classroom: Feeding the turtle, greeting families, serving breakfast, working on projects with children, reading stories, outdoor playtime, lunch family-style—the hours and days go on! Every day, children are observed and progress notes are saved to share with families. Using children's changing interests as well as state learning guidelines, the teaching team researches and develops curriculum and translates it into Chinese so all parents can read it. If a field trip is happening that week, always designed to enrich language and vocabulary, the teachers post bilingual reminders and parents are invited to join the trip. At the end of each week, Michele and Anna create developmentally appropriate, enjoyable homework that can be taken home on Friday and completed in either language.

Michele and Anna both started working with children during their high school child development class, continuing on for bachelor's degrees in Preschool/Kindergarten/Primary Education. Like many of their Acorn colleagues, they have stayed for many years because they love the work they do.

other language. Rather, they might designate certain days or periods or activities for each language (Nemeth, 2012). These programs improve the skills of both DLLs and native English speakers.

Practical Strategies for English-Only Teachers. Although dual language programs may be ideal, in reality such programs are not very common, and there are many more DLL children than there are fully bilingual teachers. Only about 10% of early childhood education teachers in the United States are fluent in more than one language (Pianta & Hadden, 2008). Yet monolingual teachers still play a critical role for children in immigrant families. In addition to cultivating the attitudes and strategies named above, such as encouraging parents to keep speaking the home language, they have practical issues to deal with to teach each child in the classroom. They can intentionally use strategies such as these to help learning come to life (Nemeth, 2012):

- Using props—for example, holding up a bowl or a ball to clarify which thing is being discussed.
- Being clear with body language and aware of facial expressions and gestures; for example, having a specific gesture that tells children to use a quieter voice; or pointing to the head when telling children to put on a hat.
- Making eye contact and being aware that young children, especially infants, are watching one's mouth and face during speech.
- Emphasizing small-group learning and individual interactions more than whole-group lessons, in which dual language learners are easily overlooked.
- Repeating activities over time and in different contexts so DLL children have deeper experiences with words, actions, items, and interactions.

Supporting Early Reading and Writing. Young immigrant children deserve both patience and the benefit of good teaching strategies when it comes to reading and writing. They should begin the reading process by focusing on the language in which they are strongest, whether that is English or their home language. Building on what is familiar helps children make connections, grasp concepts, and build confidence. In writing, teachers and parents can work together to help children practice both the characters and content of the home language and English. If teachers feel stuck or overwhelmed, they might remember this: The most important thing all young writers—immigrant or not—need to learn is that they are interesting people who have something interesting to say that others want to know about.

Overcoming Parents' Resistance. Regardless of what the research shows about the value of dual language learning, it is not uncommon for immigrant parents to say they do not want their child to speak in the home language at school; they want the child to focus only on English. Experts would say it is important to be respectful to parents by acknowledging parents' goals *and* sharing professional expertise about how language development occurs—explaining that children learn best by mastering Spanish, Mandarin, Gujerati, Persian, or whatever their home language is while also learning English.

CONCLUDING THOUGHTS:
IMPROVING SERVICES TO HELP CHILDREN
OF IMMIGRANTS CREATE A GREAT PATH IN LIFE

Edvardo is one of millions of children living with at least one adult who is an immigrant, and he is likely to share some common experiences with other children in immigrant families—learning two languages, having a parent with long working hours, maintaining roots in two places, having complex cultural identities—but he will also navigate his own unique path through life in America.

Where immigrant children end up will in part start with *where* they begin and *how* they begin. Will they begin elementary school already behind their peers? Will they be prepared to share and laugh and play and learn new things? Will they start school having to struggle, feeling hesitant or like they do not belong? Or will they have experiences with knowledgeable, caring adults outside their family who take an interest in the fort they can build, the scratch on the shin, or their new ability to draw a dog? The children who start life with the chance to learn, explore, play, and imagine in the company of friends and caring adults have better chances of getting where they want to go as they create their path.

The answers may depend on how well the network of early childhood professionals and policymakers supports and provides for young immigrant children. Policymakers have the responsibility to make sure every child in an immigrant family has space in an affordable early care and education program, and program directors should review their current enrollment requirements to ensure that all children in immigrant families, regardless of documentation status, may participate in their program. To make sure parents know their child is wanted and welcomed in a program, teachers and program directors should reach out to immigrant families with information about enrollment, eligibility, and cost requirements to encourage participation.

Bilingual teachers are a much-needed gift to the field. Administrators should try to recruit more bilingual teachers—and increase training for all teachers on working with young immigrant children. It is important to use culturally appropriate instruction and assessment practices, and support learning and assessment in both the home language and English for dual language learners. And for immigrant families, it is particularly necessary to encourage parent involvement and find ways to make welcome and include parents and other family members who do not speak English.

For Edvardo, the path that started in the muddy blueberry fields could end up on the green campus of a university where he is a professor or behind a stainless steel counter where he serves as head chef or on the worn wooden floor of Congress where he represents his district. Another child in another family of immigrants might live in San Francisco's Chinatown, Chicago's South Side, San Antonio's Edgewood neighborhood, or a nameless suburb of any city in America, and will take a completely different journey. Yet all of them face endless possibilities in America, especially when they have a strong start that includes high-quality early childhood services.

REFLECTION, DIALOGUE, AND ACTION

1. Talk to someone you know—perhaps even a family member—who is a first- or second-generation immigrant with a young child. What options did they consider for early childhood services for the child? Did they enroll the child in a program, and why or why not? Write down what you learn about their experiences.

2. With permission, visit a Head Start, pre-K, or other program that serves immigrant children. How many children in the program are immigrants and what countries are they from? What challenges and benefits do teachers experience from having them in the program? Ask teachers what supports they need to help the children succeed.

3. Check the Internet for a congressperson or senator in your state and search for his or her stance on immigration policies. Note whether you find any information related to early childhood policies for immigrants, perhaps for Head Start or public pre-K. Do you agree or disagree with their position and why? Find a way to communicate that to their office.

INFORMATION TO EXPLORE AND SHARE

National Migrant and Seasonal Head Start Association

Migrant and Seasonal Head Start was created in 1969 under the umbrella of the federal Head Start program as a response to meet the unique needs of migrant farm worker families. It operates in 40 states and serves more than 37,000 migrant and seasonal farm worker children, 75% of whom are infants or toddlers. www.nmshsaonline.org

Center for Early Care and Education Research–Dual Language Learners

Based at the Frank Porter Graham Institute at the University of North Carolina-Chapel Hill, the Center aims to improve assessment, child care, and education for DLL children from birth through age 5. The goal is to support children's development and learning. The Center's website includes links to resources developed by the Center and other experts in DLL research. cecerdll.fpg.unc.edu

FirstFocus

FirstFocus is a bipartisan children's advocacy organization launched by America's Promise. The purpose of the organization is making children and their families a priority in federal policy and budget decisions. An important area of attention is children of immigrants, with resources available online. www.firstfocus.net/our-work/children-of-immigrants

United States Committee for Refugees and Migrants

USCRI is an international advocacy and domestic refugee resettlement organization that aims to help forced and voluntary refugees worldwide by advancing fair and humane public policy, facilitating direct professional services, and promoting the full participation of migrants in community life. www.refugees.org

CHAPTER 10

The Early Years Matter
for Children in Developing Countries

Photo by Heather Biggar Tomlinson

Nani is a stout, smiling woman who lives in Jakarta, the capital of Indonesia. She is Irwan's grandmother, and she takes care of Irwan with her daughter-in-law Ati, a widow. Irwan is a shy boy, prone to illness, fond of sweets and fried food, and a doting big brother. Ati and Nani want a good life for Irwan, and they would love to enroll him in kindergarten (in Indonesia, kindergarten is for children ages 4 to 6), but they cannot find one they can afford. Kindergartens in Indonesia, like early childhood programs in many other developing countries, are privately run, have registration and tuition fees, and require uniforms and school supplies before starting. Nani and Ati do not have the money.

They are hard-working and resourceful—Nani does laundry for two families, and Ati sells things at a small *warung* (shop)—but between them, they earn about $4 a day. The amount is above the national poverty line, but it does not go far in the expensive capital city, and kindergarten seems out of reach. Nani and Ati visit various programs, but none are affordable for them. Also, the program needs to be within walking distance of their house. They do not own a motorbike, the normal mode of transportation in Jakarta, and using the public buses would be expensive and time-consuming in Jakarta's dense traffic.

In the end, they cannot find a kindergarten close by that they can afford, so Irwan will stay home until he can enter primary school the year after next. He struggles with learning, and there are few opportunities for him to gain school readiness skills. Grandmother Nani has a 4th-grade education and cannot read; mother Ati can read, but it has not occurred to her to read to her boys—even if she owned any children's books, which she does not. All their money goes toward rent and food, so they are not able to buy books, crayons, or toys. Irwan wants to go to kindergarten—he sees other children in their uniforms—but Nani and Ati cannot think of any solution. So for now, he will play in the alleys around their house and help his grandmother watch the baby.

THE CHARACTERISTICS OF A DEVELOPING COUNTRY

Early childhood is a time of life overlooked and underappreciated in many countries, and this is even more the case in developing countries, which have many urgent competing demands on their limited budgets, as well as often-limited expertise in early development and learning.

Although the term is widely used, there is no single definition of a *developing country*. Generally, developing countries are those in which most people live on much less money than people living in highly industrialized countries. Developing countries often lack many of the basic services that are taken for granted in affluent economies—such as access to free education, high-quality health services, public libraries, and adequate nutrition for the poor.

World Bank economists explain that if a country has a gross national income of less than about $1,000 per person (United States equivalent), it is considered a low-income country. A middle-income country has up to about $4,000; an upper-middle-income country has up to about $12,000; and a high-income country has over $12,000 per person (World Bank, 2012). Developing countries are generally those in the low- and middle-income group.

While income is a very important aspect of a country's level of development, it is only one component. What is the quality of life like in a country? How much education do its citizens have? Do citizens enjoy a long and healthy life? These kinds of components are measured and combined to create a score called the Human Development Index (HDI). Although there are exceptions, usually a country's income and its HDI are related. Developing countries are both relatively poor and relatively difficult places for young children like Irwan to thrive.

As illustrated in Figure 10.1, the majority of the world's children (92%) live in developing countries (UNICEF, 2009). The risks to children living in a developing

Figure 10.1. The World's Developing Countries

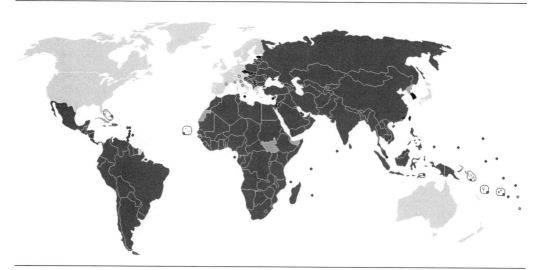

Source: Adapted from the International Monetary Fund. Data for South Sudan are not yet available.

country mean it is especially important to have good early childhood policies in place to ensure children survive, stay healthy, live in safe and peaceful places, and have access to education.

RISK FACTORS FOR CHILDREN IN DEVELOPING COUNTRIES

Most children who live in developing countries face multiple and simultaneous risk factors (Engle, Rao, & Petrovic, 2013). Most often, poverty is the greatest risk factor, from which many other problems arise to affect children's development.

Poverty

The poverty line in Indonesia and many other developing countries is around $2 a day, an amount that is hard to imagine living on even for the poorest of Americans. Some people assume that to live on so little means that the cost of living is adjusted. That is not necessarily so; the price for a gallon of gasoline or a bag of rice is the same for Ati as for her wealthier neighbors. The disparity between rich and poor is one of the most challenging issues in developing countries because gaps in income only continue to grow larger—which leads to gaps in education and achievement levels.

Although we usually think of poverty as related to how much money a family has, being poor is not only about material assets and health, but also about a lack of *social capital*. Many people in developing countries are both materially poor and socially poor, meaning they are not considered important and valuable participants in society. Irwan's mother, Ati, is an example. As a young widow, she has few material resources, and she is often excluded within her community.

Families with young children tend to be among the poorest globally. Similar to the situation in the United States (see Chapter 5), families with young children in developing countries make up a large share of the total population of the poor, and their risks and stressors tend to accumulate. Families like Irwan's generally have to manage many problems simultaneously. These include issues similar to those in the United States, such as competing demands for family income for food, rent, medical, child care, and transportation needs.

Irwan's mother, Ati, and Anna's mother, Ruby (Chapter 5), face similar concerns. Having a small income makes it more likely they will live in an unsafe and sometimes violent neighborhood. The stress of that environment, in turn, may contribute to getting sick more often and having feelings of depression, anxiety, and anger. When parents do not feel well, it can be difficult to provide children with appropriate nurturing and stimulation. Lack of money also means making difficult choices: Should the mother buy eggs, take Irwan or Anna to a doctor, or pay for an early childhood program?

The problems in developing countries may also include factors such as lack of safe drinking water, poor infrastructure like unsafe roads and school buildings, high exposure to unclean environments and disease, lack of medical care, irregular electricity, and high exposure to natural disaster and violence. When poverty exists at the family, community, and country levels, it is hard to contain its ripple effects, which touch all domains of child well-being.

Poor Nutrition and Health

Starting before birth, good nutrition is vital for healthy development. When children do not get what they need in the womb, they are at risk for significant developmental delays, a problem for about 1 in 10 children in developing countries (Engle et al., 2013). And after birth, the most important means of good nutrition for babies comes from breastfeeding, yet almost half of all children in developing countries are not breastfed. If poor nutritional experiences continue over long periods of time, children stop growing normally for their age, both physically (they are short for their age) and mentally (they have low cognitive levels and may be socially different from other children). This is called stunting, and 28% of children under 5 in the world (171 million children) are stunted (UNESCO, 2012).

Both Irwan and his brother experienced poor prenatal nutrition–Ati did not eat enough protein or fruit or take prenatal vitamins–and have lacked dietary diversity, sufficient protein, and dairy products since they were born. Irwan's baby brother could still avoid stunting with improvements in his diet. However, Irwan became stunted before age 2, and the effects are mostly irreversible, although improved nutrition and a stimulating environment can help to some extent. Paradoxically, Irwan is overweight for his age, which is not uncommon since he eats too many high-energy but low-nutrition foods, like fried chips.

Diseases and toxic environments also pose problems for children's development. Malaria and diarrhea are known to cause developmental delays, for example, as are pesticides, pollution, arsenic (common in well water), and high lead levels–all of which are prevalent in developing countries. For example, in developing countries as much as 15% to 20% of the mental retardation that occurs is related to lead exposure

(Fewtrell, Kaufmann, & Prüss-Üstün, 2003). And children are affected both directly and indirectly by adults' heavy smoking and alcohol use, which are increasing problems in many developing countries (World Health Organization, 2003, 2004).

Lack of Intellectual Stimulation

Besides these health risks, young children in developing countries are often at risk because they lack sufficient stimulation and learning opportunities. Between 60% and 90% of parents in developing countries do not read books to their children, take them to places and events in the community, play with them, tell stories, or sing to them on a regular basis (Engle et al., 2013; Hasan, Hyson, & Chang, 2013). Irwan's story shows how even children of very loving families may lack simulation. Through no fault of their own, many parents do not know how important it is to talk to and respond to their babies. Lacking this responsiveness, children may feel less secure and have lower cognitive abilities. Out-of-home learning opportunities are also missing in most young children's lives: The majority of children in developing countries never attend preschool.

Violence

Imagine putting gas masks on children or trying to explain why someone the children know was shot and killed yesterday. Exposure to armed conflict and other violence affects millions of young children every year; children are attacked, bullied, sexually abused, trafficked, forced into labor, forced to become soldiers, and more. Experiencing or witnessing traumatic violence causes difficulties with behavior, mental health issues, and post-traumatic stress disorder (examples of the effects of violence on children are described and discussed in Chapter 6). Sometimes children are the direct victims of violence, and sometimes parents are the victims. There are over 7 million orphans under age 6 in sub-Saharan Africa alone. Without parents, children's survival is in danger, and even if they survive they often suffer from a deep sense of depression and vulnerability.

Combined, these risk factors make it difficult to survive the early years in developing countries, where 7 out of 100 children do not live beyond the age of 5 (UNICEF, 2009), as compared with fewer than 1 out of 100 in developed countries. Early childhood teachers work, often unpaid, to ensure that children in developing countries not only survive but flourish. The next section explores how early childhood development programs can make a difference.

HOW EARLY CHILDHOOD PROGRAMS CAN HELP CHILDREN IN DEVELOPING COUNTRIES

In the United States, we usually refer to child care, preschools, and similar programs as early childhood education programs, or sometimes early care and education–both ECE. People who work in developing countries usually use the term *early childhood development* (ECD) programs to place additional emphasis on the broad range of services that children need, especially health and nutrition services from the prenatal period to age 5. Early education services are one aspect of ECD programs, ideally integrated with other services, as is also the case in some American programs such as Head Start and Early Head Start.

By themselves, community-based ECD programs cannot overcome poverty, malnutrition, violence, low levels of parental education, or environmental toxins, problems that must be addressed through broad public policies and extensive resources. But early childhood teachers do make a critical difference in their own communities. It is through family education and support programs, health clinics that immunize and feed young children, and early childhood development services such as playgroups and preschools that families learn more about what they do that is great for their children and how they can enhance children's well-being and development.

Children in developing countries who attend preschool, which is not the norm, are more likely to go to primary school, to get to 2nd grade, and to learn more in primary school (OECD, 2011). Experiences in preschool teach children how to navigate the basics needed for school, such as when to speak, when to play, how to hold a pencil, how to hold a book, and how to sing songs or say rhymes. Preschool experiences also make children more confident entering primary school and more eager to learn. As in the United States, children from the poorest and most disadvantaged backgrounds within developing countries benefit the most from preprimary programs (Hasan et al., 2013).

Cognitive and Academic Development

Looking first at effects on cognitive and academic outcomes, one sees that preprimary program participation benefits children in developing countries from around the world, as shown in Figure 10.2. Children have been shown to make gains in test scores, language skills, class participation, memory skills, classifying skills, reading, writing, mathematics, and more.

As found in studies of low-income children in the United States (Chapter 5), the positive effects of ECD programs for children in developing countries last into children's teen years and beyond. In a study of children from 65 countries, 15-year-olds in 58 of those countries outperformed their peers if they had gone to at least 1 year of school before 1st grade—and this was after taking into account the effects of a family's wealth and education (OECD, 2011).

Social, Emotional, and Motor Development

Beyond these cognitive and academic benefits, do ECD programs positively affect other areas of child development and family well-being? The answer is an emphatic yes. Many studies document the effectiveness of programs that integrate health, nutrition and feeding information, and parenting education to improve parent-child interactions (Engle, Fernald, Alderman, et al., 2011). Consider the following examples (summarized from Walker et al., 2011):

- Babies between 6 and 12 months in Chile with iron-deficiency anemia were given oral iron supplements for a year, and their mothers received home visits every week from a professional educator. Mothers learned how to promote their

Figure 10.2. Cognitive and Academic Gains Associated with Participation in Early Childhood
Development Programs

Children Participating in the Study	Impact of Having Gone to an ECD program
3rd-graders in an urban area of Argentina	Higher test scores, improved attention, effort, class participation, and discipline; effects were twice as large for students from poor backgrounds
4- and 5-year-olds in rural China (Gansu, Shaanxi, & Henan)	Scored 20% higher on school readiness
Children entering primary school in Chile	Higher cognitive skill scores
4- to 6-year-olds in Integrated Child Development Services in rural India (Maharashtra)	Significant positive effects on development and cognitive outcomes
Primary school children in Madagascar	A 2.7-month benefit in cognitive development and a 1.6-month benefit in language and motor skills
1st-graders in Mozambique	Scored 12.1 percentage points above other students on a cognitive development test, including memory, classifying objectives, and counting to 20; preschool participation increased the probability of enrolling in 1st grade by 24%
4th-graders in Brazil	Higher scores in mathematics
2nd-graders in rural Bangladesh	Performed better in speaking, reading, writing and mathematics
1st-graders in rural China (Guizhou)	Literacy and mathematics scores significantly higher than other children's
4-year-olds in 310 poor and rural villages in Indonesia	Improved language and cognitive scores, with the greatest gains among the poorest children
15-year-olds in Uruguay	0.8 years more education, 27% more likely to still be in school, and less likely to repeat a grade compared to siblings who had not attended

Sources: Adapted from a 2012 Education for All global monitoring report by UNESCO; Hasan et al. (2013).

child's development and improve their relationship with their baby. Besides health benefits, children's social-emotional development improved significantly.

- Pregnant women in South Africa learned how to have more sensitive, responsive interactions with their future infants and learned more about how their babies develop. By the time their babies were 6 months and then a year old, mothers had indeed become more sensitive and less intrusive. And by the time the babies were 18 months old, those babies were more securely attached to their mothers than babies of mothers who did not participate in this program.

- In a group of Chinese villages, some families with children under age 2 received two parent counseling sessions (about 6 months apart and following the World Health Organization's Care for Development guidelines). In each session, parents saw demonstrations of play activities and had time to practice and to discuss how to do the activities at home. Children's adaptive, language, and social skills improved.

- In a special-care nursery in India that served many babies born prematurely or with low birth weight (indicating high risks for later development), some mothers in a group of 800 learned how to stimulate their babies. Besides spending a year learning individually and in groups, the mothers also received home visits. One and two years later, babies of all birth weights showed better psychomotor developmental levels and mental development scores compared to babies of nonparticipating mothers.

These studies are especially convincing because all the researchers randomly chose some participants to receive the intervention (such as a parenting class), while others did not receive the intervention or received it later on. This research design raises confidence in the results and provides more evidence that ECD can make a difference across many areas of children's development and learning. This is the good news. The not-so-good news is that in many developing countries (as in the United States), there are not enough ECD programs to reach all families, and the programs that do exist are often poor-quality.

BALANCING RESOURCES TO ACHIEVE QUANTITY AND QUALITY

Education is one of the biggest budget items for developing countries, yet programs for children below the primary grades get a very small percentage of the total education funds. That tiny fraction of money gets divided into many tinier pieces, and policymakers sometimes have to make tough choices about whether to put money toward increasing the number of young children who have access to programs or toward improving the programs that exist. Quantity and quality both tend to be low in developing countries.

Access to Preprimary Programs

Increasing numbers of children are enrolled in preprimary (preschool) programs in developing countries. In 2009, 157 million children in developing countries were enrolled in some kind of ECD program (UNESCO, 2012); this is a 40% increase over

PROFESSIONAL PROFILE

Yulianti Siantayani, Director,
Bukit Aksara Pre- and Primary School, Semarang, Indonesia

Yulie's deep love for young children and her interest in learning more about early child-hood motivate her to engage in a range of activities in her typical week. In any public place, young children instantly capture her attention. As the head of *Bukit Aksara*, Yulie spends substantial time in the office, yet she sees her role not just as a manager but as a "mother" to her large staff, encouraging them to work together to help children develop and learn. During the day, Yulie renews herself by visiting classrooms, marveling at how the children—including those with special needs—make friends, share, take responsibility, and create new things. Beyond her own program, Yulie serves as a speaker and trainer. Village teachers are starved for knowledge, Yulie finds, and so she helps them learn more about high-quality early childhood practices. Other time is spent on publications—besides writing children's books, she's recently begun to write books for parents and teachers. Yulie often travels to provide guest lectures at a college in the Indonesian province of Papua, a region distant not only geographically but also culturally from her home in central Java.

Yulianti Siantayani, M.Pd., is the founder of Bukit Aksara Pre- and Primary School in Sema-rang, Indonesia, and is currently a doctoral candidate at Jakarta State University. Through an initiative supported by the World Bank and the Government of Indonesia, Yulie was formerly a consultant with the National Early Childhood Specialist Team.

the decade and represents 46% of eligible children. However, this reported number may be somewhat higher than is really the case. Government officials sometimes in-clude children who were brought to an occasional health clinic or parenting class, or who are enrolled in a program focused exclusively on rote memorization of religious texts, rather than only counting children attending early care and education programs on a regular basis. However the numbers are calculated, the majority of children–certainly more than half–are left out of early childhood services.

Enrollment rates vary greatly by country and region. The region farthest behind in enrollment rates is Sub-Saharan Africa, which has shown gains in recent years but still has a very low rate, and the Arab States, where enrollment rates are approximate-ly 21% (UNESCO, 2012). The fastest increases in rates since the 1980s have occurred in Latin America and the Caribbean, where enrollment rates are now almost at 70% (Engle, Rao, & Petrovic, 2013).

Even within regions, there are big differences by country. A child in Bangladesh has very little chance of attending preschool, regardless of whether the child is a boy or a girl, rich or poor, or urban or rural; only about 18% go to preschool. On the other hand, 61% of 3- and 4-year-olds in Thailand go to preschool (UNESCO, 2012). It is important to emphasize that not all families in developing countries are poor: In almost every country, wealth is the dividing factor in terms of ECD access. Families with more wealth can send their children to ECD programs, whereas some moderate-income families, and most poor families like Irwan's family, often cannot. The ob-stacles include more than just the costs of registration and tuition, which are hard to pay in many cases, but also school supplies, uniforms (expected in most developing countries), lost work time, and transportation.

As in the United States, in developing countries older children are more likely to be enrolled in preprimary services than younger children. Babies and toddlers and their parents are very unlikely to receive any organized early learning experience other than health services, and children ages 5 and 6 are the most likely to participate. This, of course, raises questions about adequate support for the very youngest children and their families during a critically important period of development, as emphasized in Chapters 2 and 5.

Program Quality

Even with experience in preschool, success in school is not assured; it depends on both the quality of the preschool program the child attended and the quality of the primary school. In many developing countries, both are of low quality. Infant-toddler, preschool, and kindergarten teachers are usually the least-qualified teaching personnel, they are often unpaid volunteers, and they may have received little to no training. The early grades of primary (elementary) schools are often not much better. They frequently are overcrowded, lack basic supplies and teaching materials, sometimes lack electricity for lighting and temperature control, and apply developmentally inappropriate teaching practices that rely on passive listening and rote memorization. Poor program and classroom quality is reflected in children's lack of progress. For example, a 2010 study showed that more than 90% of 2nd-graders in Mali, West Africa, could not read a single word either in French or the local language; many other countries showed similar results (Gove & Cvelich, 2010). As a result of early failure experiences, lack of parent awareness, and lack of appropriate training, mentoring, and compensation for teachers, the highest dropout rates in developing countries occur in 1st and 2nd grade (O'Gara, 2013).

One program quality indicator that is relatively easy to measure is the ratio of adults to children. In developing countries, many programs have high numbers of children compared to numbers of caregiving adults. In the United States, many states require 1 adult for every 10 4-year-olds or every 15 5-year-olds. In South Africa, one can find centers with 1 adult and 60 children (Manyike, 2012). Dealing with those numbers, teachers understandably find it difficult or impossible to create quiet spaces, promote active learning, find teachable moments, or focus children's attention.

Teacher Quality

Teacher qualifications are not the whole story of quality, but, like child-staff ratios, they are another easy-to-track program indicator. Using those data, research suggests that many educators in developing countries lack specific knowledge and skills related to young children. Only 12% of early childhood teachers in rural China, for example, have any special training related to teaching in early childhood (UNESCO, 2012).

There are professional development success stories, though. For example, the Madrasa Resource Centre is a low-cost, innovative program to train staff in Kenya, Uganda, and Zanzibar. Teachers are required to have 8 years of schooling, 1 year of teacher training, and 6 months of early childhood development training, in which they learn to use locally available, low-cost materials to teach children. After graduation, the Centre continues to provide teachers with support. The children who get these teachers do better than other children in their verbal, nonverbal, cognitive, and other school readiness skills.

The Importance of Good Public Policies in Developing Countries

Public policy is a term that can be difficult to understand in practical terms. What does government policy have to do with the current or future early childhood professional who is concerned about what happens to children like Irwan, living in developing countries? Depending on legislative language, funding to carry out policies, and enforcement, public policies can take different forms; public policy can mean laws that may not be broken without a penalty, incentives that reward ideal behavior, or guideposts that point the way to the desired goals. Regardless, these policies indicate an issue's level of importance and set the lead for people to follow. For early childhood, public policies in developing countries (as well as in the United States) are likely to provide answers to basic questions such as how many families can find a preschool and afford to enroll their children, how many educators will be hired, and how many years of education or days of training someone needs to qualify to teach.

For example, if the Indonesian government decided to make kindergarten free so that all 4- to 6-year-old children including Irwan could enroll, it would have to change its policies: It would need to empower districts to create the physical buildings to hold the classes; train and pay thousands of new teachers; hire people to decide the standards for program safety and quality; and monitor programs to make sure they achieve the standards.

Countries have different mixes of national, state, and local control over education in general and early childhood specifically. However the country divvies up responsibilities, establishing comprehensive ECD policies is a challenge because multiple government departments must be involved, including departments that oversee education, health and nutrition, child protection, social affairs, women's empowerment, religious affairs, and so forth. In addition, involving interested international development agencies, nonprofit organizations, and private sector companies is often helpful or necessary in developing countries. Because so many stakeholders are involved, policy and planning can become complicated. In some cases, if ECD is everyone's "baby," it becomes no one's responsibility in the end.

Nonetheless, more and more developing countries are trying to do better by their youngest citizens, recognizing both the human and moral responsibility to do so, and the economic and human-capital benefits of investing in early childhood. Coordination can be challenging, but governments now generally agree that it is worth it.

That was not always the case.

HISTORIC EARLY CHILDHOOD DEVELOPMENT MOVEMENTS AND MEASURES

1990 was a landmark year for young children around the world. Delegates from 155 countries met together in Thailand, under the organization of the United Nations

---

PROFESSIONAL PROFILE

Amer Hasan, Education Economist, The World Bank, Jakarta, Indonesia

Based in Jakarta, Amer works on early childhood development in Indonesia and is the World Bank's focal person on early childhood development for the East Asia and Pacific region. In Indonesia, the focus of his work is on evaluating whether and how early childhood services have improved poor Indonesian children's readiness for school. A recent week started with a flight to Kunming, China, where he participated in a workshop with the Yunnan Ministry of Education. The workshop was designed to be a brainstorming session around suitable approaches to increasing access to early childhood services in rural areas of Yunnan. Amer shared Indonesia's experiences with increasing access in rural areas and highlighted the country's achievements and challenges with early childhood issues over the past decade. Back in Jakarta, Amer and his colleagues met with the government department in charge of early childhood teacher training to design an evaluation of their training program. Later that week, he participated in a field visit in North Jakarta and observed a training session for a series of parenting education modules that are being tested before they are introduced as part of one of the country's flagship antipoverty programs.

Amer Hasan has a Ph.D. in public policy with a focus on program evaluation. He has worked on various teams while at the World Bank ranging from community-driven development to poverty and inequality to education and human development. He has lived and worked in South Asia, Latin America, and the Caribbean as well as East Asia and the Pacific.

---

and the World Bank, to sign a declaration saying that the global community would commit to providing high-quality basic education, including early education, for all children. The declaration was called Education for All (EFA). Yet 2 decades later, the majority of children in developing countries were still not participating in any type of preprimary program (UNESCO, 2012). The EFA emphasis on early education shifted countries' focus a bit, but not enough, as most of the resources have gone toward ensuring that children attend primary school.

The Millennium Development Goals (MDGs) were another critical global movement that could have shifted countries' ECD policies but ultimately did not. In 2000, 191 countries agreed to seven major goals, such as eradicating extreme poverty and ensuring that all children go to primary school, to be achieved by 2015. Increased access to preprimary programs, however, was not made a goal, in spite of its proven associations with reduced poverty and increased productivity. Early childhood experts and advocates are working to get ECD on the list for the next major global framework of common goals.

Because government policies are so important in creating more effective services, the World Bank is developing a tool called the Systems Approach for Better Education Results (SABER-ECD), which will be used to collect information on countries' ECD policies (World Bank, 2013)–their legal frameworks, funding, coordination, scope of implementation, and monitoring. The results will help each participating country see the gaps in their systems and learn from other countries in similar situations.

CONCLUDING THOUGHTS:
SUSTAINABLE EARLY CHILDHOOD PROGRAMS REQUIRE
COMMUNITY OWNERSHIP AND NATIONAL LEADERSHIP

For the global community of early childhood professionals, the goal is to help as many children as possible, especially the most vulnerable, get off to a great start in life. It is the job of governments to put in place good public policies that protect children's rights to life, health, and education, and back up those policies with the funding to make them a reality. With good policies in place, teachers and other direct service providers can do their jobs better.

In reality, many developing countries (like many highly industrialized countries) do not yet have good policies in place, nor the funds to carry out ideas or regulations. ECD teachers nevertheless carry on, with commitment, inspiration, and love for the children they serve. Many of them work for free if there is no money to pay them, which indicates just how high their commitment levels are.

Whether or not a country has strong national early childhood policies and financing, the most successful systems are those that empower parents, providers, and other leaders in the local neighborhood or community to create their own systems. When programs are organic—that is, thought of, wanted, and managed by a neighborhood or community—they tend to use local resources, both in terms of physical materials and peoples' wisdom and talent.

It does not make sense to tell infant caregivers in a remote village to buy baby rattles if they have no money. But if they know why the concept of babies connecting movement to noise is important, they can put shells in plastic water bottles to do the same job. Similarly, it does not help children to build safe, beautiful child care centers if families move all the time. In Mongolia, where children were not going to kindergarten because they live in nomadic families, teachers created mobile *ger* kindergartens (a *ger* is a traditional, easily movable felt structure that provides shelter) so that children could attend kindergarten. Enrollment rates doubled.

When people create programs using their own customs, languages, and materials, the programs are culturally and locally relevant.

However, programs tend to be most successful and sustainable when they also have financial and technical support. For example, the *ger* kindergarten program only came about because the World Bank provided support to the Mongolian government and local teachers. Or consider the Philippines, where the government has done an impressive job of increasing teachers' opportunities to interact with young children, even infants, through its Pantawid Pamilyang Pilipino Program. The program provides cash grants to extremely poor households if they take their infants or young children to early education programs.

If early childhood education and development become a significant part of the post-2015 global agenda, governments, researchers, and educators will pay much greater attention to their smallest citizens. People will be watching to see what happens to children like Irwan. The hope is not that they merely *survive* beyond age 5. The hope is that they *thrive*, arriving at the schoolhouse door with healthy bodies, a healthy sense of curiosity and wonder, and assurance that they are loved, they are smart, and they are important.

REFLECTION, DIALOGUE, AND ACTION

1. What aspects of early childhood systems in developing countries seem similar to or different from systems in the United States? What advantages might poor children in the United States have as compared to poor children in a developing country?

2. If you were in charge of the world, what are the top three risk factors or challenges facing babies and children in the developing world that you would like to see eliminated and why? Name one step you could take to make a difference for one child (or more) in a developing country—perhaps writing an email to member of Congress to support aid, using the gift catalogue of an organization like Save the Children or UNICEF, or making a small donation to a family in need (always through a reputable organization, never to an individual). Challenge yourself to carry out that step within a week.

3. Imagine a developing country you might want to visit someday (or perhaps have lived in or visited) and use one of the links in the Information to Explore and Share box to find out basic statistics about that country's ECD system: How many children are enrolled in ECD? What natural or human-made disasters affect families there? Discuss or write a paragraph describing the dreams a mother or father might have for their young child.

INFORMATION TO EXPLORE AND SHARE

Save the Children

Save the Children is an independent nonprofit organization that works to help children in developing countries with everything from survival to literacy to child protection. It especially focuses on countries facing disasters or civil conflict, helping to provide essential services to families in need. www.savethechildren.org

United Nations Children's Fund

UNICEF was created in 1946 to help provide food, clothing, and shelter for children suffering after World War II. It is a leading authority on children's rights, child survival, nutrition, children affected by HIV/AIDS, gender equality, and more. It provides global data, procures and distributes supplies in times of crisis, and advocates to government leaders. www.unicef.org

The United Nations Educational, Scientific and Cultural Organization

UNESCO works to improve peace and security in the world through programs in education, the sciences, culture, and communications. It focuses on eradicating poverty, decreasing violence, and increasing intercultural dialogue. It leads the Education for All movement. en.unesco.org

The World Bank

The World Bank was established in the 1940s as a global bank to lend money to low- and middle-income countries to reduce poverty and strengthen the services and capacities in each member country, of which there are now 188. Early childhood experts at the World Bank assess countries' needs, including through the new SABER instrument, collaborate with governments to create ECD programs, collect and analyze data, and provide advice to governments to help create stronger ECD systems. www.worldbank.org

CHAPTER 11

The Early Years Matter
for Our Future

© Goldenkb

Our central assertion in this book has is that what happens in the early years–from birth through age 8–matters a great deal. Each chapter has framed that assertion in light of different groups of young children and families, but the similarities across children and across families are more striking than the variations. The same could be said for early childhood professionals; they have different roles and backgrounds but similar missions and core values–more similarities than differences.

Common themes from the chapters of this book provide a foundation for a range of early childhood activities, from designing programs to educating teachers to improving public policies.

In discussing these themes, we keep several questions in mind. What kinds of professional practices are key to making a difference for children and their families in the early childhood years? What kinds of government policies are needed to ensure that high-quality care and education services are available to all the families who need or want them? What might the future look like if these practices and policies were consistently, universally in place? What are the long-term benefits for children as they grow up, their families, the broader education system, and society as a whole?

Throughout the book, we hope readers have kept in mind their own roles in the field, what steps are needed to achieve their professional goals, and how they can contribute to this vision of early childhood. Joining the early childhood profession allows people to make a deep and defining difference in a child's life, and in a job that is likely to be incredibly creative and dynamic, rich with interaction, and intellectually challenging.

YOUNG CHILDREN: SO DIFFERENT YET SO MUCH THE SAME

Each chapter in *The Early Years Matter* has focused on a distinct group of young children and families. They have ranged from infants to children in the early years of elementary school, they live in different communities and speak different home languages, have differing kinds of abilities and disabilities, and have different kinds of resources and challenges at home. Yet despite all these differences, the similarities are even more striking. Three common characteristics come to mind:

1. All children have enormous potential, regardless of the challenges they may face. They are at a time in their lives when development is rapid and extremely open to influence from children's caregivers and environments. Their interest in the world around them is almost limitless. Early childhood programs are places to foster learning, health, and relationships at a critical time in brain development, building a strong platform on which to add new information and future skills. The pace of an individual's change—perhaps slower for Melanie and quicker for Bree—is less important than the fact that each child *is* learning and making gains.

2. All children have families that want the best for their children. They want their children to learn, grow, and thrive, often in ways that they themselves did not. Many parents who are neglectful, managing stress poorly, lacking in parenting skills, or even abusive are mimicking what was done to them as children, acting out of a mistaken belief that they are helping their children learn to behave better. They may also live with extreme stress or mental health problems. Early childhood professionals have the advantage of frequent observation and interaction opportunities with families, opportunities to build relationships, give information, make referrals, or encourage parents to do more of what they already do well.

3. All children's potential, and parents' ambitions for their children, have a better chance of being realized when early childhood programs and teachers respond to their needs. These needs can be for reliable, affordable child care; a friendly home visitor to help adjust to parenthood; early intervention services for children with disabilities; public schools that use children's earlier learning as a stepping-stone to further engagement and mastery; programs that support a family's home language and culture while helping children learn English; or settings that go beyond education to offer comprehensive services like health promotion or parenting education.

In short, despite their differences, *all* children have potential, potential that can be nurtured and enriched by high-quality early childhood services for children and their families.

EARLY CHILDHOOD PROFESSIONALS: MANY ROLES YET A COMMON MISSION

The professionals described in this book, both the fictional and the real ones, are also different from one another in many ways—in their country of origin, education levels, career pathways, job experiences, and daily functions. For the sake of convenience, we have often called them all *teachers,* although that term does not capture the variety of work they do.

Some are teachers in group programs for children—which could mean working with newborns like Teresa or 1st graders like Carlos and Melanie; with typically developing children like Edvardo, or children with challenging behaviors like Mikey; with middle-class children like Bree or children living in stress or poverty like Anna. Others are program directors or school principals, researchers, mental health practitioners, teacher educators, parent educators, government or nonprofit staff, economists, and advocates who lobby for good early childhood-related policies. As each chapter's Professional Profiles have shown, the academic backgrounds of early childhood professionals are equally varied; child development, early childhood education, psychology, special education, social work, economics, family studies, health services, demography, and women's studies are all in the mix.

Despite these diverse roles and backgrounds, because of the nature of their work, all good early childhood professionals are committed to making a difference in the lives of young children and their families. They develop close connections with others, including with the children themselves, family members, colleagues at work, and colleagues in related fields. They apply their knowledge in dynamic, fluid environments that involve many people and audiences, combining research and their own hands-on expertise, always open to learning more as they go. As seen in the Professional Profiles, early childhood professionals are multitaskers who manage many challenges simultaneously, both within and beyond their immediate work environment. On top of all of this, they must stay aware of and attempt to influence policies at national, state, and local levels that may affect both their work with children and their own compensation and working conditions.

PUTTING IT ALL TOGETHER: PRIORITIES IN PROFESSIONAL PRACTICE

Because of early childhood professionals' diverse roles and responsibilities, people may have different opinions about the details of curricula, teaching methods, and key outcomes for children. Despite these differences, most researchers, educators, and families do have some core agreements about what works for young children. These agreements have produced a good deal of consistency about the characteristics of high-quality early childhood programs regardless of ages, settings, and services.

Among these areas of consensus, early childhood professionals stress that:

- Collaboration with families is critical;
- Instruction for each child should be individualized;
- Inclusive environments are good for everyone;
- The focus must be on both intervention and prevention of problems;
- All aspects of children's development need careful, integrated attention; and
- Professionals need ongoing support for their own learning and career development.

These priorities, reflected across all of the preceding chapters, are relevant for professionals who work with or on behalf of children at every age and grade level.

The priorities are also consistent with major research syntheses and recommendations from (a) research bodies such as the National Academy of Sciences/National Research Council; (b) position statements of leading early childhood organizations such as the National Association for the Education of Young Children and the Division for Early Childhood of the Council for Exceptional Children; (c) research syntheses such as *From Neurons to Neighborhoods: The Science of Early Childhood Development* (National Research Council and Institute of Medicine, 2000) and the *Handbook of Early Childhood Development Research and Its Impact on Global Policy* (Britto, Engle, & Super, 2013); and (d) research-to-policy organizations like the Foundation for Child Development, the National Institute for Early Education Research, the National Center for Children in Poverty, the Center for Law and Social Policy, the Children's Defense Fund, and Child Trends. In short, the research allows us to say with conviction that access to high-quality early childhood services matters for every child from every background and family environment. The more vulnerable the child, the more it matters.

RECURRING THEMES IN GOOD PRACTICE

Expanding on these priorities, four critical themes of quality professional practices recur across these chapters. These are not the only elements of high-quality practices, but they provide early childhood professionals with a foundation for excellence.

1. Using Evidence

Qualities of warmth, empathy, creativity, and organizational skills are apparent in many early childhood teachers. These qualities are necessary for good practice, but they are not sufficient. In addition to intuition and natural skills, teachers and administrators need training and education so they can implement evidence-based practices and make good decisions. The best teachers use practices based on research *and* professionals' and families' experiences and wisdom (Buysse & Wesley, 2006).

For examples of relying on research to inform practice, we can turn to the stories that introduced each chapter. The research is clear that early intervention for children with disabilities is extremely important in expanding potentials, and the earlier this intervention happens—as in Melanie's life—the better. Similarly, the research is clear that dual-language learners should continue to build a strong foundation in the home language while learning English; teachers should encourage this approach for children like Edvardo. Research also indicates that children need strong early foundations in literacy and math skills, but always taught in relevant, active, engaging ways; Ms. James's personal knowledge of Carlos's unique interests and needs (he likes all things robot-related, he needs extra encouragement in gym class) provides valuable guidance for shaping his instructional goals and project activities.

Using evidence-based practices requires keeping up with new research and new thinking about key issues in the field. As NAEYC (2009) emphasizes in its professional preparation standards, an essential part of being a professional is being a continuous learner. Countless resources are available for professional development—the internet, conferences, professional books and journals, webinars and online courses, workshops, and colleagues.

The challenge in this era of information overload is knowing what sources to trust. Well-known research-oriented websites geared toward early childhood educators are a good starting point, such as the University of Virginia's Center for Advanced Study of Teaching and Learning (curry.virginia.edu/research/centers/castl); NAEYC (www.naeyc.org), which has research summaries on selected topics and evidence-based position statements; or Child Care and Early Education Research Connections (www.researchconnections.org), which helps users search for specific topics, authors, and state-level research evidence. Each chapter has cited other credible web-based resources to help professionals keep abreast of new knowledge. Just as we encourage young children's curiosity and critical thinking, we should nurture our own so that we remain motivated, connected, and current.

2. Responding to Each Child's Strengths and Needs

Although children have certain characteristics in common, professionals must also respond to children's many individual characteristics. Some of these characteristics are developmental. Three-year-old Anna has different needs than 6-year-old Carlos—and successful programs take these into account, celebrate them, and use them to promote children's progress. Culture and language, too, shape the identities of Edvardo, Irwan, Bree, Trevor, and Tanya's son Osborne—in fact, language and culture are central to every child's identity. Beyond culture and language, children have other differences, whether in temperament (Mikey is feisty, Irwan is shy), disability status (Melanie has Down syndrome, Bree is typically developing), or simply personal preferences (Anna likes burritos, Carlos likes pizza). Individual differences do not define a child, but they are part of the child and should affect decisions about how to help that child thrive. Competent early childhood professionals respect differences and build on children's strengths.

One way to do so is through implementing what have been called tiered interventions (Shapiro, n.d.). A number of chapters, including the chapters on children with disabilities and challenging behavior, have described different versions of these strategies, which are sometimes called Response to Intervention (RTI) (Buysse & Peisner-Feinberg, 2013; Fox, Carta, Dunlap, Strain, & Hemmeter, 2010). Underpinning all of these interventions is the idea that teachers need first to assess each child's current level of development, behavior, or skill, and then use that information to make good decisions about early childhood teaching and other interventions. As the discussions of the Teaching Pyramid and Positive Behavior Support in Chapter 8 illustrate, some strategies are likely to help all children (a focus on preventing problems); some strategies are useful for children at risk for or already showing problems (intermediate-level interventions); and some approaches are highly individualized, targeting one child or a small number of children who need specialized interventions to make progress (higher-intensity interventions). Professionals use their observations and insights to determine how high up the pyramid they should go with each child.

3. Partnering with Families

Most of the preceding chapters have illustrated how important it is for early childhood professionals to create supportive relationships with children's families. Some families struggle to figure out child care and education arrangements (Trevor, Teresa, Bree, Anna, and Irwan), seek answers to difficulties with their child's behavior and development (Mikey, Melanie, and Edvardo), need friendship and support (Anna and Charlotte), and look for services beyond education alone (Carlos, Anna, and Melanie). Our research examples have shown the many ways in which high-quality early childhood services build families' competence and confidence. The terms vary—"family-centered care," "family-focused programs" or "holistic ECD"—but the theme is the same: Families are the most important influence on children's development. Both philosophically and practically, partnering with families in planning and implementing early childhood services makes sense.

4. Collaborating with Other Professionals

A fourth theme emerging from these chapters is the importance of professional teamwork and collaboration. The quality of children's educational experiences depends greatly on how well teachers collaborate and integrate activities within the broader school community. Going beyond the classroom, often children's educational needs cannot be met unless other aspects of their well-being are addressed, such as Anna's nutritional needs, Edvardo's dental care, or Charlotte's safety in her early years. Professionals collaborate with one another to address children's holistic development, including cognitive and social-emotional development, physical health and nutrition, and protection from harm.

For children with disabilities, the IFSP/IEP process depends on the involvement of professionals with different kinds of expertise, not just to meet legal requirements but also to ensure attention to all aspects of development. In Melanie's case, at various times she needed an occupational therapist to help with self-help skills and physical competence, a speech and language specialist, an in-class aide, and other specialists to support her development and learning. In Mikey's case, he, his teachers, and his parents could have benefited from the support of a skilled mental health consultant as a member of the team.

In addition to those "horizontal" collaborations, "vertical" collaborations across the early childhood years also contribute to the quality of experiences for children across the early years from birth to age 8. A vertical collaboration is one that links those working with younger children with those working with older children. One example is the collaboration between early intervention professionals helping children from birth to age 3 and professionals serving children with disabilities as they move into preschool. Another example is the need for communication and collaboration between pre-K teachers and those in later grades. As described in Chapter 4, advocates of a continuous pre-K-to-3rd-grade approach have urged better coordination and alignment from the time children begin preschool through the primary grades, consistent with the birth-to-age-8 scope of early childhood education. Teamwork makes children's transitions from one setting to another easier, and the progression of their learning is likely to be smoother and more successful.

POLICIES TO SUPPORT A STRONG EARLY CHILDHOOD SYSTEM

In one way or another, each chapter has pointed out that early childhood education matters—that it has significant benefits for children and families when the quality is good. Access to high-quality programs and classrooms takes more than the best efforts of individual teachers or specific programs. It takes good public policies. In earlier chapters we have touched on these issues, but this chapter's focus on the future of early care and education requires additional attention to current and future policy priorities. Here are four examples emerging across various chapters of suggested policy improvements.

1. Policies to Reduce Families' Child Care Costs

The repeated refrain of *The Early Years Matter,* echoed by parents, researchers, and advocates, is that high-quality early childhood programs before children enter kindergarten are beyond the financial means of most American families today. Early childhood programs are not a luxury, they are an essential need, much like bread and milk. Parents of children like Bree and Edvardo need child care in order to keep their jobs, and their children need quality early childhood programs to develop well. Although costs vary, they are uniformly high, equaling or exceeding the costs for public college tuition in 19 states. Families have time to plan and save to meet college tuition costs, but they do not have time to save up for child care. For families with two children in preschool, the costs are more than median rent in every state in the nation (Child Care Aware, 2013b). One of Teresa's and Trevor's parents may end up dropping out of the workforce if child care costs more than the parent earns, a common dilemma for parents who have more than one young child.

In a number of chapters we describe early childhood services that the government provides at little or no cost to families, such as Head Start, Early Head Start, and some state-funded pre-K programs. But often only those families under an official poverty line qualify for these services. The millions of families who are financially pressed but not technically "in poverty" are left out. They cannot afford the programs and yet they cannot afford not to work. (Their children are also among those who would most benefit from high-quality early care and education programs, so in a different sense, their children also cannot afford not to go.)

If limited access to high-quality, affordable early childhood services is not good for children, families, employers, and the economy, what can be done to increase that access? Administrators may be tempted to keep costs down for families by hiring fewer professionals, offering fewer training opportunities, paying teachers less, not offering benefits packages, or offering children fewer creative, enriching activities–but those cuts also keep program quality down.

A better option is to use public funds to help families pay for early childhood programs, rather than putting the entire cost burden on families. As a rule, most families in most developed countries have to make some contribution to paying for early care and education before children begin formal schooling. However, unlike the United States, that contribution rarely constitutes the full cost in other developed countries. Families pay only a small share of the cost in Finland and Sweden (10%), Denmark and Norway (21%), France (14–38%), and most other developed countries (Bennett, 2008). In those countries, the government pays the remainder of the costs, usually paying more for low-income families. Helping more families be able to afford early care and education experiences, as some policymakers in the United States are now considering, would contribute critically to families' well-being, children's success, and the economy's strength.

2. Policies to Support Program Quality Improvement

Yet not just *any* early care and education experience will do: Good child outcomes are invariably linked to a *high-quality* experience. The quality of programs both before and during elementary school make all the difference.

Preschool Quality. As documented in earlier chapters, the typical quality of early childhood programs in the United States is average to low. Children in 91% of child care settings receive little positive caregiving, despite overwhelming evidence that such caregiving is a critical factor in program quality and in children's development (NICHD ECCRN, 2006). Child Care Aware (2013b; formerly known as NACCRRA) rated the program requirements and oversight of child care centers across the country; the average score was 61 points out of 100, equivalent to a D on a report card.

Not surprisingly given the poor quality of programs, a year in a typical American preschool–assuming that "typical" includes the many low-quality programs–makes little difference in children's long-term achievement. Yet in other well-off countries such as Belgium, France, Singapore, and Israel, children who have a year of preschool make major gains on reading and other measures, according to a comparison study by the Organisation for Economic Cooperation and Development (OECD, 2011). These countries tend to do certain things well at the preschool level: They offer early childhood education to all or most children, do so over a long period of time, have small child-to-teacher ratios, and invest more per child. In other words, they provide consistent access to high-quality programs, with a payoff in later student achievement.

In the United States, there are very big disparities in families' ability to enroll their children in high-quality infant/toddler and preschool programs. Affluent families can much more easily find and afford high-quality programs than low- and moderate-income families. Families on the economic margins, such as Anna's and Osborne's families, often enroll children in the lowest-quality programs because these are the most affordable. Although many low-income families may qualify for free Head Start services, often though not always high quality, there are not enough spaces available. And, as we have noted repeatedly, this mismatch is especially troubling because children from poorer families are likely to gain the most from attending high-quality programs.

Some state education departments and legislators have taken steps to focus on quality, for example, by improving regulations for early childhood services (e.g., better ratios of staff to children, higher education qualifications for teachers). Many states also now have early learning guidelines to describe what children at various ages should know and be able to do. Thirty-seven states use a Quality Rating and Improvement System (QRIS; see Chapter 3), sometimes rating programs' investments in facilities, learning materials, and teacher qualifications as part of quality improvement efforts. And although Head Start evaluation data have been disappointing in some ways, officials are using the results to identify areas for improvement, and long-term gains from Head Start participation are still evident (see Chapter 5). These steps are promising, but we are still a long way from where we need to be.

K–3 Classroom Quality. As previously noted, the quality of K–3 classrooms depends largely on the overall income levels within the county or school district because governments tie school revenue to local property-tax income rather than to overall state or national income. It leads to a classic case of the rich get richer (affluent children have good education experiences) and the poor get poorer (low- and moderate-income families have weaker educational experiences because their schools receive less money). In comparison with other developed countries, the United States appears to be the only one that funds elementary schools primarily based on local wealth (Biddle & Berliner, 2002).

Money is not the only determinant of program quality, but it is consistently associated with child outcomes and achievement levels (cf. Biddle & Berliner, 2002). International studies show that children in America's highly funded schools compete at the highest levels of achievement, equal to children from Hong Kong and Japan. In contrast, children in poorly funded American schools perform at similar levels to children in the lowest-performing countries in the world, such as Turkey and Iran (Mullis et al., 2001). The contrasts in achievement levels reflect the huge disparities in American classroom environments.

How does funding affect classroom quality and child outcomes? Well-funded schools can attract the best teachers, those with high education, experience, and competency levels, through good salaries and support systems; the best teachers usually have the most successful students (Darling-Hammond & Post, 2000). In the early grades, small class size is also especially important in producing better outcomes (especially for low-income children), and this again is usually tied to the level of school funding (cf., Biddle & Berliner, 2002). The bottom line is that, while not a panacea, policies that equalize school funding levels—what Baker, Sciarra, and Farrie (2010) call *funding fairness*—would have a substantial effect on reducing achievement disparities and enhancing children's well-being.

3. Policies to Encourage and Fund Professional Development Systems and Supports

As noted above and throughout the book, the best indicator of high-quality early care and education is the quality of teachers: When teachers are good, programs are good. Many chapters have featured exemplary teachers and other professionals who make a difference for children every day. Yet at the moment, the overall level of teacher quality is not good enough. Through no fault of their own, many teachers are unable to access degree programs; the content and quality of college courses is not always adequate; teachers do not receive enough ongoing supervision, mentoring, and continuous learning opportunities; and early childhood teachers in community child care settings are the lowest-paid and most poorly compensated, earning about half of teachers working in public elementary schools.

Policies need to go further than they have in several ways: in outlining clear, evidence-based teacher education and professional development requirements; in providing subsidies for teachers to increase their education; in providing incentives and benefits for participating in higher levels of professional development; and in ensuring worthy compensation. Most early childhood teachers are deeply committed to providing the best for children and are eager to improve their own knowledge and skills, yet little is available to help them. Current pre- and in-service professional development for early childhood teachers is scattered, piecemeal, and unsystematic, part of what has been called the "non-system" of early care and education in the United States (Hyson & Vick Whittaker, 2012). Policies and accompanying funds to address these issues could make a crucial difference.

4. Policies to Support Program Innovation, Evaluation, Scale-Up, and Effective Implementation

Across many chapters, we introduced readers to promising programs, new teaching strategies, and innovative services that seem likely to promote better experiences and outcomes for children and families. Home visiting is one example. Other examples include FirstSchool (combining the best practices of early childhood, elementary, and special education with a focus on African-American and Latino students); the PreK–3rd initiative (supporting greater alignment and coordination across these critical early childhood years); mental health consultation (giving programs the support they need to prevent expulsion and promote the development of children with challenging behavior); and Staffed Family Child Care Networks (connecting isolated home-based child care providers).

The problem is that these relatively small initiatives often stay small. There are several reasons for this. Promising effects in small projects are not always evaluated using strong outcome measures and rigorous research methods. Even if preliminary evaluations show promise, advocates can have a hard time gaining support for larger-scale implementation, called "going to scale." Plans for scaling up small but successful programs are often not well developed, and the essentials of what made the smaller effort a success may not translate well when widely implemented.

The first step is evaluation so we know if an approach truly works well. Fortunately, we see some progress in emphasizing monitoring and evaluation efforts. In Head Start, pre-K, early childhood special education programs, professional development institutes, and other parts of the early childhood field, we begin to see more attention to evaluation and scaling up good programs. Grants offered by the government to researchers and program developers frequently require and fund a strong evaluation component, and the same is true of projects supported in developing countries by the World Bank, the United States Agency for International Development, and other institutions.

And then there is the question of implementation. Just because the research is clear from evaluation studies does not mean that the research is used effectively. Implementing research findings in the real, very complex world of early childhood education is not easy. Implementation depends on planners' awareness of the obstacles and opportunities involved in conducting their research, and how well the planners have engaged policymakers, educators, and families in understanding and applying the findings. Implementation also depends on awareness of how ready the country, state, agency, program, or school is to adopt new early childhood ideas. The relatively new field of implementation science (Halle, Metz, & Martinez-Beck, 2013) is beginning to have an impact on early childhood research, policies, and practices. Effective implementation of evidence-based practices that reflect the communities' needs and values will help ensure real and lasting change for young children like Carlos, Tanya, and Irwan.

In sum, small but promising approaches should be evaluated to see if they lead to improved well-being for the children for whom the interventions are intended. If they do, government agencies, school districts, non-profits, private organizations, or all of the above should put resources toward implementing these approaches on a larger scale. Instead of being content with limited success, let's aim for the best for all children.

WHY AIM FOR THE BEST?
A BETTER FUTURE FOR CHILDREN, FAMILIES, SCHOOLS, AND SOCIETY

At their core, the early years are about individual children who like to build towers from blocks, draw fairy princesses, eat sticky rice, look at books about hummingbirds, tie double knots on their shoes, or catch fireflies in glass jars. But individual children are just the starting point; early childhood services transcend the individuals to impact the wider community. Just like the child building with blocks, good early childhood programs, practices, and policies set the foundation, providing a platform from which to construct universal benefits for families, the education system, and society.

The Best for Children

Young children grow up to be older children, adolescents, and adults. As demonstrated in every chapter, experiences in high-quality early care and education are an investment in children's futures. Children of all backgrounds benefit, showing improved language, literacy, and mathematics skills equal to from one-third of a year to a full year's worth of additional learning above and beyond what would have occurred without an excellent preschool experience. Low-income children gain the most. Those who participate in high-quality, comprehensive early education programs are more likely than non-participating peers to achieve better in school, not need special education, not smoke, not get arrested, graduate from high school on time, and go to college; by age 40, they are more likely to own a home and a savings account, and earn more than $25,000 a year (Grunewald, 2013).

Of course, a good early education is no guarantee of later success, especially if children go to poor-quality schools later on; nor can early childhood services redress all of society's problems, such as poverty or violence. But the potential to change children's lives is present and powerful.

The Best for Families

Although the stories of children in this book are composites, they are based on children in real families. Many parents are isolated, economically stressed, and full of anxiety about the future. Yet each family has strengths and brings unique gifts to a program or school community. Good early childhood professionals partner with parents to recognize and nurture families' strengths. Head Start is an example of a program that, from its beginning, has respected and engaged families, connecting them with needed resources and often shifting the long-term trajectory of families living in poverty. Similarly, teachers include parents of children with disabilities as an integral part of the teams that support children's development, empowering them in ways that last well beyond the early childhood years. For all populations, professionals intentionally reduce families' isolation by connecting them with one another; raise awareness by sharing child development information relevant to children's current status; and acknowledge and model positive ways of interacting with children. Affirming and enhancing parents' beliefs in their own competence (Browne, 2009) is a long-term gift from early childhood professionals to families.

The Best for Schools

American education, and education in most of the world, is the target of concern and criticism. It is clear that we are not yet doing the best for our children: More than 60% of U.S. 4th graders cannot read or do math at grade level, and over 800,000 youth are not enrolled in high school (Children's Defense Fund, 2013). Too many, especially in low-income communities, think of school as little more than a setting for failure.

In addition to benefiting individual children, high-quality early education pays dividends to schools. Good K–3 teachers help all children learn no matter what their starting point, but they do love having children come through the classroom door with a smile, knowing how to listen and follow new rules, ready to make friends and ask questions. Experience in a quality preschool is consistently associated with better school readiness and children's improved approaches to learning (Grunewald, 2013; Vandell et al., 2010). Moreover, the benefits are multiplied if there is strong consistency and coordination with programs in kindergarten and the primary grades.

The Best for Society

Teachers and parents may look at the individual child, but policymakers look at the system and costs. High-quality early education is not necessarily cheap. Is it worth it? Economists advise that investing in early education, starting as early as possible, is one of the best investments governments and the private sector can make.

Two leading economists with the Minneapolis Federal Reserve Bank have analyzed early education as an investment prospect. They have found a long-term return on the costs of high-quality care ranging from 7% to 20%, with more than half of the benefits going to the general public (Grunewald & Rolnick, 2010).

Nobel Prize–winning economist James Heckman also has been an advocate for early childhood education as a smart economic investment (Heckman & Masterov, 2007). Heckman's analyses show that gaps in key workforce skills such as motivation, persistence, and self-control emerge early and are difficult to change later. Heckman and many other economists advise deeper and broader investments in early education, including home visits, in order to improve America's productivity and competitiveness in the global marketplace.

Beyond the economic benefits, every society needs future generations of citizens who are competent, caring, responsible, and ready to make positive contributions to their communities. Good early childhood programs, and good early childhood teachers, foster those attributes.

CONCLUDING THOUGHTS:
YOU AND THE FUTURE OF EARLY CHILDHOOD EDUCATION

We hope readers have grown in their knowledge, vision, and commitment to the field of early care and education as a result of reflecting on the issues presented in *The Early Years Matter*. We hope you are energized and excited to see what you can do and how much children, families, and communities need you.

As previewed in the first chapter, throughout this book we have tried to illustrate the many reasons why services during these important years do indeed matter for children, families, schools, and society. We have also tried to increase readers' respect for children's and families' many strengths and unique characteristics. We hope that as readers have learned more about services provided to young children, they have also gained a more realistic sense of the challenges of implementing those services effectively. Keeping all of these issues in mind, we have aimed to inspire readers to broaden their vision of potential careers and deepen their commitment to children.

There could not be a more exciting time to be an early childhood professional. We hope that *The Early Years Matter* has shown you the enormous potential of early childhood programs and services to contribute to joyful, fulfilling lives for young children and their families. Most importantly, our hope is that this book inspires your own dedication or rededication to the youngest and most vulnerable members of our society. By being the best professional, parent, or concerned citizen that you can be, you will join millions of others to make the early years matter today and far into the future.

REFLECTION, DIALOGUE, AND ACTION

As you come to the end of *The Early Years Matter*, consider how to deepen and extend your learning by creating a personal action plan.

1. Is there one area of early care and education that you want to learn more about? If so, use references and resources from that chapter, as well as personal contacts, to broaden your knowledge.

2. Are you interested in having firsthand contact with early childhood programs and services? Through your workplace, college, or colleagues, arrange to get involved—observe in a program, volunteer, start a service learning project, or find an in-depth field experience.

3. Do you want to get more involved in the world of policy? Use this book's resources to learn more about what is going on in your state, in national groups, or in international organizations. Write, advocate, volunteer—take action.

4. Do you want to be an important person in the life of one child? Make a commitment to do so, as a family member, a caring teacher, or a volunteer. Are you enticed by new career opportunities? Job-shadow someone whose work interests you, arrange for an informational interview, sign up for a course either on campus or online, or apply to a specialized program.

INFORMATION TO EXPLORE AND SHARE

Center for Response to Intervention in Early Childhood

Based at the University of Minnesota, the federally funded CRIEC studies and disseminates information about the use of tiered interventions to reduce the number of children entering school with reading difficulties and other problems. www.cehd.umn.edu/ceed/projects/crtiec

Child Care Aware

Formerly the National Association of Child Care Resource and Referral Agencies, Child Care Aware shares information about access and quality for families and professional resources for child care providers. www.childcareaware.org

Early Childhood Workforce Systems Initiative

ECWSI helps states develop, enhance, and implement policies for an integrated early childhood professional development system for everyone who works with and on behalf of young children. www.naeyc.org/policy/ecwsi

National Implementation Research Network

NIRN provides extensive resources and links to information and practical tools on all aspects of implementation research, with the goal of improving outcomes across the spectrum of human services, including ECE. nirn.fpg.unc.edu

References

1,000 Days Partnership. (2013). Why 1,000 Days. Available at www.thousanddays.org/about/

Alanis, I. (2013). Where's your partner? Pairing bilingual learners in preschool and primary grade dual language classrooms. *Young Children, 68(1)*, 42–46.

American Educational Research Association. (2013). *Prevention of bullying in schools, colleges, and universities: Research report and recommendations.* Washington, DC: Author. Available at www.aera.net/Portals/38/docs/News%20Release/Prevention%20of%20Bullying%20in%20Schools,%20Colleges%20and%20Universities.pdf

Anderson, E. M. (2013). Preparing the next generation of early childhood teachers: The emerging role of interprofessional education and collaboration in teacher education. *Journal of Early Childhood Teacher Education, 34*(1), 23–35.

Art Therapy Centre. (2013). *Lefika La Phosido–The Art Therapy Centre.* Available at www.art therapycentre.co.za/

Ascend at the Aspen Institute. (2012). *Two generations, one future: Moving parents and children beyond poverty together.* Washington, DC: The Aspen Institute.

Association for Supervision and Curriculum Development (ASCD). (2012). *A whole-child approach to education and the Common Core State Standards initiative.* Alexandria, VA: Author. Available at www.ascd.org/ASCD/pdf/siteASCD/policy/CCSS-and-Whole-Child-one-pager.pdf

Astuto, J., & Allen, L. (2009). Home visitation and young children: An approach worth investing in? *SRCD Social Policy Report, 23*(4), 3–21.

Baker, B. D., Sciarra, D. G., & Farrie, D. (2010). *Is school funding fair? A national report card.* Newark, NJ: Education Law Center. Available at www.schoolfundingfairness.org/National _Report_Card.pdf

Ball, J. (2011). *Enhancing learning of children from diverse language backgrounds: Mother tongue-based bilingual or multilingual education in the early years.* Paris: UNESCO. Available at unesdoc.unesco.org/images/0021/002122/212270e.pdf

Barnett, W. S. (2013). Getting the facts right on pre-K and the President's pre-K proposal. New Brunswick, NJ: National Institute for Early Education Research. Available at www.nieer.org/sites/nieer/files/Getting%20the%20Facts%20Right%20on%20Pre-K.pdf

Barnett, W. S., Carolan, M., Fitzgerald, J., & Squires, J. (2012). *The state of preschool 2012: State preschool yearbook executive summary.* New Brunswick, NJ: National Institute for Early Education Research.

Barnett, W. S., Hustedt, J. T., Robin, K. B., & Schulman, K. L. (2004). *The state of preschool: 2004 state preschool yearbook.* Washington, DC: National Education Association. Available at www.nieer.org/yearbook2004/pdf/yearbook.pdf

Belfield, C. R., Nores, M., Barnett, S., & Schweinhart, L. (2006). The High/Scope Perry Preschool Program: Cost benefit analysis using data from the age-40 follow up. *Journal of Human Resources, 61*, 162–190.

Belsky, J. (2002). Quantity counts: Amount of child care and children's socioeconomic development. *Journal of Developmental and Behavioral Pediatrics, 23*, 167–170.

Bennett, J. (2008). Early childhood services in the OECD countries: Review of the literature and current policy in the early childhood field. Innocenti Working Paper No. 2008-01. Florence, Italy: UNICEF Innocenti Research Centre.

Bernard Van Leer Foundation. (1995). *A guide to promoting resilience in children: Strengthening the human spirit.* The Hague, The Netherlands: Author.

Bialystok, E. (2008). Second-language acquisition and bilingualism at an early age and the impact on early cognitive development. In R. E. Tremblay, R. G. Barr, & R. DeV. Peters (Eds.), *Encyclopedia on early childhood development* (pp. 1–4). Montreal, Quebec: Centre of Excellence for Early Childhood Development. Available at www.child-encyclopedia.com/documents/BialystokANGxp_rev.pdf

Biddle, B. J., & Berliner, D. C. (2002). A research synthesis: Unequal school funding in the United States. *Educational Leadership, 59*(8).

Biggam, S., & Hyson, M. (2014). The Common Core State Standards and developmentally appropriate practice: Creating a relationship. In C. Copple, S. Bredekamp, & K. Charner (Eds.). *Developmentally appropriate practice: Focus on kindergartners* (pp. 95–112). Washington, DC: NAEYC.

Bodilly, S. J., & Beckett, M. K. (2005). *Making out-of-school time matter: Evidence for an action agenda.* Santa Monica, CA: Rand Corporation.

Borge, A.I.H., Rutter, M., Côté, S., & Tremblay, R. E. (2004). Early childcare and physical aggression: Differentiating social selection and social causation. *Journal of Child Psychology and Psychiatry, 45*(2), 367–376.

Branch, G. F., Hanushek, E. A., & Rivkin, S. G. (2013). School leaders matter: Measuring the impact of effective principals. *Education Next, 13*(1), 62–69.

Britto, P. R., Engle, P. L., & Super, C. M. (Eds.). (2013). *Handbook of early childhood development research and its impact on global policy.* New York: Oxford University Press.

Britz, E., & Batalova, J. (2013, January). Frequently requested statistics on immigrants and immigration in the United States. Migration Policy Institute. Available at www.migrationinformation.org/USfocus/display.cfm?ID=931#7

Bromer, J., Van Haitsma, M., Daley, K., et al. (2009). *Staffed support networks and quality in family child care: Findings from the Family Child Care Network Impact Study.* Chicago, IL: Erikson Institute, Herr Research Center for Children and Social Policy. Available at www.erikson.edu

Browne, H. C. (2009). *Almost like family: Family child care.* Washington, DC: Center for the Study of Social Policy. Available at www.strengtheningfamilies.net/images/uploads/images/(1.2_.2)_Family_Child_Care_Study_.pdf

Bruder, M. B., & Dunst, C. J. (2005). University faculty preparation of students in using natural environment practices with young children. *Psychological Reports, 96*, 239–242.

Burchinal, M., Hyson, M., & Zaslow, M. (2011). Competencies and credentials for early childhood educators: What do we know and what do we need to know? In E. Zigler, W. S. Gilliam, & W. S. Barnett (Eds.), *The Pre-K debates: Current controversies and issues* (pp. 73–77). Baltimore, MD: Brookes.

Buysse, V., & Peisner-Feinberg, E. (Eds.). (2013). *Handbook of Response to Intervention in early childhood.* Baltimore, IL: Brookes.

Buysse, V., & Wesley, P. W. (Eds.). (2006). *Evidence-based practice in the early childhood field.* Washington, DC: Zero to Three.

California Tomorrow. (2004). *Ready or not? A California Tomorrow think piece on school readiness and immigrant communities.* Oakland, CA: Author.

Camilli, G., Vargas, S., Ryan, S., & Barnett, W. S. (2010). Meta-analysis of the effects of early education interventions on cognitive and social development. *Teachers College Record, 112*, 579–620.

Campbell, F., Conti, G., Heckman, J. J., Moon, S. H., Pinto, R., & Pungello, E. (2014). Early childhood investments substantially boost adult health. *Science, 343*(6178), 1478–1485.

Capps, R., Fix, M., Ost, J., Reardon-Anderson, J., & Passel, J. S. (2005). *The health and well-being of young children of immigrants.* Washington, DC: Urban Institute.

Carolan, M. (2013, June 3). Highly qualified teachers: The workforce early education needs and deserves. Preschool Matters. Available at www.preschoolmatters.org/2013/06/03/highly-qualified-teachers-the-workforce-early-educations-needs-and-deserves/

Cawthorne, A., & Arons, J. (2010). *There's no place like home: Home visiting programs can support pregnant women and new parents.* Washington, DC: Center for American Progress.

Center for the Study of Social Policy (CSSP). (n.d.). Strengthening Families Research in Brief: The Adverse Childhood Experiences Study. Available at www.cssp.org/reform/strengthening-families/resources/body/1.3_.1_RB_-_ACE_Study_.pdf

Center for the Study of Social Policy (CSSP). (2007). *Strengthening families: A guide for early childhood programs.* Washington, DC: Author. Available at www.cssp.org/publications/neighborhood-investment/strengthening-families/top-five/strengthening-families-a-guidebook-for-early-childhood-programs.pdf

Centers for Disease Control and Prevention (CDC). (2012). Middle childhood: 6-8 years of age. Developmental milestones. Available at www.cdc.gov/ncbddd/childdevelopment/positiveparenting/middle.html

Centers for Disease Control and Prevention (CDC). (2013a). Developmental milestones. Available at www.cdc.gov/actearly.

Centers for Disease Control and Prevention (CDC). (2013b). Childhood obesity facts. Available at www.cdc.gov/healthyyouth/obesity/facts.htm

Centers for Disease Control and Prevention (CDC). (2013c). Facts about Down syndrome. Available at www.cdc.gov/ncbddd/birthdefects/downsyndrome.html

Center to Mobilize Early Childhood Knowledge (CONNECT). (2013). *Foundations of inclusion policy advisory: Rights for children, parents and teachers related to inclusion.* Chapel Hill, NC: The University of North Carolina, Frank Porter Graham Child Development Institute, Author. Available at www.community.fpg.unc.edu/

Chang, F., Early, D., & Winton, P. (2005). Early childhood teacher preparation in special education at 2- and 4-year institutions of higher education. *Journal of Early Intervention, 27,* 110–124.

Child Care Aware. (2013a). *Parents and the high cost of child care, 2013 report.* Arlington, VA: Author. Available at usa.childcareaware.org/sites/default/files/Cost%20of%20Care%202013%20110613.pdf

Child Care Aware. (2013b). *We can do better: Child Care Aware state child care center regulations and oversight.* Arlington, VA: Author. Available at www.naccrra.org/sites/default/files/default_site_pages/2013/wcdb_executive_summary_040813.pdf

Child Trends. (2010). *Child Trends data bank, early school readiness.* Washington, DC: Author. Available at www.childtrendsdatabank.org/?q=node/291.1

Child Trends. (2013). *Child Trends data bank, full day kindergarten.* Washington, DC: Author. Available at www.childtrends.org/?indicators=full-day-kindergarten

Child Welfare Information Gateway. (2012). *Mandatory reporters of child abuse and neglect.* Washington, DC: U.S. Department of Health and Human Services, Children's Bureau. Available at www.childwelfare.gov/systemwide/laws_policies/statutes/manda.pdf

Children's Defense Fund. (2012a, January). Children in the United States. Available at www.childrensdefense.org/child-research-data-publications/data/state-data-repository/cits/2012/2012-united-states-children-in-the-states.pdf

Children's Defense Fund. (2012b). *The facts about full day kindergarten.* Washington, DC: Author. Available at www.childrensdefense.org/child-research-data-publications/data/the-facts-about-full-day.pdf

Children's Defense Fund. (2013a, March). Research library: Each day in America. Available at www.childrensdefense.org/child-research-data-publications/each-day-in-america.html

Children's Defense Fund. (2013b, July). Children in the United States. Available at www.childrensdefense.org/child-research-data-publications/data/state-data-repository/cits/2013/2013-united-states-children-in-the-states.pdf

Coalition for Evidence-Based Policy. (2012). *Top tier initiative: Evidence summary for The Nurse-Family Partnership.* Washington, DC: Author. Available at www.evidencebasedprograms.org/1366-2/nurse-family-partnership

Collier, V. P., & Thomas, W. P. (2009, November). *Educating English learners for a transformed world.* Albuquerque, NM: Fuente Press.

Comer, J. P., Haynes, N. M., Joyner, E. T., & Ben-Avie, M. (1999). *Child by child: The Comer Process for change in education.* New York: Teachers College Press.

Commonwealth of Massachusetts. (2013). *Parent engagement and family support.* Available at www.mass.gov/edu/birth-grade-12/early-education-and-care/parent-and-family-support/

Copple, C., & Bredekamp, S. (Eds.). (2009). *Developmentally appropriate practice in early childhood programs serving children from birth through age 8* (3rd ed.). Washington, DC: NAEYC.

Cost, Quality & Child Outcomes Study Team. (1995). *Cost, quality, and child outcomes in child care centers. Public Report* (2nd ed.). Denver, CO: Economics Department, University of Colorado at Denver.

Craik, F. I. M., Bialystok, E., & Freedman, M. (2010). Delaying the onset of Alzheimer disease. Bilingualism as a form of cognitive reserve. *Neurology, 75,* 1726–1729.

Currie, J., & Kahn, R. (Eds.). (2012). Children with disabilities. *The Future of Children, 22*(1, special issue).

Currie, J., & Thomas, D. (1995). Does Head Start make a difference? *The American Economic Review, 85,* 341–364.

Damme, L. (2011). *Paid family leave. A Next Social Contract Series.* Washington, DC: The New America Foundation. Available at www.newamerica.net/publications/policy/paid_family_leave

Darling-Hammond, L., & Post, L. (2000). Inequality in teaching and schooling: Supporting high-quality teaching and leadership in low-income schools. In R. D. Kahlenberg (Ed.), *A notion at risk: Preserving public education as an engine for social mobility* (pp. 127–167). New York: The Century Foundation Press.

De Feyter, J. J., & Winsler, A. (2009). The early developmental competencies and school readiness of low-income, immigrant children: Influences of generation, race/ethnicity, and national origins. *Early Childhood Research Quarterly, 24,* 411–431.

Desai, S., Chase-Lansdale, P. L., & Michael, R. T. (1989). Mother or market? Effects of maternal employment on the intellectual ability of 4-year-old children. *Demography, 26,* 545–561.

Devereux Foundation. (2012). *Devereux Center for Resilient Children.* Available at www.centerforresilientchildren.org

Di Lauro, E. (2009). *Reaching families where they live: Supporting parents and child development through home visiting.* Washington, DC: Zero to Three. Available at www.main.zerotothree.org/site/DocServer/HomeVisitssing_Mar5.pdf?docID=7889

Division for Early Childhood and National Association for the Education of Young Children. (2009). Early childhood inclusion: A joint position statement of the Division for Early Childhood (DEC) and the National Association for the Education of Young Children (NAEYC). Chapel Hill, NC: The University of North Carolina, FPG Child Development Institute. Available at www.naeyc.org/files/naeyc/file/positions/DEC_NAEYC_EC_updatedKS.pdf

Duncan, J., Bowden, C., & Smith, A. (2005). *Early childhood centres and family resilience.* New Zealand: Ministry of Social Development, Centre for Social Research and Evaluation.

Dunlap, G., Strain, P. S., Fox, L., Carta, J., Conroy, M., Smith, B., et al. (2006). Prevention and intervention with young children's challenging behavior: A summary of current knowledge. *Behavioral Disorders, 32,* 29–45.

Early, D., Maxwell, K., Burchinal, M., Alva, S., Bender, R., Bryant, D., et al. (2007). Teachers' education, classroom quality, and young children's academic skills: Results from seven studies of preschool programs. *Child Development, 78*(2), 558–580.

Ehrle, J., Adams, G., & Tout, K. (2001). *Who's caring for our youngest children? Child care patterns of infants and toddlers.* Washington, DC: Urban Institute.

Engle, P., Fernald, L., Alderman, H., Behrman, J., O'Gara, C., & Yousafzai, A. (2011). Strategies for reducing inequalities and improving developmental outcomes for young children in low-income and middle-income countries. *The Lancet, 378*(9799), 1339–1353.

Engle, P., Rao, N., & Petrovic, O. (2013). Situational analysis of young children in a changing world. In P. L. Britto, P. L. Engle, & C. M. Super (Eds.), *Handbook of early childhood development research and its impact on global policy* (pp. 35–64). New York, NY: Oxford University Press.

Epstein, A. S. (2014). *The intentional teacher: Choosing the best strategies for young children's learning* (rev. ed.). Washington, DC: NAEYC.

Erikson Institute. (2013). *Fussy Baby Network.* Available at www.erikson.edu/fussybaby

Espinosa, L. M. (2010). *Getting it right for young children from diverse backgrounds: Applying research to improve practice.* Upper Saddle River, NJ: Pearson.

Espinosa, L. (2013). *PreK–3rd: Challenging common myths about dual language learners. An update to the seminal 2008 report.* New York, NY: Foundation for Child Development.

Farrington, D. P., & Ttofi, M.M. (2009). School-based programs to reduce bullying and victimization. *Campbell Systematic Reviews.* DOI 10.4073/csr.2009.6

Federal Interagency Forum on Child and Family Statistics. (2013). America's children: Key national indicators of well-being. Available at www.childstats.gov/americaschildren/famsoc1.asp

Fewtrell, L., Kaufmann, R., & Prüss-Üstün, A. (2003). *Lead: Assessing the environmental burden of disease at national and local level.* Geneva: World Health Organization.

FirstSchool (n.d.). Available at www.firstschool.fpg.unc.edu/

Fortuny, K., Capps, R., Simms, S., & Chaudry, A. (2009). *Children of immigrants: National and state characteristics. Brief 9.* Washington, DC: Urban Institute.

Foundation for Child Development. (2010). Pre-K–3rd education. Components. Available at fcd-us.org/our-work/prek-3rd-education/components

Fox, L., Carta, J., Dunlap, G., Strain, P., & Hemmeter, M. L. (2010). Response to intervention and the Pyramid Model. *Infants and Young Children, 23*, 3–14. Available at www.journals.lww.com/iycjournal/Fulltext/2010/01000/Response_to_Intervention_and_the_Pyramid_Model.2.aspx

Fox, L., Dunlap, G., Hemmeter, M. L., Joseph, G., & Strain, P. S. (2003). The Teaching Pyramid: A model for supporting social competence and preventing challenging behavior in young children. *Young Children, 58*(4), 48–53.

Fox, L., Dunlap, G., & Powell, D. (2002). Young children with challenging behavior: Issues and consideration for behavior support. *Journal of Positive Behavior Interventions, 4*, 208–217.

Fox, L., & Smith, B. (2007). Promoting social, emotional, and behavioral outcomes of young children served under IDEA. Policy Brief. Technical Assistance Center on Social and Emotional Intervention for Young Children (TACSEI). Available at www.cpin.us/fcab_resources/fcab_res_sed/fcab_res_sed_mod/fcab_res_sed_mod_sr/HO9Children%20with%20special%20needs.pdf

FPG-UNC Smart Start Evaluation Team. (1999). *Smart Start: A six county study of the effects of Smart Start child care on kindergarten entry skills.* North Carolina, NC: Frank Porter Graham Child Development Center Smart Start Evaluation Team.

Genesee, F. (2008). Early dual language learning. *Zero to Three, 29*(1), 17–23.

Gilliam, W. S. (2005). Prekindergarteners left behind: Expulsion rates in state prekindergarten programs. *FCD Policy Brief, Series No. 3.* Available at www.fcd-us.org/resources/resources_show.htm?doc_id=464280

Gilliam, W. (2008). Head Start, public school prekindergarten, and a collaborative potential. *Infants and Young Children, 21*, 30–44.

Gormley, W., Gayer, T., Phillips, D., & Dawson, B. (2004). *The effects of Oklahoma's universal pre-K program on school readiness: An executive summary.* Washington, DC: Georgetown University Center for Research on Children in the United States.

Gormley, W., Gayer, T., Phillips, D., & Dawson, B. (2005). The effects of universal pre-K on cognitive development. *Developmental Psychology, 41*, 872–884.

Gormley, W. T., Phillips, D. A., Newmark, K., Welti, K., & Adelstein, S. (2011). Social-emotional effects of early childhood education programs in Tulsa. *Child Development, 82*, 2095–2109.

Gove, A., & Cvelich, P. (2010). *Early reading: Igniting education for all.* Research Triangle Park, NC: Research Triangle Institute.

Greene, R. (2008). *Lost at school: Why our kids with behavioral challenges are falling through the cracks and how we can help them.* New York, NY: Scribner.

Greico, E. (2004). Educational attainment of the foreign born in the United States. Migration Policy Institute. Available at migrationpolicy.org/article/educational-attainment-foreign-born-united-states

Grindal, T., Bowne, J., Yoshikawa, H., Duncan, G. J., Magnuson, K. A., & Schindler, H. (2013). *The added impact of parenting education in early childhood education programs: A meta-analysis.* Manuscript under review.

Grunewald, R. (2013, February 8). *Early childhood education "fade out" in context.* St. Paul, MN: Federal Reserve Bank, Achievement Gap Committee. Available at www.minneapolisfed.org/publications_papers/studies/earlychild/Fade_Out_Grunewald_020813.pdf

Grunewald, R., & Rolnick, A. J. (2010). An early childhood investment with a high public return. *The Regional Economist.* Available at www.stlouisfed.org/publications/re/articles/?id=1987

Guralnick, M. J., Connor, R. T., & Johnson, L. C. (2011). The peer social networks of young children with Down syndrome in classroom programmes. *Journal of Applied Research in Intellectual Disabilities, 24*(4), 310–321.

Halle, T., Anderson, R., Blasberg, A., Chrisler, A., & Simkin, S. (2011). *Quality of Caregiver Child Interactions for Infants and Toddlers (QCCIIT): A review of the literature,* OPRE 2011-25. Washington, DC: Office of Planning, Research and Evaluation, Administration for Children and Families.

Halle, T., Metz, A., & Martinez-Beck, I. (Eds.). (2013). *Applying implementation science in early childhood programs and systems.* Baltimore, MD: Brookes.

Hamre, B., & Pianta, R. (2001). Early teacher–child relationships and the trajectory of children's school outcomes through eighth grade. *Child Development, 72*, 625–638.

Hamre, B. K., & Pianta, R. C. (2007). Learning opportunities in preschool and early elementary classrooms. In R. Pianta, M. Cox, & K. Snow (Eds.), *School readiness and the transition to kindergarten in the era of accountability* (pp. 49–84). Baltimore, MD: Brookes.

Hanline, M. F., Wetherby, A., Woods, J., Fox, L., & Lentini, R. (2004). *Positive beginnings: Supporting young children with challenging behavior* [CD-ROM]. Available at www.pbs.fsu.edu/return.html

Hart, B., & Risley, T. R. (1995). *Meaningful differences in the everyday experience of young American children.* Baltimore, MD: Brookes.

Hasan, A., Hyson, M., & Chang, M. C. (Eds.). (2013). *Early childhood education and development in poor villages of Indonesia: Strong foundations, later success.* Washington, DC: The World Bank.

Hebbeler, K., Spiker, D., Bailey, D., Scarborough, A., Mallik, S., Simeonsson, R., & Singer, M. (2007). *Early intervention for infants & toddlers with disabilities and their families: Participants, services, and outcomes.* Final report of the National Early Intervention Longitudinal Study (NEILS). Available at www.sri.com/neils/pdfs/NEILS_Report_02_07_Final2.pdf

Heckman, J. J., & Masterov, D. V. (2007). *The productivity argument for investing in young children.* Presentation paper, University of Chicago, Department of Economics, Chicago. Available at www.jenni.uchicago.edu/human-inequality/papers/Heckman_final_all_wp_2007-03-22c_jsb.pdf

Hemmeter, M. L., Ostrosky, M., & Corso, R. (2012). Preventing and addressing challenging behavior: Common questions and practical solutions. *Young Exceptional Children, 15*, 31–44.

Hemmeter, M. L., Santos, R., & Ostrosky, M. (2008). Preparing early childhood educators to address social emotional development and challenging behavior: A survey of higher education programs in nine states. *Journal of Early Intervention, 30*, 321–340.

Heymann, J., Earle, A., & Hayes, J. (2007). The work, family, and equity index: How does the United States measure up? The Project on Global Working Families. Available at www.mcgill.ca/files/ihsp/WFEI2007FEB.pdf.

Horton, C. (2003). *Strengthening families through early care and education. Protective factors literature review: Early care and education programs and the prevention of child abuse and neglect.* Washington, DC: Center for the Study of Social Policy.

Howes, C., Galinsky, E., Kontos, S., & Shinn, M. (1995). *Quality in family child care and relative care.* New York: Teachers College Press.

Hyson, M. (2008). *Enthusiastic and engaged: Approaches to learning in the early childhood classroom.* New York: Teachers College Press.

Hyson, M., Horm, D. M., & Winton, P. J. (2012). Higher education for early childhood educators and outcomes for young children: Pathways toward greater effectiveness. In R. C. Pianta, W. S. Barnett, L. M. Justice, & S. M. Sheridan (Eds.), *Handbook of early childhood education* (pp. 553–583). New York: Guilford Press.

Hyson, M., & Vick Whittaker, J. (2012). Professional development in early childhood systems. In S. L. Kagan & K. Kauerz (Eds.), *Early childhood systems: Transforming early learning* (pp. 104–118). New York, NY: Teacher College Press.

Johnson-Staub, C., & Schmit, S. (2012). *Home away from home: A toolkit for planning home visiting partnerships with family, friend, and neighbor caregivers.* Washington, DC: Center for Law and Social Policy (CLASP).

Johnston, C. A., Moreno, J. P., El-Mubasher, A., Gallagher, M., Tyler, C., & Woehler, D. (2013). Impact of a school-based pediatric obesity prevention program facilitated by health professionals. *Journal of School Health, 83*(3), 171–181.

Jones, M., & Shue, P. (2013). Engaging prekindergarten children dual language learners in projects. *Young Children, 68*(1), 28–33.

Jordan, E., Szrom, J., Colvard, J., Cooper, H., & DeVooght, K. (2013). *Changing the course for infants and toddlers: A survey of state child welfare policies and initiatives.* Washington, DC: Child Trends. Available at www.childtrends.org/changing-the-course-for-infants-and-toddlers

Kaiser, B., & Rasminsky, J. S. (2012). *Challenging behavior in young children: Understanding, preventing, and responding effectively.* Upper Saddle River, NJ: Pearson.

Kennedy Krieger Institute. (2005). *PACT: Helping children with special needs.* Available at www.pact.kennedykrieger.org/nursery.jsp

Klein, L., & Knitzer, J. (2006, September). Effective preschool curricula and teaching strategies. *Pathways to Early School Success.* Issue Brief 2.

Lally, R. (2013). *For our babies: Ending the invisible neglect of America's infants.* New York: Teachers College Press.

Laughlin, L. (2013). Who's minding the kids? Child care arrangements: Spring 2011. *Household Economics Studies.* Washington, DC: U.S. Census Bureau. Available at www.census.gov/prod/2013pubs/p70-135.pdf

Lombardi, J. (2003). *Time to care: Redesigning child care to promote education, support families, and build communities.* Philadelphia, PA: Temple University Press.

Love, J. M., Chazan-Cohen, R., Raikes, H., & Brooks-Gunn, J. (Eds.). (2013). What makes a difference: Early Head Start evaluation findings in a developmental context. *Monographs of the Society for Research in Child Development, 78* (special issue).

Magnuson, K., Lahaie, C., & Waldfogel, J. (2006). Preschool and school readiness of children of Immigrants. *Social Science Quarterly, 87*(5), 1241–1262.

Manyike, T. V. (2012). Assessment of the norms and standards for day care centres for pre-school children in South Africa. *Anthropologist, 14*(6), 593–606. Available at www.krepub-lishers.com/02-Journals/T-Anth/Anth-14-0-000-12-Web/Anth-14-6-000-2012-Abst-PDF/Anth-14-6-593-12-762-Manyike-T-V/Anth-14-6-593-12-762-Manyike-T-V-Tx[12].pmd.pdf

Masten, A. S. (2013). Risk and resilience in development. In P. D. Zelazo (Ed.), *Oxford handbook of developmental psychology: Self and other* (Vol. 2, pp. 579–607). New York: Oxford University Press.

Matthews, H., & Ewen, D. (2006). *Reaching all children? Understanding early care and education participation among immigrant families.* Washington, DC: Center for Law and Social Policy.

McCabe, L. A., & Frede, E. C. (2007). *Challenging behaviors and the role of preschool education.* Preschool Policy Brief. New Brunswick, NJ: National Institute for Early Education Research. Available at nieer.org/publications/policy-matters-policy-briefs/policy-brief-challenging-behaviors-and-role-preschool

McCartney, K., Burchinal, M., & Grindal, T. (2011). The case for public preschool. In E. Zig-ler, W. Gilliam, & W. Barnett (Eds.), *The pre-K debates: Current controversies and issues* (pp. 116–120). Baltimore, MD: Brookes.

McWilliam, R. A. (2010a). *Routines-based early intervention: Supporting young children and their families.* Baltimore, MD: Brookes.

McWilliam, R. A. (2010b). *Working with families of young children with special needs.* New York, NY: Guilford Press.

Meisels, S. J., & Atkins-Burnett, S. (2005). *Developmental screening in early childhood: A guide* (5th ed.). Washington, DC: NAEYC.

Melhuish, E. C., Sylva, K., Sammons, P., Siraj-Blatchford, I., Taggart, B., Phan, M. B., et al. (2008). Preschool influences on mathematics achievement. *Science, 321,* 1161–1162.

Moiduddin, E., Aikens, N., Tarullo, L., West, J., & Xue, Y. (2012). *Child outcomes and classroom quality in FACES 2009.* OPRE Report 2012-37a. Washington, DC: Office of Planning, Research and Evaluation, Administration for Children and Families, U.S. Department of Health and Human Services.

Morrison, G. (2012). *Early childhood education today* (12th ed.). Upper Saddle River, NJ: Pearson.

Morrissey, T. W., & Banghart, P. (2007). Family child care in the United States. Research Brief. National Center for Children in Poverty, Columbia University Mailman School of Public Health. Available at www.nccp.org/publications/pub_720.html

Mullis, I. V. S., Martin, M. O., Gonzalez, E. J., O'Connor, K. M., Chrostowski, S. J., Gregory, K. D., Garden, R. A., & Smith, T. A. (2001). *Mathematics benchmarking report: TIMSS 1999–Eighth grade achievement for U.S. states and districts in an international context.* Chestnut Hill, MA: Boston College.

Murphey, D., Cooper, M., & Forry, N. (2013). *The youngest Americans: A statistical portrait of infants and toddlers in the United States.* Washington, DC: Child Trends.

Myles, B., & Simpson, R. (1998). Aggression and violence by school-age children and youth: Understanding the aggression cycle and prevention/intervention strategies. *Intervention in School and Clinic, 33*(5), 259–262.

National Association for the Education of Young Children (NAEYC). (n.d.). *Research reports and summaries.* Available at www.naeyc.org/resources/research

National Association for the Education of Young Children (NAEYC). (1996). Prevention of child abuse in early childhood programs and the responsibilities of early childhood pro-fessionals to prevent child abuse. Washington, DC: Author. Available at www.naeyc.org/files/naeyc/file/positions/PSCHAB98.PDF

National Association for the Education of Young Children (NAEYC). (2009). *NAEYC standards for early childhood professional preparation: Position statement.* Washington, DC: Author.

National Association for the Education of Young Children (NAEYC) & National Association of Early Childhood Specialists in State Departments of Education (NAECS/SDE) (2003). Early childhood curriculum, assessment, and program evaluation: Building an effective, accountable system in programs for children from birth through age 8. Available at www.naeyc.org/files/naeyc/file/positions/CAPEexpand.pdf

National Association of Elementary School Principals. (2008). *Leading learning communities: What principals should know and be able to do* (2nd ed.). Washington, DC: Author.

National Center for Children in Poverty (NCCP). (2012a, February). *Basic facts about low-income children, 2010: Children under age 6.* Available at www.nccp.org/publications/pub_1054.html

National Center for Children in Poverty (NCCP). (2012b). Children in poverty. Available at www.nccp.org/topics/childpoverty.html

National Center for Education Statistics. (2010). *Digest of education statistics.* Washington, DC: Author. Available at www.nces.ed.gov/pubsearch/pubsinfo.asp?pubid=2011015

National Dissemination Center for Children with Disabilities. (n.d.). All about the IEP. Available at parentcenterhub.org/repository/iep-overview

National Dissemination Center for Children with Disabilities. (2010). Autism spectrum disorders. Fact Sheet. Available at parentcenterhub.org/repository/autism

National Dissemination Center for Children with Disabilities. (2011). Intellectual disabilities. Fact Sheet. Available at parentcenterhub.org/repository/intellectual

National Dissemination Center for Children with Disabilities. (2012). The Common Core State Standards. Available at parentcenterhub.org/repository/commoncore

National Dissemination Center for Children with Disabilities. (2013). Resources especially for child care providers and preschools. Available at parentcenterhub.org/repository/childcare

National Forum on Early Childhood Policy and Programs. (2010). Understanding the Head Start impact study. Center on the Developing Child, Harvard University. Available at www.developingchild.harvard.edu/

National Governors Association Center for Best Practices and Council of Chief State School Officers (2010). *Common Core State Standards.* Washington, DC: Author. Available at www.corestandards.org

National Infant & Toddler Child Care Initiative. (2010). Credentials for the infant/toddler child care workforce: A technical assistance tool for Child Care and Development Fund administrators. Available at http://www.zerotothree.org/site/DocServer/ITC_TA_Tool.pdf?docID=4245

National Institute on Out-of-School Time. (2008). *Making the case: A 2008 fact sheet on children and youth in out-of-school time.* Wellesley, MA: NIOST.

National Professional Development Center on Inclusion. (2011). *Research synthesis points on early childhood inclusion.* Chapel Hill, NC: The University of North Carolina, FPG Child Development Institute, Author. Available at www.community.fpg.unc.edu/npdci

National Research Council and Institute of Medicine. (2000). *From neurons to neighborhoods: The science of early childhood development* (Committee on Integrating the Science of Early Childhood Development; Board on Children, Youth, and Families; Commission on Behavioral and Social Sciences and Education; J. P. Shonkoff & D. A. Phillips, Eds.). Washington, DC: National Academies Press.

National Scientific Council on the Developing Child. (2007). *The timing and quality of early experiences combine to shape brain architecture: Working Paper No. 5.* Available at www.developingchild.harvard.edu

National Women's Law Center. (2013). Expand access to high-quality early care and education for infants and toddlers. Fact Sheet. Washington, DC: Author. Available at www.nwlc.org/sites/default/files/pdfs/infanttoddlerfactsheet.pdf

Nelson, C. A., Furtado, E. A., Fox, N., & Zeanah, C. H., Jr. (2009). The deprived human brain. *American Scientist, 97,* 222–229.

Nelson, C. A., Zeanah, C. H., Fox, N. A., Marshall, P. J., Smyke, A. T., & Guthrie, D. (2007). Cognitive recovery in socially deprived young children: The Bucharest early intervention project. *Science, 318,* 1937–1940.

Nemeth, K. N. (2012). *Basics of supporting dual language learners.* Washington, DC: NAEYC.

Ng, J. C., Lee, S. S., & Pak, Y. K. (2007). Contesting the model minority and perpetual foreigner stereotypes: A critical review of literature on Asian Americans in education. *Review of Research in Education,* 31, 95–130.

NICHD Early Child Care Research Network. (1996). Characteristics of infant child care: Factors contributing to positive caregiving. *Early Childhood Research Quarterly, 11,* 269–306.

NICHD Early Child Care Research Network. (2002). Early child care and children's development prior to school entry: Results from the NICHD Study of Early Child Care. *American Educational Research Journal, 39,* 133–164.

NICHD Early Child Care Research Network. (2003a). Child care and common communicable illnesses in children aged 37 to 54 months. *Archives of Pediatric and Adolescent Medicine, 157,* 196–200.

NICHD Early Child Care Research Network. (2003b). Early child care and mother-child interaction from 36 months through first grade. *Infant Behavior and Development, 26,* 345–370.

NICHD Early Child Care Research Network. (2006). *The NICHD Study of Early Child Care and Youth Development (SECCYD): Findings for Children up to Age 4½ Years.* DHHS, Eunice Kennedy Shriver National Institute of Child Health and Human Development, NIH. Washington, DC: U.S. Government Printing Office. Available at www.nichd.nih.gov/publications/pubs/documents/seccyd_06.pdf

Odom, S. L. (2009). The tie that binds: Evidence-based practice, implementation science, and outcomes for children. *Topics in Early Childhood Special Education, 29,* 53–61.

Odom, S. L., Buysse, V., & Soukakou, E. (2011). Inclusion for young children with disabilities: A quarter century of research perspectives. *Journal of Early Intervention, 33*(4), 344–356.

O'Gara, C. (2013). Education-based approaches to early childhood development. In P. L. Britto, P. L. Engle, & C. M. Super (Eds.), *Handbook of early childhood development research and its impact on global policy* (pp. 227–259). New York, NY: Oxford University Press.

Olds, D. L, Kitzman, H. J., Hanks, C., Cole, R., Anson, E., Sidora-Arcoleo, K., Luckey, D. W., Henderson, C. R. Jr., Holmberg, J., Tutti, R., Stevenson, A., & Bondy, J. (2007). Effects of nurse home visiting on maternal and child functioning: Age nine follow-up of a randomized trial. *Pediatrics, 120,* 832–845.

Organisation for Economic Co-operation and Development (OECD). (2011). *Does participation in pre-primary education translate into better learning outcomes at school?* Paris: PISA in Focus. Available at www.oecd.org/pisa/pisaproducts/pisa2009/47034256.pdf

Orthner, D. K., Jones-Sanpei, H., & Williamson, S. (2004). The resilience and strengths of low-income families. *Family Relations, 53,* 159–167.

Ounce of Prevention Fund. (n.d.). Why investments in early childhood work. Available at www.ounceofprevention.org/about/why-early-childhood-investments-work.php

Patrinos, H. A., & Velez, E. (2009). Costs and benefits of bilingual education in Guatemala: A partial analysis. *International Journal of Educational Development, 29,* 594–598.

Payton, J., Weissberg, R. P., Durlak, J. A., Dymnicki, A. B., Taylor, R. D., Schellinger, K. B., & Pachan, M. (2008). *The positive impact of social and emotional learning for kindergarten to eighth-grade students: Findings from three scientific reviews.* Chicago, IL: Collaborative for Academic, Social, and Emotional Learning.

Peisner-Feinberg, E. S., Burchinal, M. R., Clifford, R. M., Culkin, M. L., Howes, C., Kagan, S. L., & Yazejian, N. (2001). The relation of preschool child-care quality to children's cognitive and social developmental trajectories through second grade. *Child Development, 72*, 1534–1553.

Perry, D. F., Allen, M. D., Brennan, E. M., & Bradley, J. R. (2010). The evidence base for mental health consultation in early childhood settings: A research synthesis addressing children's behavioral outcomes. *Early Education and Development, 21*(6), 982–1022.

Perry, D. F., Holland, C., Darling-Kuria, N., & Nadiv, S. (2011). *Challenging behavior and expulsion from child care: The role of mental health consultation.* Washington, DC: Zero to Three. Available at www.main.zerotothree.org/site/DocServer/32-2_Perry.pdf?docID=12901

Peth-Pierce, R. (2002). *The NICHD study of early child care.* Child Care and Early Education Research Connections. Available at www.childcareresearch.org/childcare/resources/627/pdf

Pew Center on the States. (2011). *Paying later: The high costs of failing to invest in young children.* Issue Brief. Washington, DC: Author.

Pianta, R. C. (2011). A degree is not enough: Teachers need stronger and more individualized professional development supports to be effective in the classroom. In E. Zigler, W. Gilliam, & W. Barnett (Eds.), *The Pre-K debates: Current controversies and issues* (pp. 64–68). Baltimore, MD: Brookes.

Pianta, R. C., & Hadden, D. S. (2008, June). What we know about the quality of early education settings: Implications for research on teacher preparation and professional development. *The State Education Standard.* Washington DC: National Association of State Boards of Education.

Pianta, R. C., & Hamre, B. K. (2009). Conceptualization, measurement, and improvement of classroom processes: Standardized observation can leverage capacity. *Educational Researcher, 38*, 109–119.

Pianta, R. C., Hitz, R., & West, B. (2010). *Increasing the application of developmental sciences knowledge in teacher preparation.* Washington, DC: NCATE.

Posel, D., & Casale, D. (2011). Language proficiency and language policy in South Africa: Findings from new data. *International Journal of Educational Development, 31*(5), 443–451.

Powell, D., Dunlap, G., & Fox, L. (2006). Prevention and intervention for the challenging behaviors of toddlers and preschoolers. *Infants & Young Children, 19*(1), 25–35.

Preston, J. (2012, August 25). Young and alone, facing court and deportation. *New York Times.* Available at www.nytimes.com/2012/08/26/us/more-young-illegal-immigrants-face-deportation.html?pagewanted=all&_r=0

Pueschel, S. (2002). *A parent's guide to Down syndrome: Toward a brighter future.* Baltimore: Brookes.

Puma, M., Bell, S., Cook, R., Heid, C., Broene, P., Jenkins, F., Mashburn, A., & Downer, J. (2012). *Third grade followup to the Head Start Impact Study Final Report.* Executive Summary. OPRE Report # 2012-45b. Washington, DC: Office of Planning, Research and Evaluation, Administration for Children and Families, U.S. Department of Health and Human Services.

Pungello, E. P., Campbell, F. A., & Barnett, S. W. (2006). *Poverty and early childhood educational intervention* (Policy Brief No. 1). The University of North Carolina at Chapel Hill, Center on Poverty, Work and Opportunity. Available at www.law.unc.edu/documents/poverty/publications/pungelloandcampbellpolicybrief.pdf

Qin, D., Way, N., & Mukherjee, P. (2008). The other side of the model minority story: The familial and peer challenges faced by Chinese American adolescents. *Youth & Society, 39*, 480–506.

QRIS National Learning Network. (2014). Current status of QRIS in states. Available at qrisnetwork.org/sites/all/files/maps/QRIS%20Map,%20QRIS%20National%20Learning%20Network,%20www.qrisnetwork.org%20%5BRevised%20February%202014%5D.pdf

RAND Corporation. (2005). *Making out of school time matter. Research brief.* Santa Monica, CA: Author.

Raver, C. C., Jones, S. M., Li-Grining, C. P., Metzger, M., Champion, K. M., & Sardin, L. (2008). Improving preschool classroom processes: Preliminary findings from a randomized trial implemented in Head Start settings. *Early Childhood Research Quarterly, 23*(1), 10–26.

Reichman, N. E., Corman, H., & Noonan, K. (2008). Impact of child disability on the family (2008). *Maternal and Child Health Journal, 12*(6), 679–683.

Reynolds, A. J. (2000). *Success in early childhood interventions: The Chicago parent-child centers.* Lincoln, NE: University of Nebraska.

Reynolds, A. J., & Robertson, D. (2003). School-based early intervention and later child maltreatment in the Chicago Longitudinal Study. *Child Development, 74*(1), 3–26.

Reynolds, A. J., Temple, J. A., Robertson, D. L., & Mann, E. A. (2001, June). *Age 21 cost-benefit analysis of the Title I Chicago Child-Parent Center Program.* University of Wisconsin–Madison, Waisman Center. Available at www.waisman.wisc.edu/cls/cbaexecsum4.html

Ritchie, S., & Guttman, L. (2013). *FirstSchool: Transforming preK–3rd grade for African American, Latino, and low-income children.* New York, NY: Teachers College Press.

Robert Wood Johnson Foundation. (2012). Increasing physical activity through recess. Research Brief. Available at www.rwjf.org/content/dam/web-assets/2012/01/increasing-physical -activity-through-recess

Rosenberg, S. A., Zhang, D., & Robinson, C. S. (2008). Prevalence of developmental delays and participation in early intervention services for young children. *Pediatrics, 121*(6), 1503–1509.

Rumberger, R. W., & Tran, L. (2006). *Preschool participation and the cognitive and social development of language-minority students.* Santa Barbara, CA: Center for the Study of Evaluation/ University of California Linguistic Minority Research Institute.

Schmit, S., & Ewen, D. (2012). *Supporting our youngest children: Early Head Start programs in 2010.* Policy Brief. Washington, DC: Center for Law and Social Policy. Available at www.clasp. org/resources-and-publications/publication-1/EHS-Trend-Analysis-Final.pdf

School of the 21st Century: Linking communities, families, and schools. (2002). Available at www.yale.edu/21c/index2.html

Schulman, K. (2011). *Promising state child care quality and infant toddler initiatives.* National Women's Law Center. Available at www.nwlc.org/sites/default/files/pdfs/statechildcarequality initiativesapril2011_0.pdf

Schumacher, R., & Hoffmann, E. (2008). *Build supply of quality care.* Charting Progress for Babies in Child Care Project. Washington, DC: Center for Law and Social Policy (CLASP).

Schweinhart, L. J., Montie, J., Xiang, Z., Barnett, W. S., Belfield, C. R., & Nores, M. (2005). *Lifetime effects: The High/Scope Perry Preschool Study through age 40.* Ypsilanti, MI: High/ Scope Press.

Schweinhart, L. J., Weikart, D. P., & Larner, M. B. (1986). Consequences of three preschool curriculum models through age 15. *Early Childhood Research Quarterly, 1*, 15–45.

Shapiro, E. (n.d.). Tiered instruction and intervention in a response-to-intervention model. RTI Action Network. Available at www.rtinetwork.org/essential/tieredinstruction/ tiered-instruction-and-intervention-rti-model

Shonkoff, J. (2012). *The impact of early adversity on children's development.* Boston, MA: Center on the Developing Child, Harvard University.

Sidorowicz, K., & Hair, E. (2009). *Assessing peer conflict and aggressive behaviors: A guide for out-of-school time program practitioners.* Research-to-Results Brief. Washington, DC: Child Trends. Available at www.childtrends.org/?publications=assessing-peer-conflict-and-aggressive-behaviors-a-guide-for-out-of-school-time-program-practitioners

Solomon, A. (2012). *Far from the tree: Parents, children and the search for identity.* New York: Scribner.

Squires, J., & Bricker, D. (2009). *Ages & stages questionnaires (ASQ-3)* (3rd ed.). Baltimore, MD: Brookes.

Stoltzfus, E., & Lynch, K. (2009). *Home visitation for families with young children.* Washington, DC: Congressional Research Service Report to Congress. Available at www.supportingebhv. org/images/CRS%20report%20%20Home%20Visitation%20-20Oct% 202009.pdf

Stuhlman, M. W., & Pianta, R. C. (2009). Profiles of educational quality in first grade. *The Elementary School Journal, 109,* 323–342.

Suarez-Orozco, C., Suarez-Orozco, M. M., & Todorova, I. (2008). *Learning a new land: Immigrant students in American society.* Cambridge, MA: Harvard University Press.

Susman-Stillman, A., & Banghart, P. (2008). *Demographics of family, friend, and neighbor child care in the United States.* National Center for Children in Poverty, Columbia University Mailman School of Public Health. Available at www.nccp.org/publications/pub_835.html

Susman-Stillman, A., & Banghart, P. (2011). Quality in family, friend, and neighbor child care settings. *Reviews of Research Literature Review.* New York: Columbia University, National Center for Children in Poverty, Child Care and Early Education Research Connections.

Takanishi, R. (2004). Leveling the playing field: Supporting immigrant children from birth to eight. *The Future of Children, 14*(2), 61–79.

Technical Assistance Center on Social Emotional Intervention (TACSEI). (2004). Facts about young children with challenging behaviors. Available at www.challengingbehavior.org/ do/resources/documents/facts_about_sheet.pdf

Technical Assistance Center on Social Emotional Intervention (TACSEI). (2011). Backpack connection series. Available at www.challengingbehavior.org/do/resources/backpack.html

Thapa, A., Cohen, J., Higgins-D'Alessandro, A., & Guffey, S. (2012). School climate research summary: August 2012. School Climate Brief, No. 3. National School Climate Center, New York, NY. Available at www.schoolclimate.org/climate/research.php

Tomlinson, H. B. (2009). Developmentally appropriate practice in the primary grades–Ages 6 to 8: An overview. In C. Copple & S. Bredekamp (Eds.), *Developmentally appropriate practice in early childhood programs serving children from birth through age 8* (3rd ed., pp. 257–279). Washington, DC: NAEYC.

UNESCO. (2012). *Expanding equitable early childhood care and education is an urgent need.* Paris: Author. Available at unesdoc.unesco.org/images/0021/002160/216038E.pdf

UNICEF. (2009). *Tracking progress on child and maternal nutrition.* New York: Author.

UNICEF. (2012). Measuring child poverty: New League tables of child poverty in the world's rich countries. Innocenti Report Card 10. Florence, Italy: UNICEF Innocenti Research Centre.

U.S. Department of Education, Office for Civil Rights. (2014). Civil rights data collection: Data snapshot (School discipline). Available at www2.ed.gov/about/offices/list/ocr/docs/crdc-discipline-snapshot.pdf

U.S. Department of Education, Office of Special Education and Rehabilitative Services (n.d.). History: Twenty-five years of progress in educating children with disabilities through IDEA. Available at www.ed.gov/policy/speced/leg/idea/history.pdf

U.S. Department of Health and Human Services. (n.d.). *Factors that contribute to child abuse and neglect.* Child Welfare Information Gateway. Available at www.childwelfare.gov/can/factors/ contribute.cfm

U.S. Department of Health and Human Services. (2010, January). *Head Start Impact Study, Final Report.* U.S. Department of Health and Human Services, Administration for Children and Families. Available at www.acf.hhs.gov/programs/opre/hs/impact_study/reports/ impact_study/hs_impact_study_final.pdf

U.S. Department of Health and Human Services. (2011). *Annual update of the HHS poverty guidelines 76(13). Fed. Reg. 3637-3638.* Washington, DC: Author.

Valladares, S., & Moore, K. A. (2009). *The strengths of poor families.* Research Brief. Washington, DC: Child Trends.

Vandell, D. L., Belsky, J., Burchinal, M., Vandergrift, N., Steinberg, L., & NICHD Early Child Care Research Network. (2010). Do effects of early child care extend to age 15 years? Results from the NICHD Study of Early Child Care and Youth Development. *Child Development, 81*(3), 737–756.

Vick Whittaker, J. E., & Jones Harden, B. (2010). Beyond ABCs and 123s: Enhancing teacher-child relationship quality to promote children's behavioral development. *National Head Start Association Dialog, 13*(3), 185–191.

Waggoner, L. (2013, May 28). *Immigration reform 2013: 3 Waves of immigration that changed America.* PolicyMic. Available at www.policymic.com/articles/44183/immigration-reform-2013-3-waves-of-immigration-that-changed-america

Walker, S., Wachs, T., Grantham-McGregor, S., Black, M., Nelson, C., Huffman, S., . . . Richter, L. (2011). Inequality in early childhood: Risk and protective factors for early child development. *The Lancet, 378*(9799), 1325-1338.

Weber, R.B. (2013). *Improving the quality of family, friend, and neighbor care. A review of the research literature.* Corvallis, OR: Oregon Child Care Research Partnership. Available at health.oregonstate.edu/sites/default/files/occrp/pdf/Improving-the-Quality-of-Family-Friend-and-Neighbor-Care-2013-Review-of-the-Literature.pdf

Weiland, C., & Yoshikawa, H. (2013). Impacts of a prekindergarten program on children's mathematics, language, literacy, executive function, and emotional skills. *Child Development, 84*(6), 2112–2130.

World Bank. (2012). *How we classify countries.* Washington, DC: Author. Available at www.data.worldbank.org/about/country-classifications

World Bank. (2013). *What matters most for early childhood development.* Washington, DC: Author. Available at www.siteresources.worldbank.org/EDUCATION/Resources/278200-1290520949227/7575842-1365797649219/Framework_SABER-ECD.pdf

World Health Organization (WHO). (2003). *Gender, tobacco and health.* Geneva: Author.

World Health Organization (WHO). (2004). *Global status report on alcohol.* Geneva: Author.

Yale School of Medicine. (2013). *Comer School Development Program.* Available at www.medicine.yale.edu/childstudy/comer/index.aspx

Yoshikawa, H., Weiland, C., Brooks-Gunn, J., Burchinal, M. R., Espinosa, L. M., Gormley, W. T., Ludwig, J., Magnuson, K. A., Phillips, D., & Zaslow, M. (2013). *Investing in our future: The evidence base on preschool education.* Washington, DC: Society for Research on Child Development. Available at www.srcd.org/policy-media/policy-updates/meetings-briefings/investing-our-future-evidence-base-preschool

Zeanah, C. H., Smyke, A. T., Koga, S. F. M., Carlson, E., & the BEIP Core Group. (2005). Attachment in institutionalized and community children in Romania. *Child Development, 76,* 1015–1028.

Zero to Three. (2009a). Early intervention for infants and toddlers with disabilities. Available at www.zerotothree.org/public-policy/policy-toolkit/earlyintervensinglmarch5.pdf

Zero to Three. (2009b). *Seizing the potential: Quality infant-toddler child care.* Washington, DC: Author. Available at www.zerotothree.org/public-policy/policy-toolkit/child_caremar5singles.pdf

Zero to Three. (2012). *Staffed family child care networks: A strategy to enhance quality care for infants and toddlers.* Washington, DC: Author.

Zigler, E., Gilliam, W. S., & Barnett, W. S. (2011). *The Pre-K debates: Current controversies and issues.* Baltimore, MD: Brookes.

Index

About the Authors

Marilou Hyson, Ph.D., is a consultant in early child development and education and adjunct professor in the University of Pennsylvania's Graduate School of Education. Formerly associate executive director of the National Association for the Education of Young Children (NAEYC), Marilou also served as professor and chair of the University of Delaware's Department of Individual and Family Studies. At NAEYC, Marilou contributed to the development of position statements on early childhood curriculum, assessment, and program evaluation; early learning standards; early childhood mathematics; and professional preparation; she also worked on accreditation and national recognition for 2- and 4-year higher education programs. Most recently, Marilou has consulted with the World Bank and Save the Children on early childhood projects in Indonesia, Vietnam, Bangladesh, and Bhutan. A former editor-in-chief of *Early Childhood Research Quarterly* and a former executive branch fellow of the Society for Research in Child Development, Marilou's publications have emphasized young children's emotional development and approaches to learning, global efforts to develop and evaluate early childhood services, and early childhood professional development. She is the author of *The Emotional Development of Young Children: Building an Emotion-Centered Curriculum* and *Enthusiastic and Engaged Learners: Approaches to Learning in the Early Childhood Classroom,* both published by Teachers College Press.

Heather Biggar Tomlinson, Ph.D., is a consultant for the World Bank on issues related to early childhood development and parenting education. She currently studies parenting education programs in Indonesia and co-created award-winning parenting education modules for Indonesia's flagship poverty-reduction program. She also wrote a statement on behalf of the Government of Indonesia on the importance of early childhood development in the post-2015 global agenda. Previously, she served as a consultant for UNICEF and as staff for the National Association for the Education of Young Children, where she drafted policy and position statements and managed the accreditation of early childhood degree programs at 4-year colleges and universities. As a fellow for the Society for Research in Child Development, Heather worked for Senator Edward Kennedy, primarily working on the reauthorization of Head Start. She has also been a research analyst for the NICHD Study of Child Care and Youth Development. She is the author of several chapters in NAEYC's Developmentally Appropriate Practice series, as well as many empirical articles, policy briefs, institutional reports, and position statements. She serves on the Editorial Advisory Board for the *Sage Encyclopedia for Early Childhood Education.* She has a Ph.D. in developmental psychology and lives in Jakarta with her husband and three young children.